TINY TRAUMAS

TINY TRAUMAS

WHEN YOU DON'T KNOW WHAT'S WRONG, BUT **NOTHING FEELS QUITE RIGHT**

DR MEG ARROLL

Thorsons

Thorsons
An imprint of HarperCollins*Publishers*
1 London Bridge Street
London SE1 9GF

www.harpercollins.co.uk

HarperCollins*Publishers*
Macken House, 39/40 Mayor Street Upper
Dublin 1, D01 C9W8, Ireland

First published by Thorsons 2023

3 5 7 9 10 8 6 4 2

A catalogue record of this book is available from
the British Library

HB ISBN 978-0-00-853640-4
TPB ISBN 978-0-00-853643-5

Printed and bound in the UK using 100% renewable electricity
at CPI Group (UK) Ltd

For my wonderfully gentle and kind-hearted daddy
- gosh, I miss you.

Contents

Introduction

It's nothing major, nothing big ... and you can't quite put your finger on it, but somehow ... you still feel ... 'under' - underwhelmed, undervalued, underloved. You have a nice enough family, an ok enough job (it's a job after all), a good enough group of friends. There's food on the table, there's shelter, there's warmth, so, in the hierarchy of needs, you're doing just fine. But somehow, you don't quite feel ... h-a-p-p-y. And isn't that the goal that 'society' sets us all up for, whether it be enforced through our parents, teachers, friends, the workplace or virtually everywhere you look?

Nothing all that bad has happened in your life ... but that's just the thing: we are taught to ignore the 'Tiny T traumas' that gradually and insidiously leave a hollow space, with their undercurrent of constant melancholy and niggling sparks of anxiety, all wrapped up in a film of other people's Insta-perfect lives.

The vast majority of my clients haven't suffered from any major early-life trauma such as sexual or physical abuse, living in a war zone or experiencing the death of a caregiver in childhood. But there are always tiny nicks and little bumps along the way that leave an impression. Small wounds, made almost imperceptible by pervasive societal norms that teach us to 'keep calm and carry on', accumulate deep within our emotional core and compound like credit card interest. Eventually, this collection of psychological silt impacts on our wellbeing – and although this may not (yet) be all-consuming, many of us sense its gravitational pull into fatigue, low-level anxiety and lack of confidence. The culmination of Tiny T trauma should be ignored at our peril as, unchecked, it can lead to many of our modern-day mental and physical health problems.

Luckily, most of us don't experience recurrent Big T trauma, or at least not multiple traumas and abuses that could account for psychological dis-ease.

We will lose loved ones, around half of us will get divorced and many of us will have physical injuries or illnesses, and it is known that these Big T traumas can lead to diagnosable mental health issues such as anxiety and depression. But this does not account for what I see in my practice day in, day out. Rather it is the more subtle experiences, such as parent–child misattunement, frenemy bullying, classroom humiliation, instability caused by frequent geographical moves (with changes of schools and jobs), achievement culture or constantly trying to make financial ends meet, that result in a low-grade sense of 'what's the point of trying?' Feeling a bit crap most of the time, languishing, high-functioning anxiety and maladaptive perfectionism are not, however, presentations that your GP will diagnose or treat. These don't fit the neat and tidy criteria in medical encyclopaedias, and when your doctor asks if you've had any significant life events in the past year, the answer may well be 'no'. So, people are left at sea in their not-quite-serious-enough-but-utterly-life-sapping existence – this is because we do not recognise the insidious impact of Tiny T trauma.

I tend to speak about Tiny T traumas simply as 'Tiny Ts', as this pretty much universal experience has the right to be used and spoken of in everyday common language. Because it is the little things that make life matter – but it's also the small, daily things that drain our vitality, spark and potential. However, if we become aware of our own Tiny Ts, we can use them to our advantage by building a robust psychological immunity that will buffer us against the devastating impact of future Big T traumas.

Because you do matter. Listen to me – you do. Much more than you know right now. And by the end of this book, not only will you start to believe this, but those daily anxieties and frustrations will start to melt away. Trust me, I'm a psychologist – but not the kind you might imagine me to be. There's no couch, no beards, no judging nods, as there's no shame in our experiences, our mistakes or even in our darkest thoughts. This book is what I know to be true from my 20-plus years of experience in research and practice. Every single person I have worked with has some form of Tiny T, of which there are countless examples. However, the outcomes of Tiny T tend to bubble up and present themselves in recognisable ways, and in this book I will share with you the cluster of Tiny T 'Themes' I have identified. I use the term themes as these are not medical conditions per se, yet they can affect people in common patterns. One, probably more, of these themes may be familiar to you and you might feel like you're the only one who suffers from this – but right here, right now, I want you to know that these themes, ailments, or whatever else we want to call the set of signs and symptoms in each chapter, are very common indeed. As we don't have medical definitions, I can't give you exact percentages or figures about how many people feel these ways – but I can tell you from my experience and observations: if you don't have a Tiny T Theme, someone you know, someone very close to you, will.

When guiding you through these Tiny T flashpoints, such as low-grade panic, never quite feeling good enough, and even health problems like insomnia, weight gain and chronic fatigue, I will of course give you practical and tangible ways to grapple with these issues - so that you can take back control of your life and no longer be a slave to Tiny T. It's not easy to access psychological services these days but we do know from research that bibliotherapy - what you're doing right now by reading this book - can be helpful in reducing symptoms.

Because we all have to deal with life's tricky problems, which are both complex and everyday, let's make it as simple and easy as possible. To do this we will use my solution-focused, three-step method:

The AAA Approach

- **Step 1: Awareness** – Discovering your unique constellation of Tiny T, and how this is affecting your lived experience, in order to take control of your life.
- **Step 2: Acceptance** – This is often the most challenging part of the process, and the stage that I see many people try to piggy-back over – yet without acceptance, Tiny T will still unduly influence your present life.
- **Step 3: Action** – Acceptance, however, is not enough; you must take steps to actively create the life you desire.

It is important, in the beginning at least while you're getting to know the process, that you follow these steps in sequence. I frequently see people in my practice who are incredibly frustrated as they have launched straight into Action techniques, which is akin to putting a sticking plaster over a nasty scratch without first washing it out – the dirt and grit becomes trapped and eventually causes infection, leaving someone with more profound issues than the initial injury. Similarly, without first generating some Awareness of Tiny T, and cultivating Acceptance of what has happened in your life, the benefit of taking Action is often short-lived. On the other hand, some people do have a great deal of Awareness, particularly those who have tried a range of psychological and self-help techniques, but again they go directly from Awareness into Action without working through the Acceptance stage. This is by no means a shortcoming of the individual – we live in fast-paced, immediate-gratification societies so it makes sense that we all want a two-minute, TikTok-able solution. However, just as with any skill, once you become accustomed to the process, you will find it easier to move through the stages, and will become a master of the three As.

One last note before we begin properly. One of the most common questions I'm asked is 'How long will it take?' – and the only accurate answer is that it's different for everyone. Just as physical healing takes some time, emotional and psychological recovery does need to be given space and time to occur. The deeper the cut, or the greater number and degree of Tiny Ts in this case, the more work you may have to do on your recovery. And it is work, or rather effort – but I assure you it's worth it. Because *you are worth it.*

However, this does lead to a somewhat harsh reality: while Tiny Ts are not your fault, you're the only one who can do anything about them. But now, already right now, you've made the vital first step to grapple with the widespread difficulties I see every week, and I will be with you on this journey. You are not alone.

So, I'll begin with a bit more info about what Tiny Ts are, and why they matter, to start the overarching process of the AAA Approach - raising Awareness.

CHAPTER 1

Tiny T trauma and why it matters

In this chapter we will explore:

- how trauma affects physical and mental health
- the difference between 'Big T' and 'Tiny T' trauma
- the many and varied sources of Tiny T
- the psychological immune system
- how we can use Tiny T as psychological antibodies.

In this first chapter we'll look at the differences between Big T and Tiny T trauma, as every experience we have shapes us. There's no denying this. It's useful to define these as it starts to explain why so many of us feel a bit crappy so much of the time. We will also look at a number of sources of Tiny T trauma, with real-world examples to give context to this type of emotional assault, which typically hides in plain sight. Indeed, this is one of the very reasons why it can be so damaging.

Psychology is a relatively new discipline that's only been studied with robust methods for the last century, so please forgive the field for taking a bit of time to get to grips with low-level trauma. The first step is to observe what's happening on the ground floor, as it were, and ensure that what professionals like psychologists study and research is a clear reflection of people's lives. You can share your examples also with the hashtag #tinyt to help others feel less isolated in their experiences and add to the evidence base. But for now, let's get started ...

Big T Trauma and Health

Until relatively recently, researchers and psychologists have tended to focus on significant negative events that occur in people's lives. It makes sense as these are the ones that cause acute psychological illness and for which people seek professional help. These include life-limiting (and at times heartbreakingly life-threatening) mental health conditions such as major depression, generalised anxiety, post-traumatic stress disorder and a whole host of others documented in the mental health bible called the *Diagnostic and Statistical Manual of Mental Disorders* (*DSM*). In this and other earlier versions, Big T trauma was a feature in many of the listed conditions - these are the obvious horrendous situations that we know often lead to mental and physical health problems. Experiencing a war zone; childhood sexual, physical or emotional abuse; rape or molestation; being caught up in natural disasters such as fires, earthquakes, tornados and hurricanes; or being on the receiving end of acts of violence such as an armed robbery or terrorism - all constitute Big T trauma.

In the most up-to-date fifth version of the *DSM* (so known as the *DSM-5*) there are 157 separate diagnosable disorders, over 50 per cent more than when that tome was first published in 1952. Does this mean that as humans we have developed this many more mental health conditions? I'd say perhaps some, but mainly we're just getting much better at recognising and defining human experience and suffering, and now we're aware that other events, many of which are more common, can lead to emotional and functional problems.

Major Life Events That Most of Us Will Experience at Some Point

Fortunately, most of us won't experience the severe events within Big T trauma – but at some point, we will all lose loved ones, many of us will get divorced and even joyous occasions can feel awfully stressful (childbirth, weddings, Christmases even). These, instead, are what psychiatrists Thomas Holmes and Richard Rahe coined as 'major life events'. The two doctors pored over five thousand sets of medical notes to see if patients' stressful life experiences were related to later health issues and compiled a list of events from the most traumatic (death of a spouse) to something less significant but still stressful, such as a minor violation of the law (who hasn't had a traffic fine!?), with points or 'life change units' attached to each incident. Along with the severity of these events, how many happened together in the space of a year appeared to be an important indicator of health problems. By adding together patients' life change units, the psychiatrists were able to see that a total score of 300 or more put people's health at risk, between 150 and 299 there was a moderate risk of developing an illness, and below 150 yearly total units gave individuals an only slight risk of poor health.[1]

So, we can get the sense that some of the things we experience through life may make us vulnerable to both physical and mental health issues, particularly if they hit in a short space of time. But this isn't the whole picture; even though there are many studies that support this theory, some also find that people who haven't reached the magical cut-off threshold in the life events scale develop problems. Why would these things make one person very ill, but not another? This, I propose, is where Tiny T comes into its own.

Tiny T Trauma – The Missing Link?

As an academic in my early career, I was part of a research group call the Chronic Illness Research Team and we carried out studies on all sorts of illnesses, and how these conditions affected patients. This is actually why I started writing books in the first place, as students associated with our module 'The Psychology of Physical Illnesses' tended to have some history of long-term health problems or were at the time feeling pretty down and wired with anxiety (although that was not surprising for third-year psych undergrads!).

In response, my colleagues and I started writing books for the mainstream, rather than just dusty scientific journal articles. And here it really started to dawn on me that the significant Big T traumas and life events that researchers talked about couldn't account for many of the conditions we studied and worked with. I'd heard about 'small t trauma' from the work of psychologist Dr Francine Shapiro, now best known for the creation of eye movement desensitisation and reprocessing (EMDR). Dr Shapiro expanded the concept of trauma to experiences that happen frequently and to most people, such as emotional neglect or indifference, social humiliation and family issues, but that did not meet the severity bar for either Big T trauma or major life events. However, in her research and practice, Dr Shapiro saw that these smaller assaults could also result in long-term emotional and/or physical difficulties. Sometimes this type of trauma is described as 'little t' also, but I prefer to call it 'Tiny T' and will use this term throughout our journey together. But no matter what label I searched for in academic databases, I struggled to find 'small, little or tiny trauma' in scientific papers, clinical reports or even more mainstream publications. Like so many important topics, it was somewhat ignored, fobbed-off and brushed under the carpet. Until now.

One scientific paper I did locate on the topic looked at both Big and Tiny Ts in people with irritable bowel syndrome (IBS). I expected to see the same old results: that the bigger traumas caused more symptoms and had a much more significant impact on the patients' lives, etc., etc. But, contrary to this, it was minor traumas that seemed to predict IBS symptoms rather than the Big T or life events that psychologists are taught lead to ill health.[2] People whose parents had been cold or aloof were more likely to have this tummy condition than those who had experienced full-on abuse or neglect. I found this fascinating – you know those moments when fireworks ignite in your mind? Not only were Tiny Ts important ... THEY WERE MORE IMPORTANT IN THESE PATIENTS THAN BIG T TRAUMA! It was with this eureka flash that I began to become somewhat obsessed with Tiny T and how it could explain so many issues I saw in my then students and later therapeutic clients.

Because even with the 157 diagnosable conditions in the *DSM-5*, you couldn't say that we've got it all covered. The majority of people who I see in my clinic would not tick all the boxes for a particular diagnosis, but does that mean that they're not in need, or indeed worthy, of help? My view is a very loud, top-of-my-voice, NO. We all need a bit of help sometimes but we're only now scratching the surface with conversations about mental health, and of course, like any discipline, this always begins with the most obvious and severe examples. Then, in scientific study, we tend to trickle down to less striking, but just as deserving, presentations of whatever the topic of interest is – in this case emotional pain and disequilibrium.

Rock the Boat – Don't Rock the Boat, Baby

To explain why less significant occurrences in someone's life would have such a big impact, I like to use the following analogy. Imagine your life is a boat, and you're sailing along year after year. Over time, your boat knocks against some rocks, there's a heavy storm and fish nibble at the bottom of the hull. Each of these small bits of wear and tear on their own aren't a problem, especially if you are aware of the damage and have the tools to repair it. However, sailing is busy work and sometimes you don't notice a leak, particularly if you're bobbing around in the wind and rain. Usually, it is only when you start to have problems – for instance, you start losing momentum without knowing why – that you begin to realise you might be in trouble. This, in a nutshell, is Tiny T trauma.

A Journey Towards Understanding Tiny T Trauma

With this analogy in mind, I started to collate some of the experiences that appeared to be particularly troublesome for people - maybe not on their own, but when combined with other Tiny Ts and even societal pressures. The examples in the rest of this chapter are not exhaustive (as this would make for a very long book indeed!), but rather are some of the most frequent Tiny Ts I see.

Just like major life events, Tiny Ts happen at some stage, and when they make that first psychological dent, the low-grade trauma is often reinforced over the years. It's this reinforcement that starts to create a pattern - it could be a mental health pattern or a pattern of behaviour as a result. These are the Tiny T Themes mentioned in the Introduction, which we will explore in the rest of this book. But for now, let's take a quick trip through some widespread Tiny Ts that might just be familiar to you.

Tiny Ts from Childhood

Much of the research on trauma focuses on early-life experience, which makes sense as this is the time when neural networks are forming and so what happens to us can have the biggest impact. No one really gets through childhood unscathed - and nor should we, as these experiences go a long way in making us who we are.

For many people, events that happened many years ago leave an indelible mark. Here are a few examples of childhood Tiny Ts that might seem familiar to you or loved ones.

The parent trap

The bonds we form with our primary caregiver (often our mum and dad, but it could be foster parents, aunts, uncles, whoever looks after us when we're young) leads to what we call an 'attachment style'. In the late 1950s and throughout the 1960s and 1970s, famous psychologists such as John Bowlby and Mary Ainsworth observed that children seemed to develop one of four distinct patterns of behaviour and temperament in response to their environment.[3] We'll look at this more closely in Chapter 8 on love, but these attachment styles have been studied in countless experiments, which show that the way a caregiver reacts to a baby or infant determines how secure they feel in the world. A secure attachment is found in families where consistency and sensitive reactions are given to children, whereas an avoidant attachment is formed if parents are somewhat distant or distracted. This matters as we carry these templates into our grown-up, adult relationships. Sometimes it is good and sometimes not so good, as anything other than a secure attachment (the other two types are ambivalent and disorganised attachment) can lead us to the sub-optimal situations that leave us feeling a bit rubbish, a lot of the time.

This is also how Tiny T can trickle down through generations. Our caregivers may themselves have numerous Tiny Ts that they've never had the chance to explore. Or there may be practical issues that mean children feel somewhat lonely at times – many of us, for instance, were 'latchkey kids', coming home from school to an empty house, sorting ourselves out until working parents come home after a full-on day at work. There's no Big T here; many parents and caregivers just need to work unsociable hours to pay the bills and keep a roof over their family's heads because the cost of living is now so high in many countries – indeed, this is how society itself creates Tiny Ts for many people.

But before the 'snowflake' accusers start, I'm not saying this alone leaves people with profound psychological distress. However, it is relevant, as some of these patterns show up in adult relationships – not just romantic ties, but friendships and interactions with others. By understanding this programming, we can start to change the script if it's causing us problems in life.

Or it may be that you and your caregivers have quite different personalities – some people have parents who seem like aliens and are not like their kids at all. The extroverted dad taking his son to every football game and scout group when all the boy wants to do is write his stories underneath his duvet with a flashlight. No one would call this poor parenting, and indeed many would say that pushing children outside their comfort zone is beneficial, but research tells us that this mismatch can cause a few tiny scrapes in our sense of attachment.[4] It's really about feeling loved and accepted for who we are – unconditionally.

Hence, there are countless subtle ways our early years can shape us, and remember: it's not that the caregiving was in any way neglectful, abusive or 'bad', it just may not have suited our unique personalities and temperaments. But this is why Tiny T is imperative to understand – even without any overt wrongdoing, we can still be affected by our experiences, contexts and relationships. Without this Awareness (remembering that this is the first step of the AAA Approach), we're left in a perpetual state of not-quite-ok-ness that feels neither good nor bad, just some meandering, time-wasting place.

We don't need no education – Tiny Ts from school

Love it or hate it, school is a pivotal time in our development. You might have been Ferris Bueller at school - as Grace the school secretary says to Ed Rooney, the school principal and Ferris's nemesis: '*Oh, he's very popular Ed. The sportos, the motorheads, geeks, sluts, bloods, waistoids, dweebies, dickheads - they all adore him. They think he's a righteous dude.*' Or you may have been that sporto, a motorhead or a geek - school is a microcosm of the world, where we're often categorised and pigeonholed. Not just by our peers, but often by our emerging sense of personal identity.[5]

The Tiny Ts come from the more subtle interactions rather than more serious abuses; from, say, bullying. Overt bullying is a major childhood trauma and many children do sadly endure this, but for many others, the less obvious bitchiness, feeling like a round peg in a square hole, the humiliation on the playing field, the stress of exams and pressure to succeed in an environment focused on league tables rather than meaningful learning, can all result in Tiny T.

A few years ago, I was working with someone who would be classed as extremely successful - he was a top executive with a sizable pay cheque, a long marriage and two bright children. Mo was the absolute life of the party, had loads of good friends, an amazing home, fast car, etc. etc. and seemed completely content - yet he was steadily, and increasingly, piling on pound after pound with no end in sight. On the face of it, Mo explained away the weight gain as client lunches and his ability to now buy the best food and wine, which he also lavished on his loved ones. But this explanation wasn't getting him, or us, very far so I asked Mo the following:

'*Think of an event or experience which impacted or changed you in an important way, but you thought it wasn't serious enough to mention?*'

I use this exercise with almost everyone in initial sessions and, almost universally, what emerges is a form of trauma. For some people, this question triggers a positive memory, but negative events tend to stick in the depths of our minds more stubbornly than positive ones so, *usually*, the story here is about Tiny T in some form.

Here's what came up for Mo ...

'When I was nine years old my brother was diagnosed with ADHD. It's not like now; back then ADHD wasn't talked about and accepted by the school, other parents and community with everyone understanding like it is now – back then it felt like people just thought Van [my brother] was a bad, naughty child, always trying to get attention. I spent most of my schooldays with one eye on Van, making sure no one was bullying him – including teachers. I'm not talking about fistfights here; I joked them into leaving him alone. I was without doubt the class clown – the more I made the other kids and teachers laugh, the less they focused on Van. Maybe that's why I always laugh things off [laughing]. But I feel it's not right even saying this, as it's not Van's fault I'm this weight. Van's not to blame for anything – and I mean anything.'

We clearly hit on something incredibly important here and touched a tender nerve. But it was the start of learning how our experiences can collate and lead to feelings and behaviours (in Mo's case over-eating) that are unhelpful, and at times downright damaging as by this point Mo had high blood pressure and was warned by his doctor that he was pre-diabetic. He knew he had to do something to stop the mindless consumption of rich food and drink.

Tiny T Is Cumulative and Context-driven

When Mo next came to my office, he wasn't in his usual jovial mood. He sat down, shoulders somewhat hunched, and looked directly at the floor. He told me he couldn't believe how that single question could start to trigger so many lightbulb moments in his mind and he was feeling rather overwhelmed. Mo said he was finding it incredibly hard to accept that something to do with his brother's condition was impacting on him now, so we took some time to work through Mo's Tiny T maze and see how we could connect the dots.

In the introduction I mentioned the AAA Approach of Awareness, Acceptance and Action – Mo was trying to move straight past Awareness into Acceptance and this was causing some real emotional distress. We needed to do some more work on the first A of Awareness to lay the foundation for Acceptance because it didn't make sense to Mo that there was a direct correlation between Van's ADHD and his ever-expanding waistline – well, not quite. I agreed this was far, far too reductionist and so we needed to explore one of the fundamental tenets of Tiny T: that this type of trauma is **cumulative**.

This is a huge difference between Big T and Tiny T – Big T is usually a distinct and easily identifiable event (or series of events such as abuse) that we can all immediately agree is highly detrimental to the mind and body. However, Tiny Ts are a combination of smaller occurrences, peppered in particular contexts that build up over time.

As Mo mentioned, if he and Van were growing up now and in present-day schools they both would have had very different experiences. Our knowledge of disorders like ADHD changes all the time and we are much better at supporting individuals and their families these days. The situation was different 40-plus years ago, so it was vital that we place the Tiny T within its historical and chronological context. This enabled Mo to shift his mindset from thinking that the Tiny T implied that his dearly loved brother was somehow to blame. This Awareness of the context of Tiny T can be transformative in allowing space for the second A in our approach: that of Acceptance.

Connecting the dots ...

Often when we start our detective work around Tiny T, the connections appear in a rush – a bit like the floodgates opening for the first time! Mo began to link Tiny Ts together in that he would binge-eat during breaks, lunchtime and after school as a way of burying his feelings and fears. Food was a big deal in his family and associated with love and comfort, but it wasn't just this association that drove his over-eating behaviour. As Mo piled on the pounds, he developed a persona of the funny kid, and this was like his superpower – it protected not just Mo but his entire family from the hurtful things people could say and do. Everyone seemed to love Mo and when he left school and secured his first sales position, taking potential clients on expensive meals seemed to always win him the contract. This was a win-win situation! Wasn't it ...? Humour and food now led to success and financial security, not just a buffer from bullying. What started off as a Tiny T now became a pattern so extraordinarily ingrained that even when Mo's doctor told him time and time again that he needed to make some dietary and lifestyle changes, it felt impossible.

I hope it's becoming clearer that this is why understanding Tiny Ts is so important but often overlooked. First, the shame that Mo felt mentioning his brother and how Van's diagnosis might have impacted on him essentially prevented Mo from ever letting the awareness of these events come into his consciousness. But then, playing the classic game of Reverse Misery Trumps, in which Mo discounted his own feelings because what he experienced wasn't as bad as what his brother must have felt, is again a stark characteristic of Tiny T and makes us feel unworthy of care and compassion. This mind game also stops people from moving from Awareness to Acceptance in the AAA Approach as, by its very nature, Tiny T doesn't *seem* as bad as Big T.

It's so much easier to put your finger on one Big T event and believe that only such significant traumas or major life events are worthy of our attention - but that simply isn't the case. For Mo, it wasn't just the situation at school that led him to my office - he is a complex being like the rest of us - yet it was notable, telling and had an impact on the intervening years. The love for his brother and instinct to protect Van led Mo to become hypervigilant of teasing or bullying, so much so that it was just easier to always play the role of the class clown. This illustrates why it's so useful to start with one particular episode and work back from there - but it can be useful to find more Tiny Ts too.

Tiny Ts from Relationships

Our bonds with primary caregivers are not the only key and transformative relationships we have with regards to Tiny T - adult bonds including platonic and romantic relationships can leave our psyche with nicks and cuts. Because you never get over your first love - right? A quick head's-up here: this book is peppered with clichés - not by design, simply because clichés are clichés for a reason. They denote a shared understanding of universal phenomena, easily understood and identified. We'll explore how Tiny T can impact on future relationship choices and success in Chapter 8, but for now let's touch on overall relationship Tiny Ts.

The one that got away ...

The way in which we love, aforementioned as attachment style, is developed in childhood, but the story doesn't end with our parents or caregivers. While these relationships often go on to dictate our adult attachments, the scripts are not set in stone. Even if we were fortunate enough to form a strong, secure bond with those who cared for us early on, difficult relationships can cause Tiny T and skew our internal compass.

Is there someone who still plays on your mind? You might not have gone as far as social media stalking, but occasionally you think of them, usually when your life is feeling particularly below par. This can be Tiny T even if you ended the partnership, as all intimate relationships require us to open ourselves up and be vulnerable. Perhaps it is the event that materialised in your mind at the start of this chapter. I'll tell you right now, whatever the reason for the relationship's ending, there is learning to be found. But this can be a strikingly painful one to explore, so be patient and gentle with yourself.

In another session with Mo he said that the biggest challenges he had in his adult life were in his relationships. He was happily married now, but there was another Tiny T that still stung to his core:

> *I was in my early twenties and at uni when I met Sarah - we were in the same group so spent pretty much all our spare time together and did 'get together' if you know what I mean. So I thought we were going out. Then one day, after a few beers, I asked if she'd come with me to visit my parents and I'll never forget the look of horror on her face. Then she burst out in laughter and said, 'You know the girls ranked all the lads and you came LAST!' I didn't date again, for a very long time.*

Mo was certain this rejection was due to his weight and role as the funny guy in their social group - and, like many vicious cycles, the emotional pain sparked yet more over-eating. Furthermore, this rebuff didn't just affect his relationship with Sarah, it made him pull away from his friendship circle all together, although gradually over time.

This is the thing with Tiny T - the paper cut on your heart might have been from a ten-year relationship just as much as from a short dalliance. There is no more or less 'worthy' Tiny T - it depends on how it affected *you*, and your feelings are valid. More than valid - they're all that matters, as you are you and the indents you carry through your life not only influence your future, they programme (to some extent at least) daily and momentary emotional states. The encouraging part of this is that through the exploration of Tiny Ts, Mo was now not only raising his Awareness of Tiny T, but also moving into a state of Acceptance of how these cascading events, feelings and behaviours steered him into a world of comfort eating. Connecting the Tiny T dots was becoming a source of empowerment and psychological training for Mo, rather than a millstone around his neck. I'll share details of how we progressed Mo into the Action phase of the AAA in the chapter 'Eating Your Heart Out', as the remaining chapters of this book are about these Tiny T Themes and the actions you can use to take control of your past, present and future and live a life in which you thrive, not just survive.

Mean girls and frenemies – Tiny Ts from friendships

Although we mostly speak of the pain and hurt experienced by unrequited love or the end of a romantic relationship, friendships, acquaintanceships and colleague interactions can also cause their fair share of Tiny T. In my practice, I've particularly found female friendships to affect individuals' emotional health - both positively and negatively. There is an evolutionary reason for this that we tend to overlook in our efforts for equality, based on men and women's survival response.

The classic 'fight-or-flight' stress response is well known and discussed. In order to make it out alive when faced with a predator, our ancestors had to either fight with all their might or flee like the wind. To do this our bodies engage in a complex cascade of physiological processes that give us the best chance of survival - our hearts pump more blood to our muscles, glucose is released for an intense boost of energy, our pupils dilate to spot danger. But this isn't the only type of stress response.

The vast majority of early medical and psychological research studies were conducted in men only, including research that looked at how we cope with stress. Later studies, however, thought to investigate this vital process in different groups, and it was found that while women do have an acute fight-or-flight response, they also follow a pattern of 'tend-and-befriend'. If we think about our predecessors, females would have had the traditional role of caring for young and developing social ties for safety. If a female offended a higher-status woman in the group, this could cause problems and, at worst, end in rejection from the clan completely. In these times, this expulsion would be catastrophic for the individual and her immediate family. Which is why, in general, women often avoid direct confrontation and seem to be more affected by fall-outs with their mates and families. This constant second-guessing, people-pleasing and tiptoeing over eggshells to maintain social order (i.e. 'keeping the peace') may lead females to hide some of their culturally undesirable feelings, or in extreme cases to repress their true selves. Males can of course do this too, but the female 'tend-and-befriend' hardwiring within the brain and nervous system as a way to survive in complex group dynamics makes this sociobehavioural response much more likely in women.. On the other hand, men can have a row, duke it out and then behave as if nothing happened! This is of course quite reductionist and I'm not for a minute trying to invalidate the complexity of human behaviour, but if we start at this point, some perplexing phenomena begin to make sense. Then we can layer on top the Tiny T to construct a more detailed picture and understanding of why we do what we do, and feel the way we feel.

If a tree falls in the forest ...

Both men and women, however, are at their core social beings - the need to belong to a group and be accepted by those around us is as crucial to our survival as water, air, food and safety. I am not over-egging this pudding, I promise. Even after we're big enough to look after ourselves, our sense of identity and security is based on our interactions with other people. Rather than pondering the thought experiment of whether a tree makes a sound after it falls in a forest if no one is around to hear it, I would pose the question: who would you be if you couldn't see yourself in relation to others?

Tiny Ts from Work

Is your work just a job, a career or a calling? If you feel it's simply a way to pay your bills, the chances are you're less happy than someone who says that their work is a nurtured career or a vocation. If you're doing a job, you may spend the vast majority of your nine to five daydreaming about selling seashell necklaces on a beach, writing the next bestseller, or winning the lottery and not having to work at all. If this is the case, it's likely that Tiny T is etching away at you every ... single ... day ...

We all need to keep a roof over our heads, so the difference between a career and pay-cheque job is generally that when you're on a work path you've chosen, you're doing it for yourself - in a job, you're less in control of your ambitions and goals. A calling is in addition to this when your core beliefs and sense of identity are keenly aligned with what you do for work. Traditionally we think of these types of occupations as doctors, clergy and professions in which we help others in need. But sadly, even these roles have fallen foul of the drudgery of work in modern life, as a GP was suffering from chronic anxiety found:

> *Being a doctor is my life – it's all I ever wanted to do but I wake up every morning with a sense of dread. If I've slept at all – that's a problem too. The workload is unrealistic and patients come in so angry as they've had to wait weeks for an appointment. We have a clear sign in the waiting room that states patients should only present one health issue, but some have waited so long, it's impossible for them not to want to tell me everything. Then there's the endless pile of paperwork and meetings that we don't have time (or money) allocated for. I constantly feel like I'm drowning, and I simply don't feel like a physician any more.*

Anita was not only experiencing work strain and veering towards ill health herself, she was also afflicted with the Tiny Ts that arise from layers of bureaucracy. This has the effect of morphing what should have been a calling or career back into an unsatisfying job. I've seen this in many professions – academia, journalism, law, engineering, you name it. This soul-destroying metamorphosis has resulted in a wave of work-induced Tiny Ts that we used to only see in traditional 'jobby-job' positions. Most work now is a conveyor belt, with solicitors having to note every minute of their time, teachers having to deal with piles of paperwork, nurses box-ticking to justify their employment – I could go on but I'm sure you get the drift here and, probably, it's too close for comfort.

They're gonna find out ...

So what about those people out there lucky enough to still have the benefits of fulfilling work? Are they sailing through life? Ummm ... not quite. Because careers are characterised by opportunities for advancement such as further training and promotion, leading to higher status, social standing and usually more money, the greasy pole of the career ladder can create a specific reaction to Tiny T - the Imposter Syndrome. Continuous appraisals (judgement), fierce competition and a clear pecking order represent the perfect storm, causing people to feel like they're not at all good enough, with the prickly anxiety that someone will surely figure this out one day. You know that person who seems to be at the top of their game, supremely confident and amazing at their work - chances are, they have that echoing self-doubt in their heads and the reason why they appear so immaculate is the fear that someone might find out they've been winging it all along. Maybe this is you - the secret here is that many of us also feel like this, and the Tiny T often comes from not realising this as most of us are too afraid to talk about it. It's such a sizable issue that I've dedicated a complete chapter to it - if you don't have Imposter Syndrome, the likelihood is that you know someone who has, and is terrified of being 'found out'.

Tiny Ts from Society

This leads nicely onto some of the wider, macro sources of Tiny T. There are so many great aspects of modern societies - in fact, we really wouldn't want to go back a few hundred years *at all* in terms of both physical and psychological health. But there are still components of modern society that can result in Tiny T. We now live in a global economy that has led to higher standards of living for many, but the flipside of this is that today we have not just millions, but billions of people to compare ourselves with. This can feel overwhelming, there's no doubt about that - so, at this point I want to reassure you that the solution-focused tools in this book will enable you to manage all of these sources of Tiny T.

Wheel of Striv(f)e

'I'll be happy when ...' - how many times has this thought popped into your head? When you make a bit more money, when you get the promotion, when you find the perfect partner, when you have kids ... it goes on ... and on ...

This is what I call the Wheel of Striv(f)e. While we *strive* for all these accomplishments or milestones in life, working our backsides off and rarely taking a moment to reflect, what we're actually doing is running a hamster wheel of *strife*. It's perpetual, never-ending and utterly exhausting unless we take a leap of faith and focus on now, rather than 'when'.

This is not to say that goals are unimportant; rather, the fallacy is that we can have it all if we just work a bit harder, earn some more money or fall in love, and that these are the things that make us happy. Our modern, consumerist societies do constantly and subliminally whisper this promise into our ears. I'm not the first, and certainly won't be the last, to comment on the destructive nature of such environments - in which our worth is often intertwined with wealth, possessions and status. And while we may not be able to change this culture, we can be aware of the impact it has on how we think, the self-beliefs we hold and how this triggers Tiny T.

Digital Tiny T

We don't live merely in the physical world any more - there is an entire digital world in which Tiny T can occur. This world is new, and as such it is a bit like the Wild West, with fewer rules and consensus about what is acceptable - and what are unacceptable forms of behaviour towards our fellow human beings. From the surge of disinformation to personal information security issues, along with online bullying, trolling, stalking, revenge porn and cancel culture, we have developed a whole new universe to experience Tiny T. Of course, there are countless benefits of this technological advance, but I would contend that we are only beginning to understand some of the harms that can be suffered in this virtual world. Also, knowing that whatever we do, including the idiotic mistakes we all make, may be uploaded and held online forever with little chance of a clean slate has changed the nature of existence into a much more fearful state of being. I can't tell you how often I've heard someone say, 'I'm so glad I didn't go through my teenage years with social media!' The fact of the matter, though, is that this is the very world that young people are learning their way in.

Your teeth are so white

The phenomenon of what I call 'impossibly flawless teeth' can, in and of itself, lead the young and old to feel utterly inadequate and, at times, inconsequential. Yes, this is about social media, but not individual platforms per se; rather, it's about the odd way we as the human race use them as a source of constant comparison. Research shows that even when we know photos are retouched, filtered or even downright distorted, the emotional impact on our own self-worth is just as significant as if we thought these 'perfect' images were untouched. We'll dig deeper into this trend in Chapter 6, but suffice to say, there is now an agreement that this global world of ours, where we can compare ourselves to countless people who we do not know and will probably never meet, has had an impact on our emotional health.

The loneliness epidemic

Although we have never been more connected, we've never felt more alone. Loneliness and social isolation were already on the rise before the coronavirus pandemic, but Covid-19 pushed many people to the brink of a mental health crisis. I've said it before and I'll say it again: we are social creatures. So, although it's fantastic that we have the technology to make it through a challenging viral pandemic with WFH, endless Zoom calls and e-commerce, the lack of physical contact for many creates Tiny T.

Chronic loneliness is as bad for our health as smoking 15 cigarettes a day. Until Covid-19 this was a topic normally considered in terms of older people, but even before 2020 we saw younger people presenting with problems associated with loneliness. What's important to distinguish here is that loneliness is a symptom, not the cause of social isolation. It's pretty easy to see this with the social restrictions brought about by the coronavirus, but pre-Covid-19 we had developed a world in which countless people could go days without seeing another soul, let alone having a hug or a supportive pat on the back.

Back again in the 1950s and 1960s, American psychologist Harry Harlow decided to separate some baby rhesus monkeys from their mothers – ugh, the photos are heart-breaking but the work was central in our understanding of the importance of feeling comfort. In their cages, Harlow left either a wire 'surrogate' mother with a food source, or a surrogate covered in soft terry cloth. Which do you think the helpless little monkeys were drawn to? It was the latter, even though at the time scientists believed young mammals primarily developed attachments with carers that provided food. What Harlow and his colleagues discovered was that infants have a biological need for 'tactile comfort' to survive – they, and we, must have something to touch and cling to for comfort, which is why a Zoom call just isn't ever going to cut it when it comes to emotional health.

Vicarious trauma and the permacrisis

There is a type of Tiny T that emerges from watching others experience Big T or major life events, known as vicarious trauma. You could be thousands of miles away from people's suffering and still feel a sense of emotional pain – especially if these events extend over a long period of time, such as the Covid-19 pandemic. Doomscrolling, that addictive-like behaviour when you're drawn to read endless news headlines, can play into vicarious trauma in our 24/7 media-frenzied world. We also appear to be within a time of permacrisis, which is a state of ongoing political, cultural and socioeconomic disruption with no foreseeable end. Whether this is actually true, or merely our perception of the world, is rather academic as it certainly feels to many people that we're in a permacrisis at the moment, leading to a form of collective trauma. With such easy access to world events, it's unsurprising that many people have reported becoming overwhelmed by severe worries over the future of our planet, known as eco-anxiety. This can affect motivation if someone falls into the mindset of a hopeless, dystopian future, leading to a form of eco-depression that can impact not just on environmental actions, but on all areas of one's life.[6]

Tiny Ts and the Psychological Immune System

I like to demonstrate how even some of the very tough Tiny Ts you have gone through can be reframed by comparing them to the physical immune system and what I refer to as the 'psychological immune system'. By the time we reach adulthood, our physical immune system is made up of the innate immunity that we were born with, and adaptive immunity that we acquire over time. Our innate immune system is encoded in our genes, but it needs to be switched on and fine-tuned in response to all the microbes that surround us in the natural world. This is why we encourage children to play outside, interact with others and generally allow them to pick up some coughs, colds and bugs. These pathogens will trigger an immune response so that, in future, we have the antibodies to fight off greater threats. In essence, our immune system has adapted because it's had to cope with some assaults - it would not be so robust if it had avoided every single harm out there.

The psychological immune system works in exactly the same way - we all have an innate survival instinct in the form of the hardwired stress response from birth. But this is quite a crude tool and so, over time, we learn other coping mechanisms to help us navigate the trials and tribulations of life. However, this can only happen when our psychological immune system has to put up a battle against a threat – say, being told 'no' as a young child. To the infant this may feel excruciating and result in tears or a tantrum, but this experience will strengthen the psychological immune system when housed in a loving and supportive environment. Then, later in life, boundaries are comfortable and respected and don't feel like assaults – because we have been able to develop what I call **emotional antibodies**. In this example above of a kid not getting exactly what they want when they want, the psychological pathogen of a boundary is housed in a safe and secure environment, and this is what makes the difference between Tiny Ts that harm and Tiny Ts that can help us throughout life – and is the reason why some people appear well equipped to deal with the major life events we face at some point.

None of us get through life unscathed, but there always seem to be some people who can weather any storm; people who are inevitably asked, 'How did you cope?' when they have endured what seems to be the unbearable. Countless articles in magazines, autobiographies and life stories on the telly tell us about people who have borne untold trauma, and somehow come out of the other side without completely falling apart. When you look a little closer at these extremely personal accounts, it is not only those who have experienced severe trauma who emerge with a stoic and grounded perspective, but also those who have experienced numerous, smaller yet not insignificant, psychological scrapes and bruises throughout their lives. Hence, for these people their experiences of Tiny T acted as emotional antibodies, protecting them when they came into contact with major life events.

Can Tiny Ts help us 'vaccinate' against emotional trauma?

For serious viruses and pathogens, such as measles, mumps and rubella, we immunise children with a vaccine that imitates the viral infection. This is how vaccines work - we're given a small dose of pathogen because our immune system will wage a response and develop antibodies - i.e. build a bit of immune muscle. The antibodies are our minuscule internal army that remember and develop a strategy for each invader - and crucially know how to defeat it when faced with the threat again.

In the same way, small 'doses' of challenging experiences or hardships during our lifespan can act as emotional vaccines, providing us with important coping strategies that will help us deal with more significant life events in the future. This is why I feel it is so important to investigate Tiny T, as emotional vaccines should be small or medium sized, just as a physiological jab mimics the virus rather than giving us an all-out infection.

Often, we berate ourselves for our 'failures', perceived wrongdoings and rejections, but by learning to see these misdemeanours as necessary to build up psychological immunity, we can let go of negative feelings towards ourselves. By viewing negative events as emotional vaccines, it is possible to take something positive from difficult experiences and galvanise our emotional antibodies.

Some people call this 'bouncing back' after a crappy thing has happened - as if human beings are made out of rubber - and sometimes this is referred to as 'resilience'. But the concept of resilience isn't merely bouncing back unaffected - rather, building a strong, resilient psychological immune system is about having developed personalised coping skills that help you deal with future difficulties in life. It's inevitable that we will experience challenges at some point in our lives - we will lose someone we love, maybe a relationship will fall apart or get made redundant - so to weather these storms we can start now by figuring out our Tiny Ts and becoming mindful of these unique flashpoints and triggers through the Awareness phase of the AAA Approach, and turn these assaults into our very own emotional antibodies.

A Note on Acceptance – It's Not Resignation

When moving forward with the AAA Approach in life, it can be helpful to recognise the differences between acceptance and resignation. I've had many people challenge the second phase of my method as a form of victimhood in which one has to passively grin and bear life's challenges - or even as a type of giving up in the face of life's difficulties. But this is not what acceptance is at all. Acceptance is an open mindset in the journey on this third rock from the sun, with the willingness to experience all the ups and downs, good and bad, with the confidence that you can cope with the troughs and genuinely find joy in the peaks. Acceptance, therefore, is not the same as resignation. Here are some examples of the differences:

Resignation	Acceptance
Psychological rigidity	Psychological flexibility
Feeling disempowered and frozen	Feeling empowered to act
Self-judgement and recrimination	Curating a deep sense of self-compassion
A mindset of scarcity	A mindset of abundance
Giving up/giving in	Recalibrating to take positive action
Tolerating difficulties	Learning from difficulties
Soldiering on	Up-skilling
Avoidance of change	Open to change
Resistance	Recognition
Judgement-led	Value-led

By developing the centre phase of the AAA Approach and accepting life's diverse experiences, we can use Tiny T proactively to build a strong and robust psychological immune system for our future self.

And Why Exactly Does This All Matter?

I would contend that it is a very fortunate person indeed that does not experience the Tiny T Themes that we will discuss in the following chapters: problems such as perfectionism and procrastination, difficulty finding that 'one true love', frustrations over the very nature of being, sleeplessness, emotional eating and feeling depressed. These are quite universal snags in the course of life that was never meant to run smoothly. The reason it matters is that it is only when we understand our own unique constellation of Tiny Ts and how these have impacted on us that we can take steps to turn the page and write our own story. In other words, we can use the AAA Approach and go from Awareness to Action, via a profound sense of acceptance (that's the magic sauce!).

At the end of the day, it's up to us to tackle Tiny T. The examples in this chapter are not intended to lead to accusations of blame or victimhood; instead, it's only once we're aware of our emotional and cognitive drivers that we can make true changes to our beliefs, thought patterns and behaviours. Which will, I assure you, result in a life less controlled by anxieties, self-doubt and low-grade depressive symptoms.

A client once said to me: 'I can feel depressed, but this doesn't mean I have depression.' This is what Tiny T is all about. But there isn't a great deal of help on offer for this more prevalent type of shadowy inner struggle that drains life of its joy. So it's up to us to work through Tiny T and come out the other side with a robust psychological immune system.

Let's Start ...

Sit down, get comfortable (are you comfy? if not, shift position, put some warm socks on or whatever makes you feel safe and secure) and explore the key Tiny T question:

'Think of an event or experience which impacted or changed you in an important way, but you thought it wasn't serious enough to mention?'

Try not to rush your response; be still with yourself and let the image come to you.

What did this introspection bring up for you? Hold this in your consciousness while you read on, and its importance will start to emerge from the heavy mist of your combined memories.

It can be profoundly helpful to write these reflections down – we know from a wealth of research studies that emotional writing and journaling can act as a form of therapy, so in every chapter there will be further journaling prompts. You may want to purchase a Tiny T journal or diary to accompany you on this journey – being able to look back on how we felt and the beliefs we held before starting any therapeutic practice can also aid the process. But if you'd prefer to just think about the Tiny T journaling questions, this is fine too. Take your time.

A note here – if anything in this book makes you feel uneasy, take a moment to sit with that feeling. It's important – vital really – as that feeling is your internal guide trying to give you directions. We all too often ignore or drown out these messages with the noise of life such as chronic 'busyness', distraction or focusing on others' needs, but we do this at our peril. We wouldn't ignore the satnav when trying to get to a certain destination. It's just the same for this journey, so we need to listen to, and follow where possible, the tinny voice of our internal satnav, particularly when it says 'recalculating'. So, before we even get under way, know that you can take a pit stop whenever you need to, and if your mind and body are screaming for you to run away, try the breathing exercise below to help put yourself back in the driver's seat.

Once you're comfortably in this seat we can start to get to the core of why you're not truly flourishing by understanding the common Tiny T Themes in the rest of this book. Throughout we'll use the AAA **Approach** of **Awareness, Acceptance and Action** in my solution-focused method so that you will come away with more than just something to chat about over the water-cooler. This will genuinely change your perspective, and life.

Breathing exercise for learning to sit with uncomfortable feelings

This is one of the simplest, yet most powerful exercises I use. Over time, we tend to get into the habit of stress breathing through our chest – check with yourself and see if you do this by placing one hand on your upper chest and one on your belly. Which hand is rising and falling? If it's the one on your chest, your body is in a stressed state, which is not at all surprising as we start to explore Tiny T. But we can manage this by activating our parasympathetic nervous system through diaphragmatic breathing.

- First, locate your diaphragm – move the hand on your belly so that your smallest finger is directly above your belly button. Now your diaphragmatic muscles should be directly under your palm.
- Keep your other hand on your chest.
- Inhale slowly and steadily through your nose and count to three, drawing the breath down towards your tailbone.
- Next, exhale slowly and steadily for four counts while repeating the word 'calm' in your mind.

- With each inhale, feel your breath expand your belly.
- With the exhale feel your stomach dip back in.
- Now the hand on your chest should be still.

A good tip is to look at the way babies breathe – before they've experienced Tiny T, tried to squeeze into skinny jeans or even become aware of such hellish things, babies naturally breathe through their diaphragm. It's glorious to see their chubby bellies protruding and dropping back – we can learn an awful lot from babies!

CHAPTER 1 TAKE-HOME TINY T MESSAGE

Tiny T trauma can arise from many areas of life, and act as a slow-burn to our emotional health. However, when we understand how these small mental cuts and scrapes have affected us, and the cumulative impact of a life of unresolved Tiny T, we can use these experiences to build a robust psychological immune system through the AAA Approach. This form of emotional strength-training creates resilience, which helps us cope with bigger issues, such as major life events, that we will all experience at some point in our lives.

CHAPTER 2

The happily never after ...

In this chapter we will explore:

- definitions of happiness
- medical gaslighting
- toxic positivity
- the hedonic treadmill
- how understanding the Big Seven can help you create lasting contentment.

When we look around at our friends, acquaintances and everyone on social media, it can seem as if they're having the time of their lives. Smiling, carefree faces appearing around every digital corner who seem to have this 'happiness' thing figured out. So, I want to ask you: are you happy? That seems like such a simple question, yet arriving at an answer can be far from straightforward. And this, of course, has so much to do with your unique collection of Tiny Ts. To unravel this reverse-image fairy tale, let's start with a story ...

Anna was smart, she was welcoming and, by all accounts, when people looked at her, they smiled inside a little. She was bubbly, helpful, friendly to everyone – in fact she was one of those people we all gravitate towards as her positivity beamed from her rosy cheeks. Never a bad word to say about anyone, so on the surface Anna seemed like one happy soul.

Yet, here she was, sitting on the slightly stiff chairs in my office being as polite as humanly possible. Anna explained to me that she had a 'brilliant, amazing, fantastic' job in a 360-degree marketing and PR firm with 'the most wonderful group of people', close-knit clusters of school and university friends, and an unreservedly supportive family. She visited her parents in the country at least once a month, with a weekly call home from her shared flat in the city, and felt loved and cared for.

But when I put to Anna those three seemingly innocuous words, 'Are you happy?', her eyes shadowed over, and a streak of pain started to spread like a rash across her delicately freckled skin.

Anna looked down at her wringing hands and quietly uttered: 'I don't know.' She went on to say she 'should' be happy, she wanted to be happy, but she just didn't feel happy. And this is why she came to see me, as the profound lack of happiness was torturing Anna to her core, and she just couldn't fathom it.

On the face of it, Anna's case seemed quite perplexing – there were no obvious Big T traumatic events in her history and even when exploring Tiny Ts, Anna insisted there wasn't a darn thing – she adamantly asserted that she had a picture-perfect childhood, wanted for absolutely nothing and could not fault her parents at all. But herein lay the emergence of a clue to Anna's Tiny Ts ...

The philosophy of happiness

Although the study of happiness is a relatively recent addition to psychological theory and research, in philosophy the greats have been exploring this emotion for some time and unpicking the different forms of good mood.

In philosophy, *hedonism* is the pursuit of happiness and pleasure, where feeling happy, excited and carefree as much of the time as possible is the primary goal of life. This is contrasted to *eudaimonism*, in which the goal of life is more about self-actualisation where we strive to achieve our personal ambition and develop our unique potential to the highest degree. Hedonism, therefore, is based on a positive feeling such as pleasure *in the moment*, whereas eudaimonism is more about finding a sense of meaning and purpose.

While you'll always find commentators arguing one side or another, most positive psychologists including myself agree that we need both to truly flourish in life.

AAA Approach Step 1: Awareness

Next, I asked Anna what she thought happiness was. 'You just know when you're happy, don't you?' was her reply. But this answer was definitely much more of a question, as her voice trembled a touch in her response, which is why it was useful to start her AAA journey by exploring the notion of happiness.

What Is Happiness Anyway?

For a long time, we didn't study happiness at all in psychology. Just as the less severe, yet still depleting mental health outcomes that are outlined in this book were ignored, positive states and emotions weren't given much attention at all during the early phase of psychology as a field of research and professional practice. It really wasn't until the development of positive psychology in the late 1990s by psychologist Dr Martin Seligman that we began to try to understand concepts such as happiness. Martin Seligman himself started his career investigating learnt helplessness, which is a characteristic feature of depression, and I remember at the time being pretty surprised that he had pivoted and was now the main proponent of this new so-called 'positive movement' in psychology.

But actually, it made perfect sense ... Dr Seligman has said that his work up to this point, which concentrated on 'the really bad stuff',[7] had positioned him perfectly to start investigating the missing piece of the mental health puzzle - namely the positive. He famously told the audience at his inaugural American Psychological Association presidential address that psychology had moved too far from its original purpose, which is to enhance people's lives, and instead had become fixated on the 'bad' rather than focusing equally on the 'good'.

And this was part of the confusion that Anna experienced - she had felt unworthy of help because there wasn't the obvious really bad stuff, as Seligman put it. She didn't think that she had a specific mental illness (and I would wholeheartedly agree with this) but all she could find when she searched online or looked for information through healthcare services and charities were serious mental health conditions. This is without a doubt because, as Seligman highlighted, we had become too focused on 'curing' mental illness – there was just no discussion of the subtleties within human lived experience. We simply didn't study happiness until relatively recently.

Isn't happiness just a feeling?

Early researchers in positive psychology referred to happiness as 'subjective wellbeing', which was simply the presence, frequency and intensity of pleasant emotions (so that's joy, serenity, pride, awe, love, among others, collectively known as 'positive affect'), the relative absence of unpleasant emotions or 'negative affect' (e.g. sadness, anger, frustration, jealousy) and an overall feeling of life satisfaction. Life satisfaction is more than a feeling, however; it's a mental judgement on how content someone is in their life and, like all judgements and perceptions, can be affected by our present situation, environment, past experiences and more. Both positive and negative affect are also influenced by many factors, including physiological and behavioural features such as hunger, thirst, whether you've had a good night's sleep – so many things!

What Makes Us Happy? The 'Big Seven'

As the field of positive psychology expanded, more and more research was being conducted to understand exactly what makes us happy. It was becoming clear that happiness was more than just a sensation, so the focus now was why some people had it, and others didn't - and why it mattered so much.

It has been suggested there are seven central factors to happiness, which are: family and close relationships (seen as the most important factor to happiness), financial situation, work (separate from finances as it contributes to self-respect and self-esteem), community and friends, health, personal freedom and personal values.[8] However, it's not merely the presence of these seven factors in your life, but how personally important they are to you that matters. This conceptualisation of happiness is often useful as it shows us what contributes towards happiness - and, in effect, what we can do to make ourselves happier.

Therefore, to help unravel a sense of confusion or dissatisfaction in someone's present life, I like to start with this simple auditing exercise to increase Awareness in this phase of the AAA Approach. You can try it too if you've been searching for your happiness pot of gold at the end of the rainbow.

Exercise: Life Assessment

Each of the following is an area of life that you may or may not feel is particularly satisfactory at the moment. For each area, give a rating out of 10, with the highest score reflecting an area where you feel particularly fulfilled, or nearer a value of 0 if it's a space that feels rather wanting. Remember, there are no judgements here at all, so take a bit of time to think about each category in terms of how it feels to *you*, right now.

- Significant other/partner
- Personal values
- Leisure and hobbies
- Personal freedom
- Career
- Money or financial security
- Health
- Friends and family

Now, have a look at your scores – does anything jump out at you? Any surprises here?

Look at your highest two *and* lowest two scores, note these down and ask yourself why you gave these ratings.

Spend a couple of minutes on this, no need to rush your response – allow it to be genuine.

For Anna, her highest scores were friends/family and personal values, and the reasons she gave these scores were echoed in what she had told me in our initial session. This finding was important of course, but not nearly as telling as her lowest scores, which were health and personal freedom – the latter of which Anna seemed reluctant, ashamed almost, to admit.

This definitely twinged something in Anna, and when we explored first why her health category was rated so unsatisfactorily her Tiny Ts began to emerge ...

When working with Anna we found that she had concentrated her life almost entirely on work and family, as these were key to her personal values, but it was becoming clear that she was finding it challenging to balance these areas of her life. When exploring Anna's Life Assessment in order to dig a little deeper into her Tiny Ts, an illuminating experience came to light. When Anna was a young teenager, she experienced a lengthy bout of ill health. Every doctor she saw fobbed her off as countless blood and other tests came back negative – to such an extent that she questioned whether she really was ill and eventually thought it must all be in her head (see the box on medical gaslighting, page 50). Anna missed quite a bit of school and started to feel like she was falling behind not only with schoolwork, but with life itself. She gradually improved but was left with a sense of never quite being able to catch up, even when objectively she was on a par with her peers. Have you ever had those dreams in which you just miss something, perhaps a bus or train, and you're shouting for it to 'STOP! Come back, that's my ride!', running, running, desperately running, but knowing in the pit of your stomach that you've missed it forever? Anna had that same nauseous feeling like the bus-speeding-away-into-the-distance-dream, which seemed to be with her no matter what she did, how many awards and promotions she won or milestones she met (more on this in Chapter 10). Her parents were supportive, although desperately worried, and repeatedly told Anna it was all ok, they just wanted her to be happy.

When Anna's health began to restore in her later teens, she dedicated all her efforts to trying to be the person she was before she became ill – the happy, carefree girl – so that she could finally measure up to her loving, patient and devoted parents' hopes. The problem was that no one actually tells us how to be happy – it's not a subject taught in school, there are no Happiness Lessons, it's assumed that everyone knows how to be happy. So, in Anna's young mind, going back to her teen-age-hood dream of a creative career seemed the best way to achieve this feat.

This is why on her monthly visits to her loving parents, a darkness hovered over Anna's heart – for she knew every day she was letting them down as she simply didn't feel happy most of the time, and was now lying to them when she gushed about the virtues of her fabulous life. All they ever told her was that they wanted her to be happy, and this was the one thing she couldn't grasp, no matter how hard she tried. Here we were in the present, where Anna felt that she had achieved what she'd fantasised about all those months when she was ill in bed, but not only did she feel unfulfilled, she also knew deep down that she had been putting her health at risk. Anna had neglected some important areas of life in pursuit of never-ending happiness, and because this was now starting to affect her health, she was essentially back full circle to the most difficult time in her life when she was unwell and couldn't find any answers.

In Anna's mind, she felt she was letting down the very people who had supported her through her gloomiest down days – in terms of both her happiness and her ability to stay healthy. In this Awareness stage, however, it was important not to gloss over Anna's experience with health issues – in particular, how difficulties in finding a diagnosis may have acted as part of her Tiny T Happily Never After Theme.

Focus on Tiny T: Medical gaslighting

The term 'gaslighting' denotes when someone undermines you to such an extent that you start to question your beliefs, experiences and even grasp of reality. Gaslighting is most commonly cited in intimate relationships and is a type of coercive control. This is a form of psychological abuse at its worst, but there are more subtle forms of gaslighting in other situations, such as healthcare. When a doctor fails to listen to a patient, their experience of symptoms, and 'psychologises' a set of medical signs and symptoms, this can be a type of gaslighting. It's a much more frequent phenomenon for women and is one reason why many conditions that either only or predominately affect females take an unacceptable length of time and struggle to be diagnosed. For example, on average it still takes four to eleven years for women to be diagnosed with the gynaecological condition endometriosis, and in this time the debilitating pain and other symptoms can cause havoc in women's and their families' lives including irreversible fertility issues.[9] Even when men and women present with the same symptoms, women tend to be less believed and have to wait longer for treatment due to gender bias.[10] Medical gaslighting is therefore all the more insidious, as it can lead people to suffer in silence and fail to seek help for treatable conditions.

Here we started to get to grips with how a constellation of Tiny Ts can slowly build over time, and why it can be so hard to pinpoint feelings of life dissatisfaction - or unhappiness. In Anna's case, one surprising revelation came to the fore - her experience with medical gaslighting had not only affected her confidence in knowing her body, it had spilled over and damaged her confidence in other areas of her life as well. As always with Tiny Ts, Anna did not feel that her experiences were severe enough to warrant attention, but her struggle to find a diagnosis had made her feel her illness was her fault. Anna tried so hard to hide this sense of shame with a veneer of happiness, via a shiny, fantastic creative career - one that was beginning to lose its sheen as it was positively toxic.

Focus on Tiny T: The curse of toxic positivity

Toxic positivity is the belief that, regardless of the situation, we should have a positive and upbeat mindset. Everyday examples of this are when people say 'stay positive!', 'keep your chin up', 'look on the bright side' no matter what you're going through. Although we know there are health benefits of happiness and other positive states such as optimism, making others or ourselves feel a sense of shame for sharing truly difficult experiences is detrimental to mental health.

However, toxic positivity is often not intentionally malicious; rather, many of us simply don't know how to comfort and support others when they are coping with life's challenges. We think it's helpful to reassure our loved ones that things will be better tomorrow, but this can make people feel isolated and unseen. Just as sitting with challenging feelings can be incredibly tough, though absolutely necessary for the individual, so is seeing someone we care for in emotional pain.

But brushing aside pain and sorrow is not the answer. Toxic positivity is harmful as it does not allow people to process their lived experience and therefore regulate their emotions. At best, toxic positivity can make someone feel rather confused, sometimes bubbling out as irritation and not quite knowing where this irritability comes from. At worst, it will result in people being wary or too afraid to speak honestly and openly about their feelings and experiences for fear of shame. This can be accompanied by feelings of anxiety and a sense of isolation, and be a form of Tiny T in itself.

So next time someone starts to tell you about a difficult experience or feeling, rather than say, 'Oh, you'll feel better tomorrow', listen. Just listen. We don't need to give advice or try to think of things to say to make someone feel better – all we need is to genuinely listen to what they are saying. We've lost the art of listening somewhat, so it can take practice – when you're with a friend or loved one who is opening up to you, you might find your mind rushing ahead, thinking and sculpting how to reply. If this happens, gently nudge your mind back to the conversation and be present with your loved one. This will help much more than any well-meaning but ill-conceived guidance on the importance of a positive mindset.

AAA Approach Step 2: Acceptance

Now that we are well on our way to connecting the dots between Tiny Ts and why we may prioritise certain areas of life at the expense of others, it's common to see people become much calmer and less frantic - there's no longer a need to put on a happy mask all the time as understanding of our emotional world increases. This is a good point to start the next phase of the AAA Approach - Acceptance - to foster this new-found awareness.

Exercise: Life plotting

I value the simplest visual techniques more than anything in my work through the AAA Approach. This is an incredibly easy way to come to terms with opposing forces in life – by plotting them against each other. Start by taking the lowest and highest scored areas on your Life Assessment – for Anna this was work and health – and plot the current state of these areas as a point that meets within X and Y axes. For Anna, her workload was high and health was low, represented by the triangle on the graph. Try to use an empty graph so that you can see the relationship between health and work, or workload, for example. Like all the exercises in this book, it does take some honesty and openness, but as you can see below, Anna was able to be candid about how, when her workload was at its highest, her health started to dimmish. Next, try to move the plot point and see what happens to the relationship between these life areas – here, when Anna lessened her workload, she could see that her health would probably improve – demonstrated by the cross on the graph.

Finally, Anna recalled her past experience when her workload was much lower, and it was during these times that her health was at its best (the star on the graph). Have a go yourself and plot a few points to see how changing the amount of one life area impacts on the other. Anna found a clear linear (straight line) correlation between workload and her health, but for many people the relationship might look like a U-shaped curve, where there's a sweet spot between two life areas – in other words, don't worry if your graph looks different from this example as we're on a journey towards Acceptance in this phase.

Now Anna was beginning to accept a couple of stark realisations: (1) that only focusing on her dream career was endangering her health, and (2) maybe the aim of being happy, in and of itself, wasn't all it was cracked up to be.

What have you discovered in your life plot? Is one area taking precedence over another to the detriment of your overall quality

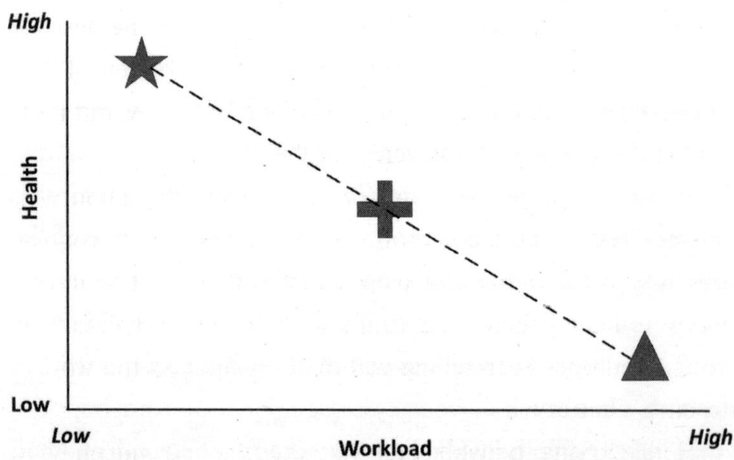

Figure 2.1: Life plot

of life? One of my clients, Cleo, found this exercise challenging as it demonstrated that she had spent the vast majority of her time, energy and resources on her family, and now that her children didn't need her so much, she found other areas of her life wanting. Cleo wouldn't have changed her parenting style for the world, but it had been hard for her to accept that in the hustle and bustle of child-rearing she kinda lost herself. This emotional and psychological work can be tough, darn tough, so take a moment for the breathing exercise in Chapter 1 if any of the techniques we explore hit you particularly hard.

The problem with just wanting to be happy

It's such a universal phrase – 'I just want you to be happy' – and it seems to be not merely innocuous, but warm, caring and supportive. However, this statement may be one of the most damaging sentiments of modern times. Although some people would perhaps look on in horror at my saying so, there is a fundamental problem with just wanting someone else, or ourselves, to be happy. It's akin to saying to children, 'I want you to go and capture a beautiful, exquisite butterfly, put it in a jar and keep hold of it forever.'

While butterflies do exist (we're not talking about rare species here, just the common winged insects) and it would be possible to catch one and keep it in a container, it would not live very long – then, once again, you'd be butterfly-less when your loved ones keep telling you the best thing in the world is to have a butterfly.

Hence, trying to just be happy all the time can morph into a form of Tiny T as it surely sets people up for a lifetime of not feeling good enough. If all your parents ever wanted for you was something you never seem to be able to keep hold of, then you must be a complete and utter failure – right?

Well, no, and this is why it's so helpful to understand exactly how happiness works.

The hedonic treadmill

The theory of hedonic adaptation,[11] also known as the hedonic treadmill, is all about trying to capture that butterfly. Some people describe it as chasing rainbows, but that's not quite right, because on the hedonic treadmill you can experience happiness, i.e. capture the butterfly, whereas if you're chasing rainbows you can never quite hold in your hands the colourful illusion. Happiness is not an illusion; it is a true experience, but the hedonic adaptation principle states that we will always revert back to our baseline level of happiness after a brief burst of pleasure. Furthermore, we get somewhat accustomed to the feeling of happiness when it comes from the same source, and so it wears off over time.

There are some amazing studies that have looked at this, including what happens to people's level of happiness after both incredibly fortunate and conversely life-limiting events. A year after winning the lottery, winners are only on average slightly more satisfied with their lives than they were before the windfall – sometimes they are actually unhappier and say they wish they'd never won the money. On the other side of the coin, people who had been in life-changing accidents and became paraplegic or quadriplegic report only marginally lower levels of happiness than their peers.[12]

This also illustrates another secret about happiness: we tend to overestimate how favourable *and* unfavourable events or life changes will make us feel. Known as the impact bias, things that we believe will make us feel over the moon do spike happiness, but not as much or for as long as we thought. Similarly, with those circumstances that we fear may not be as devastating as we imagine. But there's also another secret I want to share with you ...

... we're basically not meant to be happy all the time

Take one minute and soak that in - we are not meant to be constantly happy.

But surely we're supposed to be happy, right? If not, what's the point in existing? As boring as it is, we're really just supposed to survive long enough to breed and keep the human race going. This thought can at first seem rather defeatist, but I actually think it's liberating - because once you let go of the desire to be happy all the time, you can start to live an authentic and present existence. With this, it's possible to create a life where calm, profound contentment is your norm, rather than the boom-and-bust of the hedonic treadmill.

The happiness cash cow

The global wellness industry, which includes positive and motivational thinking, all manner of classes and products to make you happier, and countless mind–body practices, is now worth many trillions of US dollars. A trillion – that's one million million. That's a whole lotta aspirational quotes slurping up our hard-earned cash. In a sense, the wellness industry is the new, more politically correct face of the beauty industry – and it uses the same psychological tricks to keep us coming back for more. The central illusion is that we should be happy – all of the time.

The very reason why so much is being made on 'wellness' is the precise fact that we're not programmed to be constantly and consistently happy, so it will always be a futile quest. But along this brave expedition through life, we are constantly and consistently told that we must be happy – and if we aren't, there's something fundamentally wrong with us that needs fixing.

So we want to be happy – and those brief moments of pure bliss are absolutely lovely. But they are few and far between, which is why it's vital to savour each and every spark of joy.

AAA Approach Step 3: Action

Actions here are all about appreciating those fleeting moments of happiness and other positive emotions, while working on the longer-term balancing act of the Big Seven factors (family and close relationships; financial situation; work; community and friends; health; personal freedom; and personal values) to produce sustainable contentment.

Quick tips to brighten your day

Sprinkling your day with small moments of happiness will enhance your wellbeing, with the acceptance that we need to experience the entire range of human emotion for a fully lived life (more on this in the next chapter). Here are some short sharp ways to lift your mood without getting caught back on the hedonic treadmill:

Make yourself a compliments jar: Get an empty jar and every time someone gives you a compliment, jot it down on a piece of paper and pop it in your personal compliments jar. You can also write down qualities that you like about yourself (hard, I know, but it gets easier with practice) or ask a loved one to tell you the qualities they value in you and add these to your jar. Think about minor achievements too – these needn't be significant feats; it can be better to focus on the little things such as finishing a piece of artwork or replying patiently to a rude email! Then, next time you need a pick-me-up, close your eyes and grab a compliment to brighten your day and build self-confidence.

Smile: Yes, it's as simple as that! You don't even have to feel like smiling to create the positive benefits of a frown turned upside down. Researchers at the University of Kansas found that even manufactured smiling can make you feel better.[13] But genuine smiles are more powerful in their mood-boosting effects, and I find the best way to elicit a real smile is by making someone else smile. French neurologist Guillaume-Benjamin-Amand Duchenne found that genuine smiles – known as the 'Duchenne' smile – use muscles around the eyes and mouth for expression, whereas a polite smile only changes the shape of the mouth. So, give yourself the challenge of making someone truly smile a Duchenne smile to ignite a flash of happiness in both your and someone else's day.

Posture-up: Take a moment and consider how people's bodies look when they're happy – how they stand and hold themselves; in other words, their posture. Perhaps open-chested, back straight, head up, welcoming the world? Now compare this to how people look when they're experiencing somewhat more unpleasant emotions. Are they hunched maybe, emanating a sense of being closed off and unapproachable? It's often said that where the mind goes the body will follow, but this works both ways - changing our posture and body language can directly impact on how we feel. Next time you feel in need of a lift, copy the posture of happiness.[14]

Longer-term contentment prescription

To work more on sustainable personal wellbeing, which includes life satisfaction, we can go back to the Life Assessment earlier in this chapter. By working on the areas of your life that are lacking, it's possible to move from a hedonistic, in-the-moment experience of happiness to the more profound sense of self-actualisation within eudaimonism (see the box on page 43). Look again at your scoring and ask:

- Which area do you feel motivated to work on right now?
- Why did you choose this category?
- What would a score of 10 look like in this life area *to you*?
- If the score is low, what would it take to raise it by just two points?

It is now after progressing through the first two phases of the AAA Approach - Awareness and Acceptance - that motivation is highest, and this is why the process is so important to follow the AAA Approach. Making changes to your life requires effort, but know you have the knowledge and compassionate self-support to be able to target the areas of your Life Assessment that need a little TLC. In this final stage, Anna was in a place where her Tiny Ts no longer had such a hold over her and she came up with the following action points to move the life area that was lacking, her health, from a score of 3 to a 5:

- Be honest with her family about her life – that there are good and happy moments, but that work can be hard and challenging sometimes.
- Manage some people-pleasing tendencies, both at work and with family.
- Schedule some rest breaks into the day, even if it's just a walk outside during lunchtime.

There are some more suggestions about balancing the Big Seven later in this book, so that you may travel towards a more contented life.

Dr Meg's journaling prompts for sustainable contentment

1 Bring to mind three everyday, simple things that bring you a sense of joy and explore these in your journal.

2 In what ways do you prioritise self-care on a daily basis? If the answer is 'I don't', think of three small acts of kindness you could create for yourself and note these down.

3 What makes you feel most alive, inspired and motivated?

CHAPTER 2 TAKE-HOME TINY T MESSAGE

Wanting to be happy all the time is about as useful as a chocolate teapot, but we can develop a more profound sense of wellbeing that doesn't rely on the never-ending hedonic treadmill. By creating balance in the life areas that are important to us, we don't have to rely on hedonistic happiness hits – instead, we can grow a firm foundation of contentment to build a sustainable emotional life.

CHAPTER 3

Comfortably numb

In this chapter we will explore:

- the differences between depression and languishing
- the mental health continuum
- emotional literacy and the Emotobiome
- toxic masculinity
- how experiencing a wide range of emotions feeds the Emotobiome and strengthens the psychological immune system.

We hear the term 'depression' thrown around as if these three syllables hold the problem, solution and everything in between for all to see. Even though the rates of depression have, and still are, increasing, most people, thankfully, will not experience this diagnosable mental health disorder. Rather, we suffer from a type of emotional detachment, more often than not due to Tiny Ts. In this chapter we will explore our comfortably numb existence, and how we can break free from this anaesthetised state.

A new client came to me, with his shoulders hunched over, eyes to the floor and voice energy-less. Noah didn't want to be here, he said as much, but:

> *I was having a pint with one of my oldest mates, and he told me I had to do something. He said our drink was awkward, like he was sitting with a stranger, and God love him, he actually said outright he's worried about me. So here I am, I don't know what else to tell you.*

Some people come into my office and start sharing even before we've had a chance to say hello, and don't stop until the clock strikes an hour. Others, though, find it difficult to verbalise what they're going through - and Noah was part of the latter group of people. However, Noah did state in a moment of space and silence (where a great deal of therapeutic work is achieved): '*You think I'm depressed - I'm not depressed. I'm too intelligent to be depressed.*'

Hence, here we started our journey together. Apart from the fact that mental health issues are still stigmatised - we've done really well to talk about mental health in the past five to ten years, but there is still a long way to go - it was significant that Noah could say what he was *not*, yet struggled to identify in meaningful terms the emotions he was experiencing.

We sat with this a little longer and finally Noah said he was 'numb' - and had been this way for so long now, he couldn't find any other way to describe it.

What is depression?

It's completely and utterly normal, indeed part of being human, to feel a bit low sometimes. In fact, we're more wired to experience negative emotions than positive ones. This is because, in evolutionary terms, it was best to notice the worst situations, in order to survive. Even though life is much safer than it was for early humans, our brains haven't ditched this negative hardwiring. So how is it possible to tell if feeling rather *Eeyore-like* is a sign of something more serious and in need of treatment, such as clinical depression? These are the signs that the way you're feeling may be related more to an underlying depressive disorder than to Tiny Ts:

Over the past two weeks have you been:

- Feeling sad, empty or hopeless most of the time.
- No longer interested in daily activities that used to give you enjoyment.
- Unable to sleep or seem to sleep too much, including during the day.
- Feeling tired and low on energy more than usual.
- Either not bothered about food at all, or eating more than usual with weight gain or loss of 5 per cent per month.
- Feeling like you've let yourself or others down, and that you're a failure.
- Finding it hard to concentrate, even on easy things such as watching a regular TV show.
- Feeling fidgety or restless, or the opposite, that your movements and speech are slower than usual.

- Having suicidal thoughts or repeatedly thinking about death, with or without overt suicide attempts.
- Finding it difficult to carry on your usual daily activities and responsibilities such as work, school and family roles because of the above symptoms.

Could it be high-functioning depression?

You may have found some of the symptoms above a touch too familiar for comfort, but they haven't stopped your normal activities as per the final identifier. This may be a sign of 'high-functioning depression', a mental health manifestation that can often be undiagnosed or misdiagnosed. This is because the way depression is spotted often comes with observable difficulties in keeping up with family, friends and the house, maintaining performance at work and engaging in much-loved hobbies or sports. In other words, you might be suffering terribly on the inside, but on the outside everything seems fine. By no means does this ability to carry on equate to a less severe form of depression, but it does make it harder to recognise. If you're finding all your 'activities of daily living', as we like to call them, a monumental effort and have been experiencing the other listed symptoms in this chapter, do seek out help. All too often it's only when the house of cards starts falling and we can't seem to grasp our foundations that the possibility of a mental health issue is recognised. Early intervention truly can improve depressive symptoms, whether you are high-functioning or not – I know it's much easier said than done but do reach out, as there are arms to catch you before you hit the bottom.

Mental health issues such as depression are incredibly common – in fact, if you don't or have never experienced difficulties with your mental health, it's pretty damn likely that someone you know has. But ... if instead you just feel rather rotten, quite a lot but not all of the time, we need to take a closer look at Tiny Ts and the topic of **emotional literacy**.

AAA Approach Step 1: Awareness

Although Noah didn't meet the criteria for depression, he was certainly still struggling with the Tiny T Numb Theme – and hence we needed to start with the first step of the AAA Approach, that of Awareness. As mentioned in the introduction, there's a wide gap between mental health and mental illness, and we tend to only give treatment for the most serious cases in conventional medicine. This leaves huge swathes of people who are not thriving, yet not quite depressed enough to merit professional help. This is unacceptable in my view, as we all deserve a life in which we are flourishing, rather than languishing.

The topic of languishing became popular during the first year of the Covid-19 pandemic, but it has been used in the field of positive psychology for some time. If we look at the continuum below, we can start to unpick the differences not only between mental health and illness, but also between levels of engagement.[15] When Noah and I looked at this model together, and I asked him to pinpoint how he was experiencing life at the moment, he said somewhere in between languishing and coasting, but he was functioning on a day-to-day basis. He could function in the sense of going to work, feeding himself,

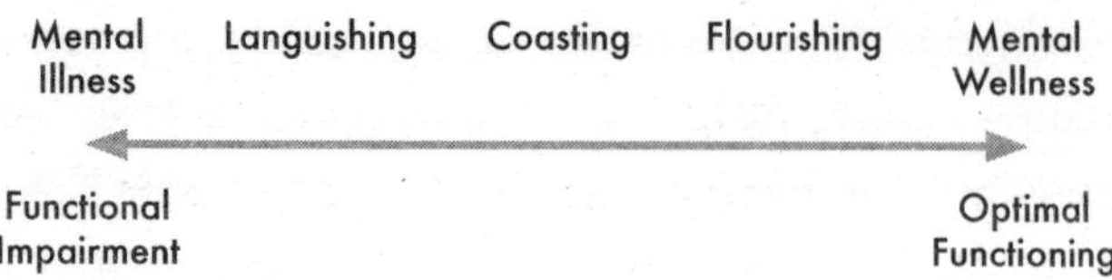

Figure 3.1: Mental health continuum

and so forth, but it was a wake-up call when his mate said he was acting like something out of a low-budget zombie movie. He admitted that he never thought of mental health in this way, and it was at this point that I posed the Tiny T question to begin to unravel Noah's constellation of Tiny Ts.

As Noah found it tough to talk about his emotions, a smoother way to get to the bottom of his Tiny T was by focusing first on the practical aspects of his life. Noah revealed that he wanted to find a partner but didn't think it was feasible any more to meet someone in a bar or at work - the usual places people used to hook up. So he decided to try online dating, with high expectations as he felt that at least this way he could save himself the embarrassment of being rejected in public. 'How wrong I was - instead of getting blown out once on a night in town, I was blown out ten or more times *a day*.' The belief that this enormous pool of potential dates would increase his chances of finding someone he clicked with turned into the sourest experience of a seemingly unending number of rebuffs. While it was exciting at first because there was no one in his immediate or extended social circle that he could see himself with, Noah said that after a while it felt frankly depressing. I asked if he shared this experience with his friend - 'Of course not, he'd rip the p*ss out of me!' In addition to the online dating Tiny T, this was also an important clue to Noah's numbness.

Focus on Tiny T: The horrors of online dating

Dating apps have boiled down human courtship to a swipe of a finger – and although this might work for some people, for many others this appearance-only process misses out all the nuance, complexity and multifaceted texture of meeting a romantic partner. While we would evaluate someone visually in a bar or at a work meeting within a few seconds, we would also have the opportunity to interact with them. They might be funny, have your same rather extreme taste in *Star Wars* backstories, or you might just be able to see something in their eyes that a filtered photo could never capture. Online dating not only strips courtship down to its bare bones; it does so in a brutal fashion – often leaving people feeling insecure, negatively preoccupied with social media and exhibiting some of the symptoms of depression.

Why Does Tiny T Make It So Hard to Describe Our Feelings?

Noah and his mate were clearly close, so why was it so hard for him to share his feelings? As children, many of us were told 'not to make a fuss', 'please just be good', 'there's no point crying over spilled milk!' or, perhaps worst of all, 'man up'. In a sense, this type of behaviour modification is useful when a child is throwing a tantrum for no apparent reason, but when it teaches us to associate a sense of shame for feeling and expressing our 'negative' emotions, Tiny T is formed. Another client named Lilly mentioned that her mum had experienced major depression, and so she went to great lengths as a child to try to 'make Mum better' - which was impossible of course - and so she felt fearful of sharing any of her darker thoughts or feelings with anyone, even now as an adult. Hence, in both cases, Tiny T indentations came early in home life where anything but a stoical outlook was perceived as unacceptable, or dangerous in Lilly's example. Keep calm and carry on, best foot forward, chin up, etc. etc. ... ad infinitum.

Let's take a pause here though and consider for a moment that perhaps there are no inherently 'good' or 'bad' emotions; rather, all feelings are useful information. What if our caregivers were aware of this and were able to help us to also understand it. Would their caregiving methods and the subsequent outcome on our lives have been different? Everyone gets angry, sad and frustrated from time to time, but rather than hide these emotions, what if we had learnt how to process them in a healthy and adaptive way? The secret here is that the difference between a fulfilling life and one that constantly feels like a let-down is all about how we manage these emotions - not the exclusion of 'bad' feelings.

In extreme cases, difficulty in pinpointing how we're feeling is known as emotional blindness, or by the more medical term 'alexithymia'. Emotional blindness has been linked to the above type of emotional blunting during childhood and adolescence as well as to frontal lobe brain injury (luckily, very few of us will suffer the latter). In some people with alexithymia, positive emotions can be identified but negative feelings are a mystery, whereas for others there is universal emotional blindness. In general, though, the vast majority of people can describe very strong emotions, but the more subtle and understated ones are harder to label. This is what I call 'emotional literacy', and it matters a great deal, as being well versed in emotional vocabulary can help with navigating Tiny Ts and getting the most out of life.

But it's hard if you've never been taught how to discuss feelings, or if, as in Noah's case, this type of expression was actively shut down. Indeed, Noah noted that he did find talking about emotions difficult – 'men just don't do that, ya know' – which links into another piece in his Tiny T puzzle.

Focus on Tiny T: Big boys don't cry – toxic masculinity

Although there is targeted support now for men, help-seeking behaviour such as talking to someone about their difficulties is still far lower than in other groups. Toxic masculinity, wherein ultra-male characteristics such as toughness, aggression and certainly no tears are prized, is still alive and kicking in many societies. In fact, I would suggest it's getting worse – just take a look at cultural media such as movies, music and social posts and it's easy to see that although there is evidence of a more nuanced approach to what it means to be a man, the cartoon version of 'maleness' is there for all to see. We know that societal norms such as this have an impact on help-seeking behaviour.[16] It is in this way that toxic masculinity acts as a Tiny T, making it hard for men to talk about their lived experience and feelings with others, or even recognise some emotions at all.

AAA Approach Step 2: Acceptance

For many of us, it can be incredibly tricky to verbalise our feelings - in essence, our emotional literacy may be low - so it's useful to start slowly with the following exercise to explore emotions non-verbally. Here, we can start moving onto the second phase of the AAA Approach: Acceptance. Working with emotions can be quite confronting, so this is a good place to start if you are feeling overwhelmed by any feeling, whether it is one that is typically deemed positive or negative.

Exercise: Emotion caricatures

Have you ever been on holiday and had your caricature drawn? Your slightly crooked teeth sketched out to look goofy and delicately frizzy hair depicted as if you just stuck your finger in an electrical socket? I can't draw for sugar, but this exercise always reminds me of those unbelievably expensive holiday treats and how magnifying a feature of an emotion can bring it to life in a way that many of us find difficult with words.

To start, think of the last 'positive' intense emotion you experienced. We all represent feelings differently, so there is no right or wrong here – it's simply what comes to you.

- Next, grab a piece of paper and draw a simple outline of a body.
- Now, explore where this emotion resides in your body and draw it there.
- Think about exactly what the emotion looks like – what are its contours? Prickly or soft, for example? Draw this.

- What colour is this emotion? For example, spicy red or deep blue? Draw this.
- What direction is this emotion headed towards in the body? Outwards or inwards? Up or down? Draw this.
- What temperature is this emotion? Tepid or warm, scalding or freezing? Draw this.
- What speed is this emotion travelling? Fast or slow? Draw this.
- Now do exactly the same but this time with a 'negative' emotion.
- Observe the difference between the two images.
- Now, tweak the colour, shape and so forth, and see how this feels for each one.

What your two sketches will (hopefully!) show is that emotions differ in many respects. We call these 'sub-modalities', and once located they can be adjusted – think of it like zooming in and out with a camera lens. You have control, so go back to your drawings and alter their temperature, speed, colour, and such like. How does that feel now? You can use your auditory sense here also and conjure up the sounds and volume associated with emotions, and then turn up or down their volume, pitch and tempo.

For Noah and Lilly, using this exercise helped them to make the first tentative steps to raising their emotional literacy. In the early stages of making the connection between feelings of 'nothing-ness', beliefs about the self and how our experiences have affected both our feelings and perceptions of the world, patience and self-compassion is paramount. You may start to see that, over a lifetime, the reinforcement of certain beliefs has acted like a slow-burn, until all that is left is, well, nothing – just a numb void.

The Emotobiome – It's All About Variety

Low levels of emotional literacy, which have become so prolific, are damaging because as human beings we need to experience and express a wide range of emotions - and accept that it's unreservedly 'ok' to **feel our feels**. I like to make the comparison to the gut microbiome - in the past few years we've all become rather obsessed with our tummy flora and fauna, feeding it probiotics, kimchi and a vast assortment of fermented foods (or perhaps just reading about these things while stubbornly chomping on a chocolate bar!). Researchers, scientists and TV docs have told us that munching down on homemade kefir and sauerkraut helps the seat of our immune system, which resides in the gut, flourish with a diverse population of microscopic and beneficial organisms. We need these little guys as much as they need us. What the boffins used to tell us was there are 'good' and 'bad' gut bacteria, but now we're coming to realise that there are no demons chilling out in our bowels. Instead, we all have a unique universe down there and if this miniature world gets out of kilter, we can develop health problems. Our emotional microcosm, which I call the **Emotobiome**, is much the same - by allowing ourselves to experience a whole range of feelings, we can feed our Emotobiome so that the 'good' and 'bad' live in harmony.

Emotions are only coloured with the hues you paint into them - a text from your ex may trigger red-hot frustration, and noticing how brightly this red feeling glows will provide you with useful information. Anger, envy, sadness - these have all been vilified but they are normal and essential emotional reactions. To ignore or bury them is to walk onto the train tracks - even uncomfortable emotions are useful; they are telling us what we need to hear. Remember, emotions are just messages - if we pause to listen, we may be given a roadmap for a future, more grounded self. Otherwise, we'll end up like a dormant volcano - calm on the surface but bubbling with uncontrolled fury when Tiny T triggers hit. So, I'll say it again to be loud and clear - there are no 'bad' emotions. Instead, understanding the Emotobiome just as we now do the gut microbiome in terms of diversity is key for emotional health and literacy. We need emotional variety just as much as our bodies need the trillions of organisms that sit within our bowels.

Exercise: The Emoji game

To further help develop emotional literacy, and prevent yourself from sitting back in comfortable numbness but missing out on life, I suggest this next quick exercise that you can do on a smartphone anywhere.

Start by opening whichever smartphone app you use most to communicate with people – texts, WhatsApp, Facebook, whatever. Now look at your most frequently used emoji – it's usually the first one that comes up.

Ask yourself:

- What does this emoji emotion mean to you?
- When was the last time you truly experienced this emotion?
- Take a moment here to check in with yourself, as this can be a much more emotionally challenging exercise than it first looks. Feel your feels, breathe deeply through your belly (as per Chapter 1) and know that you're ok.

- Now, if this is a feel-good emotion, explore and think about what you can do to actively bring more of this feeling into your life.
- If it's a less pleasant emotion, explore the circumstance, context and people surrounding you when you last felt this way.

This simple game can help you move from Awareness to Acceptance, as you may recognise that in real life there is some disconnect from what you portray and your emotional microworld. Crucially, at this stage of Acceptance, there is no judgement or blame, and the newly formed understanding of how society and early-life experiences have affected the ways in which you were taught to keep your feelings in check can be explored further. Because, of course, you are not alone in this type of emotional blunting – and if you're living within this Tiny T Numb Theme, extend patience to yourself. It can take some time to bring about diversity to your Emotobiome as it is a learning process. As such, I wish we could teach this at school from an early age, right through to graduation, as it is one of the most important life skills to have.

More than Words ...

But we are rarely taught emotional literacy at school - and in some cultures we don't even have the range of words for the full scope of the human Emotobiome. For those of us who live in countries where English is the first and primary language, we've been given a pretty raw deal. Even though English has more individual words than many other languages, it is a fairly blunt tool when it comes to emotional and relational terms.[17] There are hundreds of words and phrases from other dialects that are incredibly vivid and accurate, of which there are no direct expressions in English. Here is a very short list of some:

Word	Language of origin	Meaning
Kanyininpa	Pintupi (Aboriginal)	A relationship between holder and held, akin to the deep nurturing feelings experienced by a parent for their child
Asabiyyah	Arabic	A sense of community spirit
Bazodee	Creole (Trinidadian)	To be dizzy and dazed, in euphoric confusion – sometimes used in the context of romantic love
Fjaka	Croatian	A deeply relaxed state of body and body and mind, or the 'sweetness of doing nothing' and a 'day-dreamy state'
Krasosmutněn	Czech	Beautiful sadness, or a state of 'joyful melancholy'
Arbejdsglæde	Danish	Happiness, pleasure or satisfaction that comes from work
Gezellig	Dutch	Feelings of cosiness, friendliness, comfort, intimacy, all in relation to a shared experience with others
Myotahapea	Finnish	Vicarious embarrassment, the feeling of cringe
Suaimhneas croi	Gaelic	Peace of heart, for example the feeling of having finished a day's work
Sitzfleisch	German	The ability to persevere through difficult or tedious tasks as a type of stamina
Vacilando	Greek	The idea of wandering, where the experience of travel is more important than the destination
Firgun	Hebrew	Sincere delight and overt pride in someone else's achievements or something good that has happened to them

continued overleaf

Word	Language of origin	Meaning
Jugaad	Hindi	To be flexible when problem-solving with limited resources – to 'make do'
Iktsuarpok	Inuit	The heady anticipation when waiting for someone and looking up or going out to check if they've arrived yet
Sprezzatura	Italian	A studied carelessness or concealed yet effortful nonchalance
Nakama	Japanese	Closest friends who feel like family
Sarang	Korean	A love so strong that you wish to be with someone until death
Xīn rú zhǐ shuǐ	Mandarin	A sense of peace with oneself and a still mind without distracting thoughts
Desenrascanco	Portuguese	The ability to gracefully disentangle oneself from a troublesome situation with improvisation
Mudita	Sanskrit	Vicarious happiness, by revelling in someone else's joy
Vemod	Swedish	A tender yet calm sadness that something significant to you is over and you will never get it back
Kilig	Tagalog (Austronesian)	The butterflies in the stomach you get when interacting with someone you like, although not necessarily in a romantic sense

Language shapes our understanding and perception of the world, so having the tools - the vocabulary - for expressing the full range of human emotions can help a great deal when working with Tiny Ts. Learning additional words and phrases can be helpful, but if your primary language is one with low emotional diversity you can also utilise creative avenues such as art and music to nurture the Emotobiome.

AAA Approach Step 3: Action

I work with real-world psychology, and as such my approach is client-centred and realistic. The goal therefore is not to become an emotional evangelist overnight, but rather to help people emerge from languishing and numbness gradually and sustainably. People often find expressing emotions difficult as we live in environments where Tiny Ts have taught us to bottle them up, so pure talking therapy from a standing start can be challenging. Hence, in this Action stage of the AAA Approach we will explore some more non-verbal types of exercises to feed your Emotobiome and you can of course follow up with a therapist if and when you wish.

The Feelings Playlist

Songs get to us, as they spark an emotional reaction. It doesn't matter what type or genre the music is, the tracks we hold close to our hearts elicit intense and powerful feelings – those with decent tunes at least! If music sings to you more than words, put together a Feelings Playlist. Instead of including only your favourite songs, choose ones that make you feel a range of emotions. Have a look at the wheel below and select at least one of the primary emotions for each song. You can use the steps from the Emoji game here, too, to further emotional literacy, as once we start to become aware and expand the Emotobiome, we can manage life's inevitable curveballs more effectively, strengthening the psychological immune system.

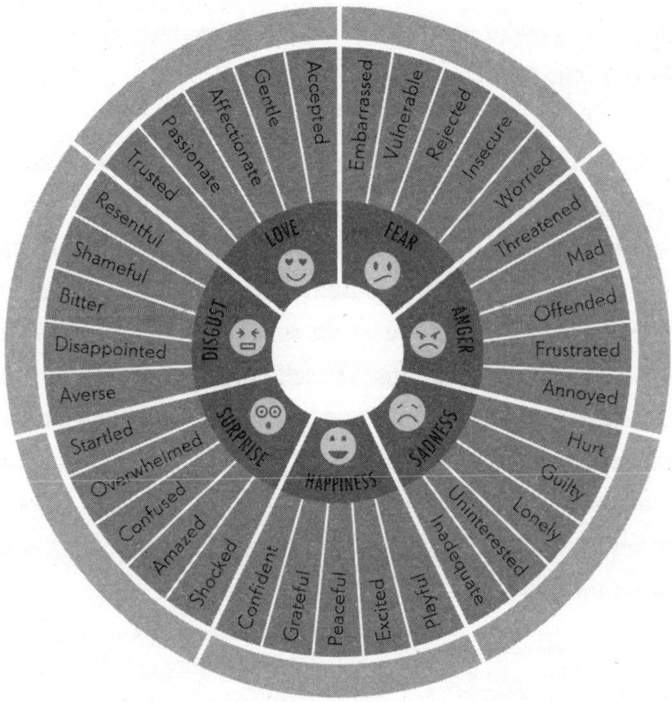

Figure 3.2: Emotions wheel

Back to the future: How you can use the power of nostalgia to enhance your Emotobiome

When we're feeling numb, we can lose our sense of time and space – so one way to manage these feelings and feed the Emotobiome is by looking in the rear-view mirror of our lives. Studies have shown that when nostalgic feelings are triggered, social bonds strengthen, positive self-regard increases and there's a boost in happiness.[18] Nostalgia can also protect us from future bouts of depression because we often find comfort in nostalgia, especially during challenging situations. These memories remind us of times when we felt safe and secure, which we know is a basic human need. Often people quite naturally engage in nostalgia when going through life's difficulties, and you may find you notice more cultural nods to the past when a society as a whole experiences troubles.

People sometimes conflate nostalgia with 'being stuck in the past' and the negative connotations of not moving on emotionally. But nostalgia doesn't work this way - rather, it enables us to connect our present lives to personal meaning and value, which again we know is a cornerstone of mental health. This gives us a sense of self-efficacy to face the challenges ahead, rather than keeping us trapped in a static state of numbness. Indeed, this boost in self-belief goes on to increase optimism,[19] which acts as a protective factor for both physical and mental health - so dust off your legwarmers and try some of these tips:

- Sniff it out with the sense of smell. Aromas and scents can trigger nostalgic feelings immediately, so if there's a smell that transports you to a particularly comforting time, for instance your grandparents' washroom, mum's cooking, or even your school canteen(!), re-create this whiff to take you back to feeling warm, safe and cared for – not only when things get tough, but on a regular basis to soothe a frazzled modern mind.
- Reminisce with photographs. It doesn't matter whether these are old-fashioned, printed photos or galleries on your smartphone, as we tend not to look at either much of the time when we're numb. You can use the 'memories' function on your phone, which will bring up a little slideshow of particular times, or take a trip to the attic and dust off some Polaroids – the important thing here is to connect with the past through photographic images. This is

beneficial when we're stuck in languishing as it reminds us how far we've come and that we do indeed have the internal resources to cope with life's hardships – now and in the future.

- Music is another powerful way to activate feelings of nostalgia and it can also get your body moving when you're in a bit of a slump – even self-confessed dance-haters still smile when they're forced to shake their boo-tay! Music-evoked nostalgia also enhances inspiration, strengthens meaning in life and buffers against the impact of chronic unpleasant emotions.[20] There are even apps that make your digital music sound like vinyl, without the need for an antique record player – if you're of an age to remember such things! But for anyone of any age, music is an incredibly strong trigger for nostalgia, so you may want to add this to your Feelings Playlist too.
- You can also spend five minutes writing down a nostalgic memory. Bring it to life with as many layers as you can recall – the people, place, and of course sights, sounds and smells of the day. You might be surprised at how much fine detail has been lurking in your memory banks. If this creates intense waves of emotion within you, use the breathing exercise on page 39 and aim to be curious about these feelings, rather than forcing them back into the recesses of your mind. Looking back may feel counter-intuitive, even uncomfortable, and your instinct may be telling you that peering in the rear-view window of your mind will only make you feel a sense of sadness that 'happier times' are behind you. You might also fear feelings of failure or that life hasn't turned out as planned,

but please trust that by connecting with nostalgia you will build resilience by allowing your Emotobiome to be populated with a healthy mix of emotional experiences. The purpose here is to strengthen your psychological immune system and you may find it interesting to witness the wide range of feelings this exercise creates – some perhaps that you haven't felt for a long time.

- Finally, practise 'anticipatory nostalgia',[21] which is the process of savouring a particularly lovely experience so that we can revisit it at a later point in time. When you next feel pleasant emotions or sensations, notice as many details about the environment and experience as you can and file it away in your brain's 'good times' folder. With practice you will become an expert at recognising those instances in life – we sometimes call them 'magic' or 'zen' moments – and by tuning into even fleeting positive events, you will give yourself a gift for future tough times *and* truly appreciate life in the present.

Shoulder to shoulder

The 'shoulder-to-shoulder' technique can be a great way to oil the wheels of more open emotional communication. I use this method called 'walk-and-talk', also known as 'eco-psychology', quite a lot because the traditional therapeutic environment of a consultation room can be a barrier to unguarded expression. Open spaces such as parks are a great option, although I sometimes venture into museums and galleries and use the artwork as a basis for conversation. Nevertheless, the key aspect here is that many people, and in particular men, find direct, face-to-face discussion more akin to a job interview and can 'perform' accordingly. Therefore, you may want to try the shoulder-to-shoulder method in this final, phase three of the AAA Approach, with a trusted friend, partner or loved one.

You may find that you are able to use some of the emotional literacy skills you've acquired so far, in terms of identifying and being able to express your experiences and emotions. Indeed, Noah scheduled a walk-and-talk with his best mate and told him about the reality of his dating experiences, and other things that he'd realised were playing on his mind. This may have been in jokey way, and there was indeed some blokey teasing, but instead of making Noah feel embarrassed, he said it simply made him feel comfortable - *not* comfortably numb. They did both agree, though, that internet dating was 'a mug's game'.

Dr Meg's journaling prompts for emotional literacy

1 Which emotions do you find difficult to accept (have a look at the Emotions Wheel if you feel stuck)? Reflect on how you manage these emotions at present.

2 In what ways can you separate your emotions from the behaviours of others?

3 I am holding on to XXX emotion because ...

CHAPTER 3 TAKE-HOME TINY T MESSAGE

In this chapter we have explored emotional numbness, sometimes referred to as languishing, as it is a common occurrence in our modern world. A range of Tiny Ts contribute to this theme, and, as mentioned, yours may differ from that of the next person. The trick is to identify your own constellation of Tiny Ts, then move with them through Acceptance and into Action in order to create emotional diversity and literacy. This will all feed your inner emotional microworld, the Emotobiome, and help you manage life's difficulties.

CHAPTER 4

Born to be stressed

In this chapter we will explore:

- the differences between stress and anxiety
- how the stress response can become problematic
- high-functioning anxiety
- how present threats and associations constitute stress, whereas worry and rumination cause anxiety
- why using different techniques for stress or anxiety is the key to overcoming this most common theme.

Are we born to be stressed ... or anxious? What's the difference and does it even matter? I would say yes, it matters a great deal, because if you know the difference between anxiety and stress and have some idea about the Tiny Ts that may be involved in both, you will be in a wonderfully robust position to overcome this most prevalent of Tiny T Themes.

Anxiety and stress are the most common difficulties that I see in my practice – I really can't express how common they are in our modern, 24/7 societies. Many people who are experiencing both anxiety and chronic stress come to me after they have travelled down many psychological treatment and self-help paths, as well as visiting their GP and sometimes specialist consultants. For some, these therapies help to a point or in certain situations, for others they arrive at my office with very little hope that there might be something that can substantially help free them from the debilitating effects of anxiety and stress.

For quite a few people, the difficulty arises because we tend to conflate and use the terms 'stress' and 'anxiety' interchangeably. However, it is my belief that if we separate out the innate, physiological stress response from the cognitive and perceptual aspects of anxiety, we will be at a massive advantage when it comes to managing these intrusive issues that can be triggered by Tiny T. Let me introduce you to Charlie to bring this into focus:

When Charlie first arrived, they had some quite visible signs of stress or anxiety - or both. Charlie was biting the skin around their nails, and I could see that their fingers had been bleeding, they were finding it difficult to keep still and their voice was trembling. I was heartened that Charlie had managed to come to me when they were in such a stressed state and knew that boded well for the future as it takes a great deal of commitment to see a professional when you feel this way. Here's what Charlie shared with me:

> *'I've tried everything, absolutely everything to get this under control. It started when I went to uni, almost as soon as I got there, I think. Well, not at first, freshers' week was sound, and I got on with everyone in halls, but when the course actually began, I started to feel so stressed. I mean really stressed, like I-wanted-to-run-out-of-the-lecture-hall stressed. So I got a referral to the mental health service at uni and had six weeks of*

CBT. It seemed to help a bit but not really; I still felt like I was going to have a heart attack when walking into a lecture.'

Charlie described the classic symptoms of the stress response (see the box on page 97) but I wondered what Tiny Ts could be driving this. Hence, we started with the Awareness phase of the AAA Approach and discussed the differences between stress and anxiety, and why previous treatment might not have helped Charlie as much as we would have liked.

The AAA Approach Step 1: Awareness

What is stress?

The word 'stress' is mostly used in psychological terms these days, but it comes from physics, and means to push a material beyond its tolerance level. When we think about this definition of stress, it starts to make sense - take a paper clip for example: it's possible to bend the metal back reasonably far and it will spring back into its original form. But if you push the clip beyond its tolerance, it will be overextended and cannot revert to how it once was. We often view stress, and associated Tiny Ts, in this way - when the straining and twisting we sometimes do in life leaves us feeling rather bent out of shape.

But before this shapeshifting happens, there is quite a lot of wiggle room in the paper clip - and in ourselves. Our bodies are very well equipped to deal with difficult situations via our autonomic nervous system. The autonomic nervous system has two opposing, yet complementary arms: the sympathetic and parasympathetic nervous system. The sympathetic nervous system is what controls how we respond to stress, often called the 'stress response' or 'fight-flight-or-freeze response'. But just as the paper clip always wants to ping back into its original shape, physiologically our bodies and minds also instinctively want to return to a state of homeostasis - where everything is ticking along nicely. This is where the parasympathetic nervous system comes in and acts like a counterweight to the stress response, essentially switching back from fight-flight-or-freeze to the state of 'rest-and-digest', in which we repair, restore and grow.

Why we're hardwired for stress

This is not to say the fight-flight-or-freeze stress response is a bad or negative state - in fact, we wouldn't be alive if we didn't have it! In this sense, 'stress' is an adaptive physiological response that is essentially hardwired into our brains. What we mean by 'adaptive' is that it has allowed us to survive and evolve into the human beings we are today. It is physiological because a cascade of bodily processes are activated when the stress response is triggered - even though stress can feel as if it is a 'mental' phenomenon, it is very much physical in nature.

The famous example that is often touted is of an early human being faced with a predator like a lion. The human is of course no match for the lion under normal circumstances, but when confronted with such a threat, our brains automatically trigger the stress response, which allows a surge of adrenaline and cortisol to flood the body, resulting in some pretty awesome superpowers! Blood is pumped hard and fast, pushing oxygen around the body; glucose is released so that our muscles have supercharged energy; and our pupils dilate so that we turn into a superhuman - well, kind of anyway.

At some point in our history these physiological changes did help us to battle the lion, run away from it or keep so still that the furry beast didn't notice us as food. Or perhaps more accurately, fight, flee or hide from other humans in opposing clans. Regardless, this stress response has been extremely valuable for us as a species, so much so that it has barely changed, even though our environments are much safer in many ways. That's why, when a car pulls in front of us on the motorway, we can steer clear of a collision before consciously thinking about turning the wheel. It's also why such an experience leaves us feeling 'pumped', out of breath and rather exhausted later on.

This response is so useful to us - so adaptive - that is it hardwired and can be triggered when we're not in any overt physical danger. Have you ever felt your heart pounding in your chest during a job interview? The interviewers aren't going to actually put you on a spit roast, but the verbal roasting will trigger the exact same physiological changes as if they were bearing down on you with spears.

Knowing this - the Awareness part of the AAA Approach - is the first step to controlling this evolutionarily driven and automatic response. In Charlie's case, it was important to find out if they had any Tiny Ts that led to an association between a particular environment or interaction at university and the stress response that was being triggered while there. As always, I posed the Tiny Ts core question, and these were the clues that started to materialise:

I can't see how what I'm gonna tell you would affect me so much as it wasn't such a big deal at the time. When I was younger, say about eight years old, I was in my school play. I'd

> *never been on stage before with a crowded audience and I just froze. I completely forgot all my lines - I think they call it drying - all I could see was pairs of eyes looking at me. The teacher eventually had to come out and get me and I struggled in crowds for a while after that.*

I then asked Charlie if they ever tried to go back on stage and they said they hadn't – they actively avoided any sort of drama or theatre, and always managed to wriggle out of presentations, even in small groups. But notably Charlie hadn't considered this to be relevant to what was going on at university, as the terror they felt was at the start of the course, simply at the sight of a large lecture hall with a podium.

How the stress response can become 'conditioned'

From the late nineteenth and early twentieth centuries, researchers known as 'behaviourists' were conducting experiments to see how people and animals learn behaviour. Behaviourists believed that we learn by simply responding to aspects of our environment – that we are a passive black box dealing with input from the environment, which then leads directly to our outward behaviours. Furthermore, the behaviourists believed that we learn by associating environment cues with reactions, known as classical conditioning. For example, Russian physiologist Ivan Pavlov noticed that a dog not only salivated when it saw food, but also began to drool *just* at the sight of the feeder. Dogs obviously are not hardwired to salivate when they see a human, so this canine learnt over time that the person meant food too. Pavlov experimentally reproduced this observation by pairing food with the sound of a bell, and lo and behold the dog started to drool just on the sound of the bell. Hence, a response was created out of two previously unrelated things.

This type of experiment was repeated by John B. Watson and Rosalie Rayner in the 1910s and 1920s with a toddler known as Little Albert. The aim was to create a response (i.e. 'condition' a particular response, in this case fear and stress) by pairing a white rat with a frightening loud noise. Albert had at first quite liked the fuzzy rat but after the association with the frightening noise, he became scared not only of the rat but also of other objects with similar features, such as the family dog, a fur coat and even a Santa Claus mask; hence the associated response was generalised. This experiment would be considered completely unethical now of course, and there is much debate and curiosity over what happened to Little Albert – some say he died from acquired hydrocephalus at six years old, others suggest he lived a long and fruitful life but with a fear of dogs. When I was an undergraduate student, my textbooks confidently stated that the child was de-conditioned, but this is unlikely and there's no doubt that if the researcher had reversed the conditioned responses, they would have published the findings. I really feel for that kid and hope that wherever he ended up, he knew how important his role was in informing our understanding of stress. Little Albert taught us that it is possible to plant associations between two previously unconnected aspects of our lives – and this is invaluable when trying to unpick what is stress and what is anxiety.[22]

For Charlie, we explored whether it was possible that the characteristics of the school stage had led to a conditioned stress response. When digging deeper into the first time Charlie had the acute stress response at university, they recalled quite a few similarities between the two environments. The seating, size and enclosed nature of the hall were indeed similar to the school stage. However, Charlie was somewhat frustrated at this point and couldn't understand why their previous psychological treatment had helped partially if their Tiny Ts were all about the school play.

The difference between stress and anxiety

Stress, or rather the stress response, is about a present, in-the-moment threat, which we often call a 'stressor'. For Charlie, all those eyes staring right at them in the dark, within a large room that was difficult to escape from, would have been powerful cues to trigger an acute stress response. However, anxiety is much more about our perceptions and usually based on past or future events. Because Charlie hadn't been back on stage, there was no opportunity for them to dampen the association between the environmental features (rows of seats, emergency exit signs, enclosed space) and this stress response. Therefore, when this response was triggered automatically at university, Charlie started to worry that they were anxious about being at university overall - and began to worry extensively about how this might impact on their future, the way people thought about them and a whole host of other anxieties.

The fundamental difference between stress and anxiety has to do with our place in time - the stress response is about a present threat and/or is triggered by an association (in Charlie's case the lecture hall environment), whereas anxiety is about thoughts based on the future (worry) or the past (rumination).

The confusion arises because humans are such a clever species and can imagine a whole host of scenarios - dangerous

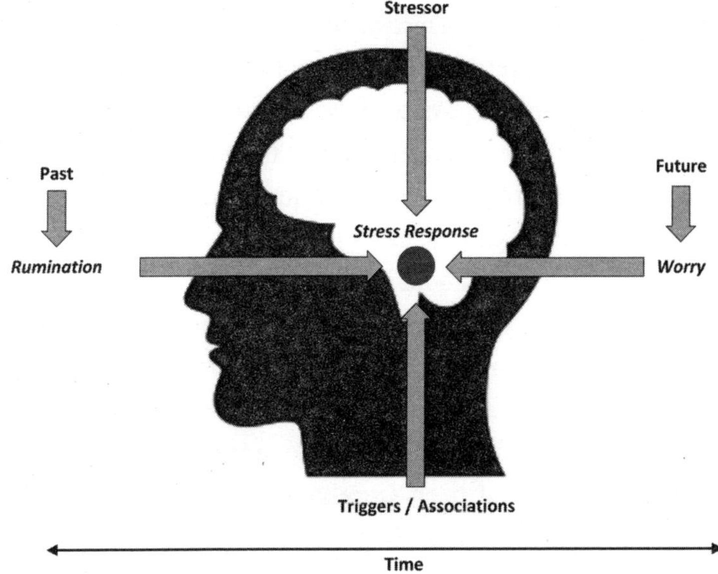

Figure 4.1: Stress, anxiety and time

and safe. This is how both worry and rumination (which are forms of anxious thinking) trigger the stress response - our minds and bodies don't know the difference between a present threat and a perceived threat, and, as such, thinking about the past and future negatively can also activate the fight-flight-or-freeze stress response. Actually, let me correct that - our minds and bodies don't know the difference until we train them to see what is stress, and what is anxiety (see below, Action stage).

It can be helpful to ask yourself the following question to find out if you're experiencing stress or anxiety:

Where do I find myself most - in the past, present or future?

Understanding the subtle differences between stress and anxiety is vital to overcoming the Tiny Ts that drive this theme, as different methods work for stress as opposed to anxiety. It can be tricky to know which is which because the symptoms are similar - a present threat, associations, rumination and worry all trigger the physiological stress response in a deep, ancient part of the brain called the amygdala. Many people call this our lizard brain as it is instinctive and somewhat automatic, rather than analytical.

However, anxiety is about higher-level cognition and thought patterns, so it has to be processed through a more evolved part of the brain known as the cortex before these thoughts can trickle down to the amygdala.[23] This is why Charlie was having so much trouble with the continuing symptoms of the stress response - they had been working at a cognitive level with previous therapy, disentangling worrisome thoughts, when at university the trigger was a conditioned association. In other words, Charlie's lizard brain was responding to the environment immediately through their survival-hardwired amygdala, whereas the techniques they'd been taught were high-order cognitive methods that were far too slow to be used in the moment.

Taken together, Tiny Ts can be involved in both stress and anxiety, as previous experience can prime your stress response in certain situations - but Tiny Ts also affect our perceptions so they can lead to anxieties and numerous mental rabbit holes that then trigger the stress response and all its physiological symptoms.

The signs and symptoms of the stress response

What the stress response feels like physically, in the moment:

- You may experience cardiovascular sensations including palpitations, when it feels like your heart skips a beat, your heart is racing, and you may even sense blood pumping through your body at an increased rate.
- Your voice may tremble and in extreme cases you may find it hard to speak properly as breathing patterns are disturbed.
- You may have gastrointestinal symptoms such as a stomach ache or an urgent need to go to the bathroom.
- You may also feel the increased need to empty your bladder – both of these mechanisms are to make it easier to fight or flee.
- You may feel jittery and restless and find it hard to sit still or feel the overwhelming need to escape.
- Blushing can occur across the neck and face, and/or your ears may start burning and appear red.
- Overall, you might feel very hot and sweaty.

What the stress response feels like cognitively in both the short and longer term:

- Concentration can be impaired during acute stress as the mind zooms in on the perceived threat.
- Other cognitive functions such as memory are worsened as cognitive resources are allocated to fight-or-flight.

- Over the longer term with chronic stress, higher-order functioning such as decision-making can be blunted.
- Also in chronic stress, you may experience temporary aphasia, where finding the right word seems difficult – it's the 'tip-of-the-tongue' feeling.

What the stress response feels like emotionally and socially, if you cannot return to a resting state:

- You may feel irritable and snappy, lashing out at little things (or people) that wouldn't normally bother you.
- On the other hand, you might feel needy and the desire for constant reassurance.
- You might feel like the world's closing in – feeling overwhelmed is a common sign of unsustainable stress.
- Sleep is but a distant dream – trouble both with falling and staying asleep are associated with long-term stress.
- Intimacy and sex can also be affected – loss of libido can be a sign that something's gotta give in your life.

Long-term stress, either caused by threat associations or by anxiety, can lead to some significant health issues including cardiovascular conditions and immune system dysfunction. Studies show that it's harder to shake off a virus, and even wound healing takes longer, if you're in a chronically stressed state[24] – so it is worth engaging in the AAA Approach to get a handle on your stress response.

The AAA Approach Step 2: Acceptance

Charlie could now see how the Tiny T incident of the school stage caused in-the-moment stress to such an extent that an association had been made in the hardwiring of their brain, and how this had been triggered at university. They were also aware that this reactivation of the stress response in this situation went on to create anxiety in the form of future worries – 'How am I going to cope if I can't even sit in a lecture theatre?' This is such a fundamental distinction that isn't generally recognised – another example is Logan, who in a sense had the opposite experience to Charlie. Logan was experiencing many of the physical symptoms of the stress response and hence attributed these to 'stress at work' – he used a range of techniques such as daily affirmations, breathing exercises and burning off steam at the gym, but these 'fixes' weren't really working any more. Here, we needed to make sure that Logan's stress response was indeed being triggered by in-the-moment stress or associations, and not any type of anxious thought patterns such as worry or rumination.

Exercise: Separate stress from anxiety

People often experience the physical, cognitive and emotional manifestations of the stress response but don't know why. One way to figure out if what's causing you difficulties is stress (or a stressor) or anxiety is to define whether it is linked to a current problem or to a hypothetical situation. You can do this by asking:

'Is there something I can do about this right now?'

If the answer is 'yes' then you are most likely dealing with a present stressor or association, for example a demanding customer. Logan was a salesperson, and he knew how to manage stressful situations at work, so this wasn't the core of his issue. Therefore, it was more likely that the reason why Logan was finding it hard to control his symptoms was more to do with a hypothetical situation – in other words, he was experiencing anxiety.

This can feel perplexing when a Tiny T is buried deep within our psyches. I posed the initial Tiny T question to Logan and watched as he carefully thought about what event or experience had impacted on or changed him in an important way, but that he hadn't thought was serious enough to mention. Logan looked me straight in the eye and said his father was a narcissist. Logan did have numerous anxious thoughts lurking in the recesses of his mind about the conflict between wanting to make his dad proud, and yet trying very hard to break free from his father's control. The hypothetical situations that edged Logan's consciousness were concerns that could not be actively resolved, as we cannot change other people. No amount of weightlifting at the gym, iron-man triathlons or 'you can do it!' affirmations could adequately overcome the sense that Logan's father didn't really notice him. This is why the Acceptance piece of the AAA Approach can be painful, as the realisation comes that sometimes we cannot change aspects of our lives – but we can learn to recognise and manage anxious thoughts. First, however, let's look at bossing the physiological stress response, something that Logan was practised at, but Charlie needed to experience.

How to learn to control the physiological stress response

This method is a way to train yourself not to immediately react to the stress response and, in time, to control it. Here we are encouraged to be curious about the physical symptoms of the stress response, so that we won't feel the overwhelming desire to escape these physiological sensations when they occur. With practice, this technique will also allow you to control the somewhat scary signs your body gives you when the stress response is in full swing, such as a racing heart, dizziness and trembling voice. Charlie and I followed these steps to enable them to first gain a sense of acceptance of the stress response, then to see it for what it is: a normal physiological mechanism.

Sit or lie down in a comfortable position – no need to rush this so take your time.

Now, imagine the situation that triggers your stress response – for Charlie we focused on a lecture hall as this was the most recent significant trigger.

Bring to mind details. Where are you? What is your position in the space? In your mind, look up, down, left and right.

As you start to feel the sensations of the stress response, know that you are ok and this is what we're here for. If the sensations haven't started for you, try to remember what this triggering situation felt like.

Now scan your body, noticing what the sensations feel like in different areas of your physical form.

Sit with these sensations for a moment, even if they feel uncomfortable.

If one sensation is particularly strong, get curious about it – explore it as if you're an alien from another planet doing research.

Think in terms of 'this is fascinating, I wonder what will come next?!'

Then, describe the feeling in your own words; e.g. 'this heart is beating as quickly as a rabbit's'.

Be curious also about any thoughts you're having; for instance, 'I really want to escape from this now!'

Rather than pushing these physical feelings aside, stay with the experience – allow it to be uncomfortable yet interesting.

Next, accept that this is your body attempting to keep you safe – and thank your body for taking care of you.

You can move on to another sensation now or bring the exercise to a conclusion by reassuring your body that it's ok, you've got it from here and can create a more adaptive response to this trigger.

Like any technique, the more this is practised the easier it becomes - and over time you will notice that your stress responses change and weaken. Indeed, although Charlie found the notion of the exercise stressful in itself at first, after a few sessions the approach of being curious about their stress response seemed to rob it of its dominance over them. And here was the point where we were ready to move on to the Action phase of the AAA Approach.

The Curse of Busy-itis: High-functioning anxiety and how it rules your life

Just as some people can have depressive symptoms but still seem to function at a high level, the same can be said of those with anxiety. People with high-functioning anxiety are often top of the class, high achievers and individuals who make you think: 'How do they do it all?' The root may be Tiny Ts fuelling what I call the 'Curse of Busy-itis', in which we constantly busy ourselves to distract from anxious thoughts.

Sometimes, distraction can be a beneficial coping mechanism, usually in the short term, but when used so much that our awareness is low (back to the first step of the AAA Approach), it can be a sign that underlying anxiety is the driving force. Do you find it uncomfortable to do nothing, to simply *be*? You may jump from one task to another mindlessly, feeling like a voyeur on your own life. If this sounds familiar, high-functioning anxiety and Busy-itis may be at play – check in with yourself and question:

- Do you find it hard to relax?
- Does your mind immediately move to the next task as soon or even before the present task is finished?
- Do you find it hard to focus on one thing at a time?
- Would other people describe you as superhuman, a high achiever and/or good under pressure?
- Do you fear letting yourself or, worse, others down if you're not on top of everything?

- Are you usually early, or the first person to arrive at a meeting or social gathering – and the last to leave as you volunteer to clean up?
- From the outside, do you appear calm and in control, but on the inside your mind is racing a mile a minute – a bit like the metaphor of a swan calmly gliding across the lake but paddling furiously below the water?
- Would you say you tend to overthink, overdo and overprepare?

This pattern and anxiety loop of distraction–anxiety–distraction can rule your life, so start on the AAA Approach and bring some Awareness to first identify if this is familiar. Then follow the tips in the chapter to address your Tiny Ts with Acceptance and Action.

AAA Approach Step 3: Action for Stress and Anxiety

As with every Tiny T Theme, these methods should be tailored to your particular needs, based on whether present stress and associative triggers are the core issue, or if worry and rumination are the drivers of your stress response. Many people experience both of course, so you can do a pick-and-mix of these techniques in this Action stage of the AAA Approach.

Quick tips and solutions for managing the stress response

These are methods to deal with a present threat, association or trigger of the stress response. As always with quick tips, it's useful to use these while also doing the longer-term work on Tiny Ts.

Shortcut stress with senses

Our senses are our superpowers, and we can use them to override the stress response. This is an excellent type of distraction for a short-term fix, just before or after a stressful situation to help you snap yourself out of the stress response and its unpleasant manifestations. Use whatever suits you best - the key here is to shock your senses so that your attention is moved from the stressor to one of the below sensations. But you can also think of your own.

- Sense of touch: plunge your hand into a bag of ice and hold it there for a few moments.
- Sense of sound: blast some loud music – using earphones is usually best so as not to annoy those around you!
- Sense of smell: put your nose in a paper bag of very strong blue cheese or another pungent food and quickly breathe in the powerful smell.
- Sense of taste: bite into a lemon and experience the extremely tart sensation of the fruit.
- The sense of sight won't usually give such an immediate effect, but you can distract yourself cognitively by reading a paragraph backwards, doing mental arithmetic in your

head (see how challenging it is to do multiplication without a smartphone calculator!) or making an alphabetical list of your favourite Netflix series/films.

Soften your vision

This is another quick tip for managing stress, but one that can be used in the moment while in public, for example in a meeting. When we are within the holds of an acute stress response, our vision is razor sharp and narrows at the (perceived) danger to help us survive – this is often called tunnel vision. Have you ever noticed that when you're in a stressful situation, you find it hard to recall the marginal details of the place or event? Perhaps after giving a presentation a colleague mentions some hoo-ha going on outside the meeting room, but you didn't notice it at all? You were so consumed in the in-the-moment stress of giving your talk that nothing else registered. However, we can reverse and activate the parasympathetic nervous system by softening our vision – close your eyes, then slowly open them to gain more awareness of the peripheral visual field. Keep looking ahead but gradually notice the broader environment. You may also want to gently massage the sides of your eyes to aid this process, but this isn't necessary if you're in a public place.

Chew it out

Researchers in Northumbria found that chewing gum has been shown to reduce acute stress and cortisol levels.[25] Interestingly, these scientists also found that gum chewing helped performance. Flavour didn't seem to matter though, so you can choose whichever type you prefer. This is a handy quick-fix if you're out and about and can't use the above senses tips – you might not have a freezer full of ice at hand, after all!

Ahhhhh ... have a good yawn

Do you tend to yawn after a stressful day? It may not be just a reflection of tiredness, but rather a way for the body to cool down the brain. During the stress response, our brains heat up – yawning is a sort of physiological air conditioning.[26] The reason why we yawn near bedtime and on waking is that brain temperature is at its highest in the evening, and rises on waking. Although there is ongoing debate about whether yawning is contagious, many people can bring on a yawn by imitating the behaviour first – this will promote relaxation and allow our hot heads to cool down.

Long-term action for managing the stress response

These are techniques that only get better with practice and that will allow you to break free from this Tiny Ts Theme for good – also enabling you to overcome similar Tiny Ts in the future.

Use the power of the parasympathetic nervous system

Regulating breathing patterns is one of the best ways to engage the parasympathetic nervous system and combat the stress response. Rather than you relying solely on the quick fixes above, training this part of the nervous system will strengthen the neural pathways and make it much easier to cope with acute stress. I like to think of the parasympathetic nervous system as our in-built 'parachute' that helps us to slow down and land softly back down onto earth during difficult times.

Consistency is what matters here; if you practise releasing your parachute regularly, you will become expert at it! Your brain will become so accustomed to engaging the parasympathetic nervous system that it will be conditioned when faced with stressors. You can use any technique you like, but this is one of my favourites that can be practised anywhere, at any time.

Handy breathing exercise

Charlie found this technique useful as it seemed more tangible and uses mental imagery to lead the inhale and exhale.

Stretch your hand out like a star and start with your smallest finger. Then, breathe in deeply so you can feel your belly expand through your nose while tracing (with a finger on your other hand) your small finger until you reach its tip. Next, exhale through your mouth while you trace the inside of your finger, so your belly dips back in on the exhale.

Move on to your ring finger, and again breathe in while you trace its outer edge, and out when moving down the inner edge.

Again, inhale while tracing the outer side of your middle finger and exhale when you move back down to your palm.

Continue with your index finger before moving to your thumb.

Repeat this process on your other hand and if any intrusive thoughts start to interrupt, acknowledge them before gently shifting back to the exercise.

This technique is often used to help children manage stress as it is such an easy method. It also engages the sense of touch, which, again, will help the mind and body to enter a rest-and-digest, rather than stressed, state.

Use physical exercise to combat stress

Do you recognise any of the symptoms in the box on page 97 at times other than when stressed? Many of the physiological outcomes of stress are exactly the same as when we exercise - racing heart, sweating, glucose pumping around the body - and one clever way to combat feeling stressed is to use exercise before a demanding situation. Types of aerobic exercise that get your blood pumping, such as running/jogging, swimming, cycling/spin and dance/body pump classes, have been shown time and time again to moderate feelings of stress.[27] Even 20 minutes will do, and the calming effects of exercise can last for many hours.[28] [29] So next time you have a big presentation, are going to an awkward family reunion or any other type of stressful event, schedule an aerobic exercise session no longer than six hours beforehand and you may find that it doesn't feel so overwhelming after all. If this isn't possible, use all that adrenaline and glucose that your body has produced in its stress response by going for a run or brisk walk after the event. This will help your body and mind return to a state of homeostasis much more quickly and it will also ease muscle tension - yet another symptom of being stressed.

Charlie enjoyed exercise and really liked this suggestion - so they scheduled in a gym session a few hours before we worked on exposure therapy below to make the process even easier. You might want to do the same.

Exposure, exposure, exposure therapy – break the associations

In the case where Tiny Ts have conditioned a stress response with a particular environmental or situational cue, exposure therapy is the best way to override this association and replace it with something that leads to a neutral or positive reaction. If you have a very severe reaction to triggers, it really is best to find a therapist who can support you in the process (for instance, if you experience panic attacks), but otherwise the theory is quite straightforward. By putting yourself in the situation or environment that triggers the stress response, your brain will learn that you're safe and it doesn't need to activate the sympathetic nervous system into a fight-or-flight response – it just takes some time and patience.

There are two type of exposure therapy: *systematic desensitisation* and *flooding*. While there is research to support the effectiveness of both,[30] I tend to err on the side of caution and suggest the former. Flooding, as you can imagine from the name, is jumping head-first into the triggering situation – for some it is quicker but, in my experience, this can backfire as it can feel overwhelming. In a sense, when Charlie entered the lecture hall in their first semester at university, this was a type of flooding – but as they didn't know this activated the stress response, it subsequently led them to engage in some cognitive distortions (see below), causing anxiety in the form of worries about the future. Systematic desensitisation allows you to build up the skills and mental muscle to manage, and in the end nullify, the acute stress response while increasing Awareness and Acceptance – so it's a win win win in terms of the AAA Approach. However, make sure not to jump past the acceptance exercise, as this type of mental imagery is a very good initial step in exposure therapy.

In Charlie's case I asked them to brain dump all of the circumstances that led to stress sensations. Then we ranked them from least to most severe. Next, we came up with a plan of how to place Charlie in these situations and which quick tips they could use at the time to manage the stress response in-the-moment. For some people this may be looking at pictures of their feared environment in a preliminary baby-step, but Charlie started by arranging dining-room chairs in a semi-circle with one chair positioned as a makeshift lectern at the front, so it felt to some extent like a school stage or lecture hall. Next, they went to a group talk in a café and gradually worked up to attending a large lecture. At every stage, Charlie's brain was overriding the association between their Tiny Ts and trigger and eventually Charlie was able to go back to their studies full-time.

Dealing with anxious thought patterns that drive the stress response

Anxiety - whether it's past-based rumination or future-focused worry - stems from our thoughts within the brain's higher functioning cortex, so it's useful to use mental strategies to overcome the negative thought patterns feeding anxiety, rather than purely relying on in-the-moment stress response management. For Logan, this area of thought patterns was the key to unlocking his difficulties with stress-related symptoms.

To start, it's helpful to identify what types of negative thought patterns (often called 'cognitive distortions' in psychology) you may be playing in your mind. Here are some of the most common categories:

Cognitive distortion	Example
Catastrophising	*If I do badly in this job interview I won't get the job and my fiancé will lose all respect for me and leave me.*
Mind-reading	*I can see that my date thinks I'm boring just by the look on her face.*
Fortune-telling	*I know my meeting will just go to pot, I can just tell.*
Negative focusing	*Even though my line manager gave me a mixture of feedback in my performance review, I can only see the criticisms of my work.*
Discounting the positive	*Yeah, I passed and got my driver's licence, but it was just luck that the traffic wasn't bad today.*
Magnification	*My situation is so awful, much worse than everyone else's.*
Minimisation	*So I managed to buy a house but most people do that as well, it's not such a big deal.*
Low frustration tolerance	*I just can't bear this diet any more!*
Personalisation	*No one's talking to me at this party – it must be the way I look.*
Labelling	*My colleague just ignored me so she must be a rude *expletive*.*
Blaming	*It's my parents' fault that I haven't moved out yet.*
All-or-nothing thinking	*If I don't ace ALL of my tests, I'm simply a failure.*
Overgeneralisation	*My relationship broke up so I must be completely unlovable.*

Next, use my three-step **ASK** process, which is based on the Socratic Disputation method of challenging negative and maladaptive thought patterns. You can use this simple process to challenge all the above examples of thoughts that feed anxiety and other cognitive distortions that initiate or maintain anxious feelings – **ASK** yourself:

A is for Accurate: Is this thought accurate? If so, what's the hard evidence for this cognition?

S is for Sensible: Is this thought sensible? Does it make logical sense objectively?

K is for Kind: Is this thought kind? If not, what function does this way of thinking have?

Let's use an example from Logan who reported cognitive distortions such as catastrophising, minimisation and all-or-nothing thinking:

Thought: My dad doesn't even notice me I must be so stupid and useless – my life will never amount to anything as I'm invisible to him.

A for Accurate: We explored the accuracy of Logan being 'stupid' – of which there was very little evidence. Of course, we all have difficulties but the fact that Logan was tackling his Tiny T meant that the evidence was much more weighted in the direction that he was far from useless, just a human who had experienced Tiny T.

S for Sensible: Logan admitted that even if his dad didn't give him the praise he so craved, it wasn't sensible to conclude that his life was worthless. Sometimes simply verbalising this erodes the loud voice of the inner critic in us all.

K for Kind: Logan immediately admitted that this thought was not kind, so we explore its function. The conclusion we came to was that this type of catastrophising thought pattern only acted to hold him in a state of stress – it wasn't actually supportive or beneficial in helping them to avoid stress sensations or harm.

Finally, we ended on one very powerful psychological coaching question:

What would your life look like without this thought?

Have a look at the table of cognitive distortions and try the ASK process yourself – better yet, write down your answers to the three questions in ASK as a record of your thoughts. Thought records can be an extremely helpful way to challenge these skewed cognitions and also act as a document to review your progress in overcoming anxiety.

Dr Meg's journaling prompts for managing stress and anxiety

If you could wave a magic wand and your feelings of the stress response drifted away ...

1 What would you be doing differently on a daily basis?

2 Is there anything you'd do more or less often than now? Describe what this would look like in your life.

3 Would you treat yourself and others differently? In what ways?

CHAPTER 4 TAKE-HOME TINY T MESSAGE

By understanding stress and anxiety as differing, yet related, concepts, we can use the correct tools for each trigger. Stress is all about a present, in-the-moment threat or an association we've made between a cue and the stress response by way of Tiny T. Anxiety is a bit like our mind playing tricks on us, as symptoms are produced when there's no actual present danger – it is rumination about past events or worries about the future. By becoming aware of which is which, accepting the associations that we have developed and then taking action to de-condition the stress response and manage anxious thoughts, we can free ourselves from this most prevalent of Tiny T Themes.

CHAPTER 5

The perfectionism paradox

In this chapter we will explore:

- the relationship between perfectionism and procrastination
- online trolling and the Dark Triad Personality Type
- burnout and how to spot the signs of exhaustion
- the benefits of strategic procrastination
- why perfectionism isn't necessary for success.

This chapter is about something I see every single day in clinic - the double-edged sword that is perfectionism and procrastination. We are not 100% born to seek out perfection, it is a drive that develops over our lifetime in response to our environment and Tiny Ts. It really is heart-wrenching how many talented, kind and intuitive people I see who self-sabotage as a result of maladaptive perfectionism, so here we will get to the root of the issue with some practical advice to break this vicious cycle.

One slightly too hot day a cool-looking woman walked into my practice. I was rather shiny of face and feeling a little muggy, but this lady seemed to not have a hair out of place and certainly did not appear ruffled by the heat. Indeed, she seemed so put-together at first, I was intrigued as to why she had come to see me, and here's what she said:

> *I can't seem to get out of a pattern of procrastination. It's become such a problem that in my latest business venture I feel like I'm losing focus ... and the confidence of my investors.*

We explored Silvia's early life and I posed the Tiny T question, and her ever-so-carefully-arranged facial expression morphed in discomfort for a nanosecond.

> *I was brought up by the strongest dad I know – he did it all on his own and worked two jobs to keep us afloat. He never even dated until I left home. I am forever grateful for my dad and everything he sacrificed for me. I was always well behaved as I knew my dad had enough to deal with at the time, so it's not that. I was a good kid and never got into any trouble at all. I'd honestly say that growing up just with my dad taught me a great deal in terms of how to be self-sufficient.*

Silvia went on to explain that she missed out on some of the fun young adult activities such as boozy late-night parties because she didn't want to give her father anything more to worry about. She did feel compelled to 'get things right – the first time'. The thought of doing anything that wasn't 'perfect' filled Silvia with a sense of dread so profound that when she was working on her new project, she found herself leaving fundamental tasks until very late at night, then rushing with an almighty panic to meet deadlines. She was exhausted, low and falling out with her collaborators, not only because the work was only just finished on time, but because she also refused to sign anyone else's sections off without a million amendments that she somehow always left to the last minute. Silvia's wicks were burning down at lightning speed, and she was about to lose the faith of her investors, so it was vital that we explored some of her Tiny Ts.

Perfectionism – Nature or Nurture?

Silvia openly admitted she was a perfectionist - with pride. She felt that this trait helped her reach her goals and was absolutely necessary to her success. When looking at the research, it does seem that perfectionism can be part of a person's innate personality, with some people having more or less of this trait.[31] This is probably in part true - but we know now that all personality types are open to change, through experience, will and, yes, with Tiny Ts.

While some people may be born with a predisposition to unrealistically high personal standards, others have this draining characteristic foisted upon them. It can be quite difficult to disentangle the nature from nurture debate here - but twin studies in which identical twins have been reared apart do show that we often have an innate tendency towards some personality traits, rather than simply learning these patterns through watching those close to us.

In Chapter 1 we explored some of the sources of Tiny Ts, and while Silvia may have been naturally inclined to perfectionism, not wanting to ever worry her father could have added to this tendency. Let's keep in mind that the way Tiny Ts work is cumulative, so there's no criticism or blame here, but rather an open-minded curiosity about Silvia's lived experience. And in this spirit, we started the first step of the AAA Approach – Awareness.

AAA Approach Step 1: Awareness

To begin, I wanted to reflect on how Silvia felt about making mistakes, and she stated that she didn't – 'I don't make mistakes.'

But doesn't everyone make 'mistakes' – I denote this word with quotation marks because its definition is *an action, decision, or judgement that produces an unwanted or unintentional result*, but in reality mistakes are a vital part of the learning process. Think back – is it easier to remember a fact or skill that you got right the first time, or one that you got wrong initially? It's usually the latter as our neural networks assimilate novel information and make new connections. Indeed, I would say that we cannot learn without making errors, miscalculations or oversights.

While we were digging deeper into this idea, Silvia started to mention an incident online, one that was clearly causing her emotional pain to talk about. As a young adult she'd forwarded a political meme on a social media platform; it wasn't directed at anyone or malicious, and she barely even thought about what she was doing as it seemed so insignificant, but the volume of abuse that resulted was frightening and shocking, making Silvia withdraw into herself. This, she said, crystallised in her mind how imperative it was not to make mistakes - and, like many Tiny Ts, compounded a behavioural tendency (perfectionism) that may not have otherwise become problematic.

Focus on Tiny T: Trolling and the 'Dark Triad'

Online trolling is a form of bullying and hence the impact on the individual is much the same – those who have been trolled report heightened anxiety, feelings of depressed mood and isolation, and in the most extreme cases there have been reports of suicide as a consequence of trolling behaviour. Research shows that people who engage in this behaviour are more likely to have what's known as the 'Dark Triad' of personality characteristics, which is a combination of psychopathy, Machiavellianism and narcissism.[32] The traits have some features in common; for instance, they share a lack of empathy and callousness. The narcissistic characteristic adds a sense of grandiosity, and Machiavellianism is associated with social engineering, coercion and manipulation. Finally, psychopathy has a strong link with antisocial behaviour – so we can start to see how destructive this Triad can be. Although trolls do tend to target high-profile individuals such as celebrities and influencers, they also seek out their friends and total strangers. Interestingly, trolls can engage in a sort of 'troll-combat', where they bully one another online. Indeed, a survey of people in the UK and US between the ages of 16 to 55 found that almost two-thirds of 16- to 24-year-olds (64 per cent) engaged in trolling online.[33] However, the rates of Dark Triad personality type are relatively rare, so what's driving this behaviour in so many people, particularly young adults? Mood and context appear to be important factors here – negative mood states such as anger and frustration in conjunction with an online environment where antisocial behaviour is prevalent (for example, outright swearing, personal attacks, veiled insults, sarcasm and off-topic statements) are even better at explaining why people troll rather than this reflecting innate personality types.[34] There is also a disinhibition effect when we're online, where people detach themselves from their real-life personality and behave out of character – a bit like being very drunk and doing something completely unlike yourself at a party.[35] This does give us a challenge, however, when it comes to our online existence, as it suggests that anyone could, in this set of circumstances, troll others.

This experience of trolling and online abuse is something I'm seeing more and more of in my practice. The sense of global humiliation can be profound, coupled with the belief that this digital trace will never be removed. We've always had public shaming – just think of stoning, flogging and being locked in a wooden pillory – but people could have left town after this and started a new life somewhere else. Now, in the time of 'cancel culture', it can be hard to believe that the sense of shame will ever go away, and that you cannot escape it. Cancel culture is the same mechanism as previous forms of public humiliation as it is used to maintain social norms to some degree, or a form of mob justice. There is no balance here, or discussion of the subtleties of a situation. Therefore, this experience significantly added to Silvia's existing reluctance to make mistakes, and hyper-charged her Tiny T Theme of Perfectionism.

Unravelling this was a pivotal first step of the AAA Approach (Awareness), in which we could start making tangible and helpful tweaks in Silvia's life to tackle the pattern of perfectionistic procrastination that she'd developed. Therefore, acknowledging an environment in which a profound fear of putting a foot wrong could leave a mental and behavioural impression started us on our journey.

Maladaptive vs Adaptation Perfectionism

It can be useful to separate adaptive from maladaptive perfectionism as many people believe that their propensity to get things just right has helped them throughout life - perhaps in securing a job, finding a partner, or simply to feel needed by others. This is a form of adaptive perfectionism, as the behavioural pattern is useful in one's life and served a purpose. However, maladaptive perfectionism, in which the fear of doing something poorly or incorrectly leads to mental tension and often behavioural delay, is one of the most common themes I see in my practice. This is why perfectionism can be so hard to crack and people often hold on to it, remembering the times it has worked in their favour but minimising the painful process to get to this outcome. Perfectionism's essential meaning is the belief that mistakes are somehow unacceptable, so great effort is expended to avoid errors at quite a high cost to the individual. An inner perfectionist can make us feel that mistakes mean we are unworthy, unsuccessful and, ultimately, unlovable. So, the stakes are indeed high. And this is why perfectionism is an underlying driver of procrastination for so many people.

Procrastination – What It's Not

It's almost easier to explain procrastination by saying what it's not - it's not being lazy, rubbish, incompetent or uncaring. In fact, it's usually the exact opposite. The procrastinators among us are generally quite conscientious - because we are worried about getting it wrong. Although we may not be aware of it, doing the dishes, sorting out a drawer or scrolling through social media is a way to distract us from the niggling feelings that we may not be good enough - and fear that everyone will soon find this out.

So we leave tasks until our stress threshold is breached and in the last hours of a day hash out something on the edge of our nerves, then convince ourselves that the end project is truly terrible, we're utterly stupid and shouldn't even be in the job. Sound familiar?

But before this point, our dear procrastinator would have spent an inordinate amount of mental energy either thinking about the task or using distraction techniques to think about anything but. This consumes such a large amount of our resources - physical, mental, emotional - that burnout can be the only way our bodies manage to get us to take note of this maladaptive pattern.

'Why can't I just get on with it!' 'I won't do this next time, I'll start early and won't get into this state again.'

Suffice to say, if you are a procrastinator, the chances are you care deeply about what you're doing, rather than not enough ... which means you might be veering into the purgatory that is perfectionism.

Can procrastination ever be a good thing?

What do you think? Can it ever be a good thing to put off today what can be done tomorrow? For some, this would be eye-twitchingly uncomfortable to contemplate but ... there are certain circumstances where procrastination *is* a good thing. 'Planned procrastination' or delaying tasks is often a very beneficial strategy – for instance, how many emails or messages do you get a day? Particularly if you're part of a parent or work group – I bet it's loads! Have you ever tried *not* responding to group messages to see what happens? The likelihood is, the vast majority of 'urgent' issues sort themselves out without your input. But it can feel hard at first as you might have a form of Tiny Ts that drives you to be the Fix-It-Person of the group. Perhaps as a kid you felt like you needed to take charge, a bit like Mo in Chapter 1 who always jumped in before anyone could tease or give his brother a hard time. You may even get a huge sense of belonging from being the go-to person, and this is fine if it's not causing you any problems such as burnout and exhaustion (see box on pages 127–8).

The reality I see every week in clinic is that this behavioural pattern, triggered by a lifetime's worth of Tiny Ts, does lead to some pretty unpleasant symptoms. But you can use planned procrastination and flip this, and I would wholeheartedly suggest this for anyone who feels they don't have enough time in the day. For some tasks, there may be logical a reason to wait awhile before progressing, such as collecting enough information before making a decision, but for many others the task just isn't as vital as it first seems. I'm talking about emails. And texts. And messages. Mostly. But there are many other micro-tasks that don't deserve the best part of your day, e.g. laundry, washing-up, countless household chores.

The reason why we busy ourselves with these types of jobs is that we feel good when something is finished, when we've actually achieved something, no matter how trivial. There's a tiny dopamine hit when the piles of laundry are sorted (honestly, how does it multiply like water-sprinkled Mogwai/Gremlins?), put away and out of sight, which is very hard to replicate when you have a crucial 10,000-word report, sales target, KPIs, and so forth to see to. But this achievement hunger is only quelled for a very short time, then very quickly comes back as we're not really making any progress on the more substantive tasks. An easy way to distinguish whether certain patterns are adaptive, such as planned delay, or maladaptive is to put to yourself these five words:

'How does this serve you?'

If hesitating to some extent when faced with a task (I am talking about replying to every email when it pings in your inbox the moment it arrives!) means that someone else will most likely reply, then give it room to breathe. We all bang on about how intrusive tech can be for our lives, but by digging deeper it's possible to see if our instant-reply nature is serving us or simply busying us enough to deflect Tiny Ts and reasons behind these behaviours.

This five-word question can be incredibly helpful to all of us in our goal-driven societies – to accept that perhaps a perfectionism–procrastination pattern was not serving us in the most beneficial way. In fact, this Tiny T Theme can quite easily lead to burnout.

How to spot the signs of burnout

In 2019 the syndrome 'burnout' was entered into the World Health Organization's bible of health and illness known as the *International Classification of Diseases and Related Health Problems Handbook* for the first time. It may seem odd that burnout has only just been officially recognised, but that's often the case with invisible illness – medical science and practice is slow to catch up with people's experience.

Burnout is listed within the category of 'factors influencing health status' and this is no joke – I've worked with people who take years to recover, have a range of associated health problems, lose their jobs, relationships and life as they knew it. Although the WHO associates burnout with workplace stress, there are countless other contexts that can cause it too, including trying to keep everyone happy, meeting our perceptions of others' expectations and simply not being a good fit with our environment. So, it's important to know the signs of this syndrome in order to catch it before serious health problems emerge.

If the following are familiar, you may be on the road to burnout syndrome:

- You cancel plans at the last minute – more and more frequently.
- You never, ever, feel like any task is completed as well as you'd ideally like and berate yourself for not achieving this standard.
- You feel you no longer have enough time in the day for friends, hobbies and/or enjoyable activities.

- You constantly feel the need to multitask – 'Who on earth does one thing at a time after all?!'
- You spend little or no time on self-care – 'self-care ... what's that when it's at home, eh?'

Signs that you might already be experiencing burnout include:

- Heightened irritability, often shown in snapping at loved ones, family members or the dog.
- Feeling overly emotional about issues that once didn't bother you – e.g. crying at an advert.
- Feeling overwhelmed and not able to cope in situations where you used to manage perfectly well.
- Some cognitive issues such as forgetting why you went in a room, not being able to focus for any length of time, even on a plot in a trashy TV show.
- Work performance is suffering.
- Bad sleep – either problems falling asleep, waking up in the night and not being able to get back to sleep, or a combination of the two.
- Feeling 'wired but tired' most days.
- Simply feeling run-ragged, exhausted but unable to switch your mind off.
- Emotional, stress or mindless eating and drinking, particularly those sweet or carb-laden foods such as biscuits, pasta and chocolate, and for those who drink alcohol, an evening glass of wine has turned into a bottle.
- Weight fluctuations (either up or down, but noticeable to you).

AAA Approach Step 2: Acceptance

Now that we are developing a good understating of certain patterns such as perfectionism that may not be serving us well, it's useful to move on to the Acceptance phase of the AAA Approach.

Perfectionism and success

One of the most common mistakes that we humans (particularly in modern societies) make is equating perfection with success: 'If I could only do this thing/that thing just right, then everything will be ok.' As we explored in Chapter 1, these competitive societal norms set us up to be rats spin-spin-spinning on the never-ending Wheel of Striv(f)e. While there's been a shift, with many prominent figures, celebs and voices telling us all how, yes indeed, they pushed the door when the sign clearly said pull, we are still programmed to think that flawlessness leads to wholeness. What is missed here, and gives me that nagging Tiny T feeling at the back of my throat, is that these life stories quite neatly follow universal story archetypes (Overcoming the Monster, Rags to Riches, The Quest, Voyage and Return, Comedy, Tragedy and Rebirth) with the protagonist usually coming out on top. In other words, although we identify keenly with these narratives, we're hearing them from people who 'got there in the end' - and if only *we* can fail so perfectly, we will, too, be successful.

Whoa, that's an awful lot of pressure! To even fail perfectly ...

So, to work through Acceptance, and overcome this unpleasant consequence of Tiny T Perfectionism, it's beneficial to do some work around the concept that *you are enough*. Start by brainstorming some ways you can remind yourself of this each day – I had one client who printed the slogan on a t-shirt, or you can use it as a password, plaster it all over the wallpaper, anything to keep this phrase in sight on a daily basis as our tricksy human brains will keep veering towards the negative.

Because as I've seen time and time again, if we don't try to tame the perfectionist monster within, anxiety, depression, ill health and burnout are genuine risks. As the old saying goes, an ounce of prevention is better than a pound of cure.

Just give up ...

... on perfectionism. Do you really need to be perfect all the time? Nope, it often doesn't do us much good and, quite frankly, perfectionism can make life pretty darn miserable a lot of the time.

Also, striving for perfectionism eats up so much cognitive energy, making it nigh-on impossible to learn from mistakes and build psychological immunity. You know that guy in the office, or the cousin/annoying friend/political leader who seems to just dust himself off and not worry when he trips up – yes him, he's the non-perfectionist. Do his blunders seem to hold him back? No! They appear to make people love him even more! Interesting eh ... While the goal isn't to be a buffoon, it's to stop all the mental replaying of an event so that (1) you can actually enjoy your time off and (2) you can figure out a lot easier what works (and what doesn't) for you in your life and be able to move on without completely battering yourself with self-recrimination.

However, people often have some reservations – 'But if I give up on perfectionism, I will never be successful!' – so the next exercise is useful within this Acceptance phase.

This is you the Perfectionist (right now)	This can be you the Success-oriented Non-perfectionist (soon)
Sets very difficult goals/ standards →	Sets realistic goals/standards →
Gives very little praise when goal is met →	Celebrates achievements →
Sets even higher bar →	Sets another bite-size realistic goal →
Just misses the mark (or thinks so) →	Sees any missteps as opportunities to learn →
Feels like a failure/berates self	Feels like a good, if fallible, person

The difference essentially is that perfectionism is doing the exact thing that's feared - setting yourself up for failure. However, it is absolutely possible to change this mindset no matter what sort of Tiny T has led to it - but you definitely have to want to summon your inner Elsa, and let that sh*t go.

AAA Approach Step 3: Action

By now, I truly hope you are energised, empowered and ready to go on to the Action stage of the AAA Approach, and these are some of the strategies you can try to break free from the paradox that is perfectionism/procrastination.

Actionable tips to beat procrastination

Find what works for you and be as kind to yourself as you would be with a good friend during the process. You can't be perfect at becoming a former-perfectionist-procrastinator!

The Pomodoro Technique

This well-known time management and productivity technique (named after pomodoro, the Italian word for 'tomato', which was the shape of its developer's timer!) is a tried-and-tested way to break down large tasks into bite-size chunks. Coaches everywhere will tell you to chunk-and-reward, chunk-and-reward but, if I'm honest, I've never personally found this useful and many of my clients reported the same. This is usually because we think about chunking work tasks by output, not time, for example finishing a report. But perfectionists can spend literally hours looking at a single paragraph, so an output-oriented mindset often plays right into the perfectionism–procrastination paradox. The Pomodoro Technique is different as it gives positive constraints based on minutes, which are defined and measured objectively, not milestones that can be subjectively arbitrated, and so are pretty much as long as a piece of string. Here's how it goes:

- Get a timer – I suggest not your phone as it relates to the next point ...
- Remove *all* distractions – put your phone on silent in a drawer, switch off all alerts on your computer if this is your type of work, or put a 'do not disturb' sign or some such other barrier to people barging in on your concentration. Unless you're an emergency medic, please do let go of all the reasons (excuses) you're about to use to justify keeping your message alerts on, as I promise you it can wait a few minutes.
- Set your timer for 15 minutes. Studies show our average concentration span is around 20 minutes, so be kind to yourself and set the timer within this concentration window.

- When the ringer goes off, take a short five-minute break and start a work-chunk tally. I do recommend standing up if you're sitting down, walking a little or stretching to remind the body that it still exists!
- Repeat the 15-mins on, five-mins off until your tally shows four work-chunks, then take a more substantial break – this can be as short as 15 minutes, but it must be long enough *for you* to feel refreshed.

For the technique to work, you really do need to use the breaks to do something that shifts your cognitive attention - looking at emails is not this! Use rituals such as making a cup of tea to having a mini-mindfulness moment, or any sort of physical movement is good.

When I first started using this technique, I was amazed at how long 15 minutes felt! Which made me think about how I always seem to get so much done just before I had a meeting/somewhere to go and so forth - these are positive constraints!

Additional tips to deal with procrastination

Schedule in 'precrastination' time

'Precrastination' is the annoying sibling of procrastination, and it denotes when you complete every small task you can find to avoid doing the thing you really need to do. Washing-up, laundry, clearing your inbox are all examples of precrastination, and I'm sure you can think of a hundred others![36] People often feel that getting all these little jobs out of the way creates headspace, and although there is some merit in this argument, the problem is that prolonged mental effort, even in seemingly easy tasks, leads to fatigue. This means that by the time you get to the important work that keeps the bills paid and family fed, you're already worn out, leading to that ever-familiar feeling of guilt that you didn't tackle your work-work first.

Some very interesting research was published that showed, when it comes to exertion, our brain is just like a muscle in the body and, if used without rest, potentially toxic neurotransmitters accumulate in the prefrontal cortex in just the same way that lactic acid builds up in leg muscles after a particularly long and intense run.[37] This slows down cognition and causes tiredness, similar to how achy and weary calves will ruin your PB time. One way to combat this and get on top of precrastination tendencies is to literally schedule these tasks in your diary. In the same way that overly restrictive diets lead to blow-outs, trying not to engage in precrastination tasks will lead to frustration and preoccupation with these everyday jobs. Ever heard of the pink elephant phenomenon? What are you thinking about now? Yep, it's impossible not to see that rose-coloured, adorable mammal in your mind's eye, which is why overly restricting a behaviour never really works - our brain knows it's still there. So if you tell yourself you won't scroll socials at all for the entire time you're on a project, as soon as you're a touch tired, irritated, hangry or such like, willpower will snap like a twig. Structured precrastination, on the other hand, is a much more realistic strategy, which keeps the pang of 'achievement hunger' at bay.

Make the short-term pain for long-term gain a bit easier by swallowing the frog in the morning

No, I didn't have a Scooby snack, as apparently Mark Twain said something along the lines of 'Eat a live frog first thing in the morning and nothing worse will happen to you the rest of the day' or 'If it's your job to eat a frog, it's best to do it first thing in the morning. And If it's your job to eat two frogs, it's best to eat the biggest one first.' It's hard to know for sure exactly what he said or even if he really did say this, as it's been attributed to various others, but the point is no one wants to eat a live frog (frogs' legs, maybe, for some ...), but if they had to they might as well get it out of the way early. When it comes to the psychology behind procrastination this is kinda important as we only have so much cognitive capacity (i.e. headspace) at a given time or on a given day, so if our heads are running worries over a task in the background, there will be less time and space to do other (more fun!) things. But if we just get it out of the way, then our minds will be freer to concentrate on the fulfilling and feel-good tasks that take rather more creativity and lateral thinking. So do 'do' the unpleasant things in the morning when energy and short-term motivation is highest after restorative sleep - assuming you've slept; if not, have a look at Chapter 9.

Reduce your expectations waaaaayyyyy down

When we care greatly about our performance or a particular output, we almost always set our expectations sky-high. We tend to be outcome- rather than process-driven and forget that a great masterpiece probably started as a series of sketches, or some ideas jotted down on the back of an envelope. Usually, whatever you do will be enough to at least move your thinking on, even though on a day-to-day basis it might not feel like you're accomplishing that much. Rome wasn't built in a day and all that.

Longer-term ways to manage perfectionism

A habit built over a life course does take some time to change, so Silvia and I also used the below exercise based on cognitive behavioural therapeutic techniques to embed a fundamental shift from perfectionism to good enough-ness, allowing for the space that we all need to live our lives.

Exercise: Give yourself a reality check

Perfectionism is basically like a magnifying glass, so big and distorted that once you start peering into it, you've already fallen down the rabbit hole. Therefore, perfectionists need regular and

Worst that will happen ...	Chances of this actually happening ...
If I don't spend every evening on this presentation working until midnight everyone at work will see that I'm actually completely crap at this job and I'll be sacked.	Hmmm ... well, I've never had a bad management review and I do get good feedback, so maybe this is a bit unlikely. And if I think about it, I can't just be sacked as I have an employment contract, so if my boss thought I wasn't up to scratch, she'd still have to give me opportunities to improve.
If I don't respond to my mates' messages straight away, they'll think I don't care and that I don't appreciate them – and ultimately, I'll have no friends at all.	I guess everyone is busy ... most friends don't respond immediately and I don't think they're bad mates, just that they must have a lot on. So, overall, I don't think I would lose any of my good friends if I took a bit more time for myself.
If I don't appear practically perfect in every way no one will like me, let alone love me.	I love the people in my life and they make f*ck loads of mistakes! And sometimes, seeing someone's vulnerable, imperfect and messy side has made me feel closer to them so maybe it's the same the other way round too ...

honest reality checks to combat this warped perception of the world. Think of the worst thing – the utterly, very worst and intolerable consequence – of not being perfectionistic.

The secret here is about moving away from a sense of self that's based on accomplishments, to one of personal worth related to our inner traits. **We can aim to be *our* best without having to be *the* best.** Because no matter how wealthy, physically flawless or successful we are, deep down we're all fundamentally fallible human beings. Which is great! How boring life would be if we were all perfect.

How to turn failure into feedback

We can turn the tables on perfectionism by seeing any slip-ups, blunders, gaffes or lapses as vital chances to look at the situation anew, with curious rather than critical eyes. Basically, #bemorecat and get as inquisitive about what happened or is unfolding by asking yourself:

- What have I achieved so far? A single blow rarely sinks an entire ship, so focus on what you've got right up till now to turn down the volume on your inner critic.
- What have I learnt from this slip-up? One oversight, even a significant one, can tell you something important about what's missing from the equation and/or what Tiny T pattern is recurring here.
- What can I take from the situation to help me move forward? You may need a boost of support/information/self-awareness in this area to shift to the next level, and if you can't see what this is, ask someone.

No one – honestly, no one – is perfect. Life would be immensely dull if we were all impeccably faultless and flawless – in fact, the most entertaining and engaging stories are always the ones where skirts are tucked into knickers or something remarkably green is stuck right in your front teeth. If there's anyone you think in your life who is near perfection, have a chat with them and ask them their embarrassing anecdotes – you might be surprised at the many gaffes they'd made in life! Biographies of respected icons can also do the trick – as long as they're self-depreciating! The open secret is that everyone has faced challenges and we can use these Tiny Ts to plump up our psychological muscles – just as long as we are as compassionate to ourselves as we would be to others. On that note ...

Make a pledge to yourself to be good enough at being good enough!

Dr Meg's journaling prompts for banishing your inner critic

1. What am I afraid will happen if I let go of perfectionism?
2. What does procrastinating protect me from?
3. If you throw away that perfectionism shield and let people know the real you, how might your life improve?

CHAPTER 5 TAKE-HOME TINY T MESSAGE

Procrastination is often driven by a fear of failure and high levels of perfectionism, frequently triggered by Tiny T. Therefore, by unpicking your Tiny T, you can manage the desire to be perfect all (or even most) of the time, allowing for a greater range of experience in life – including hiccups, mishaps and mistakes as these are usually when we laugh and learn. Perfectionism keeps us chained in expectations and puts a great deal of pressure on the individual. However, with a heavy dose of self-compassion, you can break free from this Tiny T Theme and choose what activities you want to dedicate your time and energy to, rather than feeling you have to do everything 'just right'.

CHAPTER 6

Human seemings, not human beings

In this chapter we will explore:

- why Imposter Syndrome affects some people more than others
- the evolutionary drivers of implicit biases
- the impact of microaggressions
- why we tend to compare up, rather than compare down
- empowering strategies for dealing with microaggressions.

I have had the honour of working with a wonderfully diverse range of people in my practice, and, before this, teaching in higher education and carrying out research studies. I can honestly say that I've learnt something from everyone I've met – that's the absolute magic of fellow human beings. And even though these individuals differed in their backgrounds, individual characteristics and personalities, I would say there were some striking commonalities – many felt like they're 'faking it' in some areas of their lives, usually the areas they cared most about.

I want to introduce you to Kellie. Kellie presented as a calm, collected and in control character, working as a chemical engineer, who seemed to exude serene confidence from every pore - apart from her eyes, which was so interesting to me. When we explored Kellie's life course and how she was feeling now, this is what she shared:

> *I know I'm successful and I've worked hard for it. But it doesn't seem to make any difference - I just don't 'feel' successful. People are always telling me how well I've done, particularly as a woman of colour in a STEM*[38] *field. But I constantly question whether I should even be there [in my job] and I've started to fall out of love with this career I've sacrificed so much for.*
>
> *But it's not just that - and I feel a bit embarrassed by saying this - I'm never sure if people like me, let alone respect or value me. I honestly have no clue whatsoever. I find myself searching people's faces for signs - smile lines wrinkling near eyes or a mouth ever so slightly downturned in a frown - regardless, I seem to have absolutely no idea any more what people think of me and it drives me crazy that I spend so much time caring and thinking about it. Maybe I shouldn't care ... I don't know, but I find myself wondering if an expression at work was 'ahhh' or 'ugh' from colleagues - was it good or bad? Was I good or bad? I can stay up all night thinking about it. I don't understand myself any more, I'm questioning everything I do now, and I know it's holding me back from progressing at work - I just don't want to feel this way any more.*

I asked Kellie if she had heard of Imposter Syndrome, and she nodded 'yes' - so we started our journey with the Awareness piece of the AAA Approach.

AAA Approach Step 1: Awareness

There's an imposter in our midst!

The term 'Imposter Syndrome', or imposter phenomenon, was first coined by psychologists Pauline Clance and Suzanne Imes in 1978, who saw a particular pattern in people with high personal expectations - also in those who perpetually gave themselves a very hard time at not meeting these expectations.

Although this label is bandied around in the media, on social platforms and in conversations all the time, it can be helpful to look more closely at the original definition, which includes the following components:

- You feel like in at least one primary area of your life (work, parenthood, relationships, etc.) you're faking it and are terrified of being 'found out'.
- You honestly think you're going to completely mess up a task and are then pretty shocked, not to mention relieved, when it goes well.
- You dread performance reviews, peer evaluations or accidentally hearing a conversation about you as you're sure other people's evaluations will be negative.
- When you do receive positive feedback, compliments or praise you tend to bat it away like a fly and feel slightly embarrassed by it.
- When something does go right, you'll attribute it to good luck or external forces rather than taking credit for a job well done.

- You can even feel guilty or a little frightened when faced with success or privilege – and sometimes consciously or subconsciously sabotage yourself.
- But failure itself terrifies you – so you tend to leave things to the last minute, then feel overwhelmingly stressed by the task at hand.
- You feel like everyone is naturally better than you and you strive to be as good as they are in a given situation (but don't really feel you are any good at all).
- Others may have commented that you're 'superhuman' – but you certainly don't feel it.

For those who don't struggle with this internal demon, it may seem odd that some of the highest-achieving individuals doubt themselves so much. But I would hazard an (educated) guess that a good proportion of people deemed to be 'successful' experience Imposter Syndrome - at least before they become aware of their Tiny Ts.

One issue with Imposter Syndrome is that, in the best-case scenario, it's a miserable way to live. Worst case, this mindset leads to significant mental health problems.[39] For a long time, experts thought that women had this syndrome all to themselves, but research has proved otherwise - Imposter Syndrome affects both women and men, from all walks of life, class, culture, ethnicity and sexuality, but it is fair to say that marginalised groups may experience self-doubt more keenly (more on this below). History, societal norms and cultural structures all have their part to play and can act as Tiny Ts. Indeed, as many as 70 per cent of people will experience this phenomenon at some stage in their lives[40] - and it undoubtedly results in a life less lived wherein people find it hard, or even impossible, to truly accept they are worthy of their accomplishments.

Why do some people feel like imposters more than others?

Even though Imposter Syndrome *can* affect anyone and everyone, it does seem to be more prevalent in particular groups. This is absolutely not to say that certain groups of people are weaker, more inclined to self-doubt or somehow less resilient in life – it's all down to the Tiny Ts some groups experience in society throughout their lives.

I've seen these sorts of assumptions my entire professional life – that there must be something 'wrong' with an individual, that it is their problem or failing that leads to these feelings of doubt and insecurities. However, it's far too easy to blame the individual and this doesn't help us to understand the mechanisms of an issue. But fortunately we now have more research that shows us just how societal Tiny Ts can lead to Imposter Syndrome.

A study of African American college students found that those who experienced more incidents of racial discrimination tended to feel more like imposters.[41] However, even the preoccupation with being stigmatised due to a demographic feature such as gender and race can influence whether someone feels like an imposter[42] – in other words, if you're worried that you're going to be treated unfairly due to your gender, ethnicity, sexuality, health status or any other grouping, you're more likely to experience Imposter Syndrome. This matters, as the severity of Imposter Syndrome is linked to depression, anxiety, impaired performance at work, job satisfaction and burnout.[43]

Microaggressions as Tiny Ts

This definition from professor of psychology and education at Teachers College, Columbia University Dr Derald Wing Sue sums up microaggressions to a tee: 'Microaggressions are the everyday slights, indignities, insults, put-downs, and invalidations that target groups experience in their day-to-day interactions with well-intentioned individuals who are unaware that they are engaging in an offensive or demeaning form of behaviour'[44] – and like all Tiny Ts, it is the cumulative effect that causes harm. Do any of these microaggressive statements seem familiar to you?

- 'But you look so well!'
- 'Haven't you done well, considering your background.'
- 'Yes, but where are you from originally?'
- 'Oh, it's wonderful that you can do XYZ, despite your condition.'
- 'Is your husband home?'
- 'I simply don't see colour.'

Microaggressions, then, are a type of implicit bias that are usually unintentionally harmful, yet communicate a hidden insult or invalidation. It can be helpful here to distinguish microaggressions from overt forms of oppression, often defined as the 'isms' such as racism, sexism, classism, ableism, anti-Semitism, ageism, heterosexism (or homophobia) and gender binarism, where the purpose is to dominate and maintain inequalities. In other words, the 'isms' have *both* a negative intent and impact, whereas there may not be an explicit intention to cause harm with a microaggression, although the impact can be just as damaging.

Microaggressions therefore are a more subtle form of discrimination; however, their consequence can be significant, leading to self-doubt and Imposter Syndrome, in addition to psychological fatigue as the receiver tries to figure out why such a statement made them feel so undermined. Microaggressions can furthermore affect motivation and impair professional trajectory. But the effects can be even more serious as microassaults, microinsults and microinvalidations may lead to physical health problems, shorten lifespan and increase inequality in access to education, employment and health services.

Why do we have implicit biases?

There is far, far too much information in the environment for us to compute at any one point in time – in fact, we generally only consciously process a minuscule fraction of the 11 million bits of information we take in every second of every day. In the same way as the stress response is automatic, we have other cognitive shortcuts that have allowed us to cope in a complex and ever-changing environment. Indeed, the vast majority of the brain's processes are outside our conscious awareness and operate on autopilot, allowing us to achieve high-level functions such as decision-making and reflection – basically this is so that we can get life's everyday tasks done without having to take time out to explicitly analyse every piece of information the world bombards us with. This is fantastic as it has enabled us to adapt and evolve, but it has a drawback – we, all of us, are prone to cognitive errors and biases because we have only a limited amount of mental capacity. An implicit bias is one such shortcut, where we make instant assumptions of a person or group based on the features we believe are characteristic of that group. This doesn't always lead to a negative or harmful belief, but if we have insufficient direct experience of a group, these assumptions tend to be stereotypical and caricatured and often reflect prejudice – possibly leading to unintentional microaggressions.

The back-handed compliment

When we explored microaggressions as a reason why some groups appear to have a higher prevalence of Imposter Syndrome, Kellie revealed that she had been awarded a place on an enriched programme and scholarship for her studies based not only on her grades, but on her background also. She said she always felt self-conscious about this, and that maybe she hadn't truly earnt her success. Kellie recalled the number of times someone had said to her, 'Weren't you lucky to get that scholarship' and 'Haven't you done well considering ...' – with the underlying inference that Kellie's success had little to do with academic achievements, hard work or aptitude, but rather it was unfairly attained, not the hours and hours of study or sacrifices she made during her life to commit to a career path.

Kellie also shared that her success made her feel uneasy, but she'd never been able to share this with anyone previously – certainly no one at home or work as she didn't want them to realise she had been 'faking it' all this time. Hence, she never had the opportunity to hear an alternative view, or for someone to help her challenge these thoughts triggered by the Tiny Ts of microaggressions, and so indeed whenever Kellie started to feel her most severe symptoms of Imposter Syndrome, these back-handed compliments rang in her mind.

This was a profound insight, and over the coming weeks Kellie experienced a range of emotions including anger at the microaggressions, relief that there appeared to be an identifiable reason (or reasons) for her Imposter Syndrome, and also a dose of melancholy for the time consumed by self-doubt.

Kellie stated: *'I always thought that it was something to do with me inside, like something was wrong with me, not anything to do with my experiences.'* This again highlights the way in which Tiny Ts can be almost imperceptible, and therefore insidious. Comments and interactions that on the surface appear positive, but leave a bad taste in your mouth afterwards, cause such internal tension. Microaggressions can also be behavioural; for example, my client Kai experienced constant interruptions while speaking in meetings, yet no one else appeared to be cut short like this and so self-doubt started to set its roots deeply within. The continual nature of these Tiny Ts wears people down, resulting in issues such as Imposter Syndrome, as this person being interrupted questions not only whether anyone is listening, but whether they have anything valuable to say at all. Hence, this is a form of microaggression that can turn into subtle bullying over time if left unchallenged.

In an effort to extend the Awareness and move to the Acceptance phase of the AAA Approach, I believe it's pertinent to explore how implicit biases lead people to engage in damaging activities such as microaggressions, which can contribute to Imposter Syndrome and the destruction of self-esteem.

Other Reasons for Not Ever Feeling Good Enough

Because Tiny Ts are amassed during someone's life, it's rare that uncovering just one Tiny T will lead to acceptance. When working with Kellie, like all clients, we also investigated some of her behavioural patterns that could have been perpetuating a sense of Imposter Syndrome. Again, Kellie admitted that she felt reticent about sharing some of her habits with me, especially her social media usage. She recognised that the extensive amount of time she spent scrolling through LinkedIn (*'every spare minute I get, it seems'*) made her feel even higher levels of self-doubt, but she couldn't stop doing it. When we looked closer at the chronology, a link emerged between the time she started to feel painfully like an imposter and when she started checking LinkedIn almost addictively. This illustrates how one Tiny T can snowball into another, and how we ourselves – or rather our innate and hardwired cognitive mechanisms – can perpetuate the vitality-depleting themes of Tiny Ts.

We have too many reference points

In addition to the implicit biases that we receive from others that give us Tiny Ts, we also have many in-built mechanisms to beat ourselves up with – one very common one these days is our tendency to compares ourselves to others. Yet again, this had an evolutionary advantage, as early humans would have needed this mechanism to survive – having the ability to immediately, and without much conscious thought, compare themselves against an opponent, and either conclude that they were bigger or stronger and could probably win in a fight, or see themselves as the weaker rival and flee out of harm's way, was helpful to early humans as it saved valuable seconds that otherwise could have resulted in harm or death. This is extremely reductionist of course, and there are countless traits against which we can compare ourselves with others, but even if we think about a couple of generations ago, you would typically see your family, people in your community and at work, but not many others. But now, we can compare ourselves to billions of other people in the palm of our hands. And because it would have been more dangerous in evolutionary terms to misjudge a clearly superior rival, our hardwiring directs us to compare up, rather than compare down. Hence we have an innate tendency to focus on those who we feel are better than us on some level – which was a fantastic mechanism for early humans, but is rather disadvantageous in the online world where profiles and images are tweaked, filtered and perfected.

In psychology we call these limitless points of comparison 'reference points' – and they are truly never-ending as social media algorithms are designed to make them so. Kellie felt – in the beginning at least – that a work-based platform such as LinkedIn wasn't anything like other social media apps where people edited their physical images. This was a networking platform after all, and isn't that what we're all told to do to improve our career prospects?! Exasperating as it was, we were working on the Acceptance piece of AAA, and so drilled down further to see if Kellie's Tiny Ts were driving her social media use and constant comparisons.

A case of the 'woulda, shoulda, couldas'

I was never a huge *Sex and the City* fan and can't say that I ever watched an entire series, but I found the character of Samantha such a good illustration of how to deal with the 'woulda, shoulda, couldas' - by really just not giving a flip about them! However, it's much easier said than done; as aforementioned, we are hardwired to make comparisons - not just between ourselves and other people but with our parallel-universe selves. We really can be our own worst bullies!

In a series of research studies from the University of Navarra, it was found that we tend to idealise the routes we didn't take and the choices we didn't make.[45] This can be as innocuous as food envy or as significant as regretting major career decisions, life partners or even having children. After these *sliding door moments*, because we did not go on to experience these alternative paths, we can romanticise them and ignore the fact that these choices would also be associated with difficulties, learning curves and disappointments. We consistently overestimate how good something *coulda* been - and social media adds a mighty weight to this.

Kellie said that since her Imposter Syndrome started, she found it almost impossible not to daydream about what her life might have been like if she hadn't accepted the scholarship - maybe she *coulda* done something else that *woulda* made her feel more content. Everyone on LinkedIn seemed to be having amazing careers that they were happy with - '*Why can't I be like this?*' Kellie asked.

AAA Approach Step 2: Acceptance

To help Kellie figure this out, we used the *So what?* exercise. It may sound somewhat harsh at first but bear with me as it's an amazingly straightforward and fast way to get to the bottom of a problem – and, more importantly, find the root feeling that is contributing to psychological un-ease.

To start, state the issue at hand.

The problem: I don't know if I *shoulda* taken the scholarship and pursued this career path.

So what?	Response
So what?	It doesn't seem right that I was given a scholarship and yet I question my career path.
Yeah, but so what?	Because maybe someone else could have used it and been better than me.
But like, so what?	Maybe I stole it from someone more deserving.
So what?	I didn't deserve it as I can't seem to be content with my career.

The answer: I don't feel deserving of my success.

The feelings this conclusion triggers: guilt, shame, self-loathing.

As I said, this technique can appear callous and insensitive, so you may want to inject some humour into it by imagining a good friend's voice when you use it! This really is a useful way to identify underlying feelings that perpetuate Tiny Ts Themes such as Imposter Syndrome – and once these feelings are brought out into the cold light of day, the Acceptance work can progress in leaps and bounds.

Guilt – name it, don't shame it

Here we were getting closer to this Acceptance, the central component of the AAA Approach. It transpired that the micro-aggressions that Kellie had experienced over the years had tapped into a deep, lurking sense of guilt she had about her success - or more precisely, about the assistance she had received in the form of a scholarship to get there. By finally labelling the emotion of 'guilt', we could tackle it head-on. Kellie felt guilty about the scholarship and that she didn't genuinely deserve her success as she'd has this 'leg-up'. We explored whether this guilt was warranted or unwarranted in the sense of whether she had actively done something wrong or not, and it was important that Kellie sit with this question rather than letting her inner imposter take over. It helped to discuss the Emotobiome here to enable differing emotions to be present simultaneously, even though it was uncomfortable at first.

Don't let them get you down – the art gallery exercise

Within this Acceptance phase, I also asked Kellie to choose a place she liked going, but one where other people would also be in the space - this could be a museum, cinema, art gallery, or whatever type of public place you like to visit. Kellie opted for an art gallery, so I asked her to imagine walking around, viewing art works in a time-limited exhibition. This would be the only chance Kellie would have to see such pieces; she couldn't come back another time as it was ending soon. Now, I asked her to imagine there were tons of unruly and inconsiderate people in the gallery - they're talking loudly and ignoring the usual polite behaviours of such a place. I questioned Kellie on how this made her feel - annoyed, angry and frustrated were words that came to mind. Next, I asked if she would leave this once-in-a-lifetime exhibition because others were behaving in this manner - think about this yourself in your own mental imagery.

Kellie thought about this for some time, and then said, 'No, I'd stay and take in the art regardless of what other people are doing if this was my only chance.'

The people in this exercise can be viewed as literal others, but they can also be seen in a metaphorical sense of Tiny T and the feelings Tiny T creates such as guilt. We can't change what's happened to us, but we can choose to accept these experiences and work through associated feelings. For Kellie, the inconsiderate people in the gallery were her feelings of guilt and to a certain extent shame, but recognising that this emotion needn't prevent her from enjoying her achievements was a step forward. Hence, it is this acceptance that makes it possible to truly move forwards in our lives. Because we do only get one chance at this life of ours.

AAA Approach Step 3: Action

For Imposter Syndrome it's useful to use a mix of solution-focused techniques you can do right now to turn the volume down on that inner imposter, and longer-term methods to rebuild self-confidence and a firm sense of self-worth.

Quick tips and solutions for managing the imposter inside

Text mini-survey

We're not always the best judge of ourselves and our qualities, which can feed the inner imposter. So open your phone, identify at least three people who you respect and trust, and ask them to list your three top qualities and why they think you demonstrate these characteristics. When you have the information back, see if you can find any themes - but, more importantly, drink in the positive feedback!

Power-up with a pose

Social psychologist and researcher Amy Cuddy's video of her power pose went viral because this technique is so easy and can be done just about anywhere. The theory is that we can use our body language to boost confidence, and her research found that not only did people feel more prepared to tackle the world, physiologically their levels of testosterone increased, cortisol decreased and there was even a greater appetite for risk.[46] So next time you're in a situation where you need a power-up, stand with your feet firmly placed on the ground, hands on your hips and head facing directly forward. You can do this for two minutes privately (in the loo if needs be) or adopt similar poses in important meetings to gain confidence by expanding your body to take up space and allowing your limbs to be open. You may find that you recognise this type of body language in people you view as powerful and confident and there's no harm in mimicking this.

Self-coach, rather than self-criticise

A critical internal narrative is a tell-tale sign of Importer Syndrome, often stemming from Tiny Ts. However, we can replace this self-critical voice for a self-coach. When we think of a coach, it's not someone who placates and pacifies, rather it is an individual who encourages us based on our strengths. So next time a thought such as 'You have no idea what you're doing here - you're not up to it!' enters your mind, stamp it out with a coaching roar along the lines of 'You have so much to offer here and you deserve to be here!' Finish off by repeating to yourself, 'You've got this!'

Dealing with microaggressions

Although we may long for a world in which microaggressions do not exist, the reality that we all have implicit biases means that we're a pretty long way off such a utopian existence. Even though these are societal Tiny Ts, there are still ways to manage microaggressions when they occur in order to limit their effect on you. Experts suggest making the invisible visible. Usually when microaggressions happen, people aren't fully aware that they have engaged in such an action - the intention is rarely to be discriminatory, but the impact is like any other form of prejudice or discrimination, so it's beneficial to bring it out into the open. Until others are aware of their own behaviours, they are unlikely to change, so disarming a microaggression can be beneficial all round. This is often referred to as a micro-intervention and here are examples based on the previous microaggression statements:

- In response to 'But you look so well!', **separate the intent from the statement** by saying something along the lines of 'I know you were just trying to be nice and give me a compliment, but this makes me feel invalidated as I have a chronic condition. Instead, in the future, please simply ask me how I'm doing.'
- In response to 'Haven't you done well, considering your background', **ask for clarification** such as 'What do you mean when you say that?'
- In response to 'Yes, but where are you from originally?' **disclose your own process by sharing your observations and reflections**; for example, 'I notice that you've made an assumption about my background – I've done that to others in the past but I learnt that it can be offensive and based on implicit bias stereotypes.'
- In response to 'Oh, it's wonderful that you can do XYZ, despite your condition', **target this person's values** such as 'I can see you do care about inclusivity, but this is undermined when you add a qualifier such as *despite your condition*'.
- In response to 'Is your husband home?' a **direct approach** is warranted, such as 'That is an inappropriate question'.
- In response to 'I simply don't see colour', **paraphrasing** can be used in the form of 'I think you just said that you don't recognise ethnicity; is that correct?'

However, if you are subject to microaggressions on a regular basis in a particular setting like the workplace, do seek help and report this to the appropriate person such as your line manager.

Longer-term solutions for overcoming Imposter Syndrome

Leap into feedback

People who experience Imposter Syndrome tend to be very good at their jobs as they are constantly trying to prove to themselves that they are deserving of their positions. However, because they are highly skilled and trained, often experts in their fields, they rarely receive feedback as colleagues and managers don't think they need it – this then maintains the type of signal-searching described at the start of this chapter, trying so hard to ascertain feedback in people's facial expressions and other non-verbal communication. To overcome this takes a leap of faith as the imposter inside will attempt to prevent this type of reality check with thoughts such as 'You can't ask XX what they think as they'll know you've been faking it all this time!' If you do experience these types of thoughts, go back to Chapter 4 and use the ASK technique, then arrange a time to speak with either someone at work, or an external mentor about your performance. A mentor can be a fantastic option here as their role will be to offer constructive feedback and encouragement, while allowing you to share your feelings of Imposter Syndrome and self-doubt in an uninhibited manner. Even if you're at the top of a career ladder, parallel mentors or executive coaches can offer this type of role. In my experience of psychological coaching, it is often those at the top that experience Imposter Syndrome most keenly, and benefit hugely from this sort of support, as an objective sounding-board can help everyone separate reality from your insecurities – we all need a reality check from time to time!

Be SMART

A characteristic of Imposter Syndrome is having unrealistically high expectations for the self, so a proactive way of dealing with this is to make realistic, concrete and actionable expectations - goals if you will. When our goals are vague and imprecise, there's no real way to measure progress and know if or when we've reached a milestone. Therefore, to quieten the imposter inside, think SMART when it comes to career or any other goals you may have:

Devise a goal that is **Specific**. Rather than aiming to be the top of your game, which is a vague aim, think about a goal that you can define clearly. This might be a work-related continuing professional development qualification (CPD), or something within your workload such as identifying a mentor to help with the tip above!

Decide how you will **Measure** this career goal. Because your goal is specific, it will be much easier to measure. Completion of a CPD course or securing your mentor are much more objectively measurable than working yourself into the ground to be the best of the best.

Make sure that your goal is actually **Achievable**. The great thing about SMART goals is that once you've defined an explicit goal, it's much easier to decide if it is indeed achievable. Do you have the time to fit in this CPD? Do you have the knowledge about where you can find mentors? By ensuring it's achievable you can build the self-confidence that will disperse that Imposter Syndrome.

Question yourself about whether it is **Relevant**. This may all sound great, but maybe you don't need this type of CPD! Select a goal that will help you grow and develop.

Finally define your **Timeline**. When would you like to attain this goal? Give yourself a deadline that's reasonable and realistic for your schedule.

As the nature of Imposter Syndrome makes you minimise your achievements yet maximise your near misses, it's useful to document your progress and achievements. Create a file and give it an energy-fuelled encouraging name - mine is the U ROCK file! And most importantly, celebrate each and every win, with a loved one if possible, and practise accepting compliments graciously - which can be hard at first but once the imposter inside starts to wither, it gets much more pleasant.

Those who can, teach

Imposter Syndrome makes us feel unworthy of our accomplishments, but it can also downplay how far we've come and the challenges we faced to get to where we are. However, by sharing our journey with others, we can remind ourselves that we genuinely are worthy of our achievements and at the same time we can inspire more people. Therefore, think about sharing your journey with those who may be on a similar path, and think about it from a learner's perspective.

This is a great trick to use at work if you're nervous about leading meetings or giving presentations, as it shifts the focus from 'you' to 'them'. People often report somewhat overwhelming feedback when they are more open and honest about their experiences, and frequently say how surprised they are by the number of people who tell them they felt like imposters too. This doesn't mean you have to share every aspect of your Tiny T, just the relevant parts of your story that are appropriate for the setting.

Dr Meg's prompts for self-belief

1 What compliments do you find most challenging to accept?

2 What would it mean to trust yourself unconditionally?

3 How do you want to feel tomorrow?

CHAPTER 6 TAKE-HOME TINY T MESSAGE

Although common, Imposter Syndrome is often brought about by successive Tiny Ts. However, anyone can experience the fear of 'being found out', as we are surrounded by countless reference points and have an innate tendency to compare up. Knowing how to deal with microaggressions and focusing back in on *your* progression, not in comparison to others, can help to overcome the difficulties associated with this Tiny T Theme.

CHAPTER 7

Eat your heart out

In this chapter we will explore:

- how to identify emotional eating
- how food is so much more than fuel – reward, punishment and purgatory
- it's not what you eat – it's *why* you eat
- how to practise mindful self-compassion to overcome over-eating
- how we can experiment with our behaviours to change our identities.

Over- or under-eating is another of the most frequent Tiny Ts Themes I see, but it's often misunderstood. We often call this 'emotional eating' and think of it as a way of consuming our negative emotions - the sorrowful sight of lovelorn Bridget Jones burying her heartache in a tub of Ben and Jerry's easily comes to mind - but this is only one characteristic of what I refer to as 'Tiny Ts Eating', the theme of this chapter. Excessive food consumption does indeed happen when we need to be soothed, hence the term comfort eating, but we also over-eat when we feel stressed, bored or even excited! It's such a common occurrence for a multitude of reasons, including stemming from Tiny Ts, but also due to our innate physiology that drives us to seek out energy-dense foods, modern-day priming that nudges our appetite and a society that still places so much value on physical appearance. But I digress ... let's return to Mo's story from Chapter 1. He had become a protector for his brother Val in childhood and had come to see me when his doctor warned him that he was heading for a raft of health problems if his eating behaviour didn't change. However, the pressure from looking out for his brother Val wasn't the only reason Mo turned to food as stress relief. Here he explains the family and social context in more detail:

> *I was the oldest of three, Val being in the middle, then Meera was the baby of the family. Mum was a big feeder [laughs] and was always piling on second and third helpings for her boys - but not for Meera. I felt bad for her at the time as Mum seemed like a hawk when it came to Meera and food and would tell her repeatedly, 'You'll never find a husband if you get fat!' This sounds so outdated now, but back then it seemed normal - and normal that the boys and men could eat as much as they wanted, all the time. If you turned food down it was the worst insult on my mum possible!*
>
> *So yeah, I know I find food comforting, that's no huge discovery here [laughs]. I wouldn't be clinically obese if I ate rabbit food [laughs]. But I just don't know what to do now. I've tried everything I can think of - secretly, 'cause you know, I'm a man and my mates would rip the piss out of me if they knew - the low-carb and ketosis plans which made things even worse as I stank to high heaven, not a way to get a second date I can assure you [laughs]. I've done all the fasting, 5:2, 16:8,*

all of that but it just piles back on. I think I need to just accept that I'm a fat bastard now, but I have kids and I don't want to keel over with a heart attack before I'm 50.'

Indeed, the stakes were high for Mo at this point, and he didn't lack commitment to change, but he certainly hadn't yet found the tools to do so.

What exactly is Tiny Ts Eating?

Tiny Ts Eating isn't merely devouring a pot of ice cream after a break-up, but rather can be associated with the vast range of Tiny Ts. As with every Tiny T Theme, it can be easier to identify from your pattern of behaviour, and the key here is eating when you aren't physically hungry. See whether any of these eating habits are familiar to you – if many of them touch a nerve, you are likely to have some aspects of Tiny Ts Eating at present.

- Eating to the point that it's uncomfortable or painful.
- Or alternatively, waiting until you feel you're going to pass out as you haven't eaten in many hours/all day.
- Eating zombie-like, so that you look down at an empty packet and feel surprised – like the food must have evaporated into thin air.
- Speed eating – you can eat a full meal in less time than it takes to make a cup of tea!
- Eating when doing other activities such as talking on the phone, walking, driving, working at the computer, etc.

- Finding it difficult to turn down food when it's offered.
- Eating when other people are eating, even though you're not hungry.
- Finding it hard to watch a TV show or film without snacks.
- Not really knowing you're full unless you've cleared your plate.
- Feeling like you *must* eat at set times of the day, regardless of hunger levels.
- Or tending to grab whatever's available, often convenience food, as you've not thought much about your energy needs.
- Eating when the stress response is triggered, either from in-the-moment stressors or future worries and past ruminations (see Chapter 4).
- Eating simply to pass the time or to alleviate boredom.
- Eating to escape the experience of unpleasant emotions such as sadness, guilt, loneliness, etc. (see Chapter 3).
- Eating when experiencing feelings associated with lack of control, including frustration, anger, jealousy, irritability, etc.

We all eat for reasons other than physical hunger sometimes, but if these patterns are leading to significant weight gain or loss in the form of Tiny Ts Eating, it is worth trying the AAA Approach to develop a better relationship with food.

AAA Approach Step 1: Awareness

When thinking about Tiny Ts Eating, it's important to consider the context in which it's emerged. Far from just being a means to survive, food, or rather consumption, can be associated with love, comfort and security, particularly when these emotions are derived from the primary care-giver. Mo was understandably very protective of his family and somewhat defensive, so by exploring how it's not at all unusual for food to become almost indistinguishable from feelings of comfort and love, we were able to move from a viewpoint of blame, to one of understanding. The aim of uncovering Tiny Ts is not to assign fault, but rather for the purpose of connecting the dots between current issues and our life experiences. In Mo's case, he did associate food and the act of eating with the comfort of his mother's patience and warmth at the kitchen table, where he was able to relax after a day of hypervigilance at school. Always keeping an eye on his brother was tough, especially at such a young age.

Food as Love

When growing up, we as children associate this caregiving with food, and subsequently feelings of security and safety are intertwined with eating behaviour. I shared with Mo that research shows women tend to consume less at family meals, reflecting the relative power dynamics in a family with males receiving more sustenance than females.[47] Hence, providing and dividing food for a family can be viewed not only as a manifestation of love, but also as a reflection of social roles. Mo was rather surprised at this – he always felt intensely uncomfortable and embarrassed that his sister had been treated differently from the boys in the family. He told me later that knowing that this pattern occurred in other families - many families in fact - took an enormous burden off his shoulders. Mo was beginning to disentangle some of his pent-up feelings, and we know from research that the ability to identify, regulate and express our emotions reduces the tendency to eat them away.[48]

Information is power in the Awareness phase

To help Mo further understand how his emotions impacted on his eating behaviour, I asked him to complete a food and mood diary. This is a very simple exercise that I use with all my Tiny T clients. The task is to write down not only everything you eat, but also what you are doing, who you are with and how your feel *both* before and after eating. You can use the excerpt below from Mo's diary as a template to help to remind you to jot down this important information that will raise awareness. Please be as honest as possible here - no one else needs to see this diary. Many people who have Tiny Ts Eating have developed a mindless, almost zombie-like pattern of eating and can be quite shocked when their consumption is documented in this way. Be kind and compassionate here; this is a courageous step into a more liberated life, but the process can trigger some deeply buried feelings. Complete the diary for at least a week, including weekends, as eating behaviours can vary over different days.

Food and mood diary: Date 3 January

Time	What were you doing, where, with whom?	Hunger level before and after eating[49]	Food/ drink	Feelings/ mood	Feelings/ mood after
19.30	Having a meal with extended family – mum, brother, sister and her family at restaurant	7 before 3 after	Shared pizzas, starter of garlic bread and mozzarella sticks, chocolate fudge cake as dessert	Excited to see family, been a long week at work	Happy, bit tired
23.41	Alone at home, everyone in bed	4 before 3 after	Chocolate bar, tea, biscuits	Feeling nothing, zoned out	Low, feeling guilty for eating when I already had a pudding

Mo completed his diary for two weeks, which was helpful as it allowed us to see the relationship between his feelings, Tiny Ts triggers and eating behaviour more clearly. The above is a snapshot of his diary and pinpointed the most telling aspects of his day. Mo's eating behaviour during the day wasn't especially excessive, and this was how he justified the increasing kilos as being due to something outside his control – 'I really don't eat more than other people so it *must* be down to my genes'. However, when it came to the group eating periods, Mo's Tiny T Eating came into the spotlight. He accepted that it felt almost impossible to turn down food when his family was near – it felt so natural to eat in the presence of his loved ones.

As Mo had his own family now, he saw himself not only as the protector but also as the provider, and he said it felt good to be able to buy everyone a meal and be very generous with the portions. Mo didn't want to tell everyone he needed to lose weight – he didn't want them to worry, as they all looked to him as the strong one, so even though he wasn't particularly hungry before the meal, Mo ate until he was physically uncomfortable. When we explored the feelings part of his diary, Mo could quite easily see that he had positioned himself as the caretaker and protector of everyone in his life, a pattern learnt early on when he had to fend off Val's school bullies. This identity had become such a core part of him that he felt he could never show any weakness or ask for support from his nearest and dearest. Of course, this is an impossible role to maintain 24/7 and the pressure was almost unbearable. But eating chocolate eased that pressure at the end of the day ... in the moment at least.

Can food be an antidepressant?

Certain highly palatable foods like chocolate boost the 'feel-good' neurotransmitters such as serotonin in the brain. This has a direct impact on our mood – some researchers go as far as to say that chocolate can act as an antidepressant.[50] Other foods and drinks containing a lot of sugar (including 'healthy' drinks such as fruit smoothies, as they have a high concentration of fruit sugars) will hike alertness and can also lead to over-excitability. This is commonly followed by a mood crash as the body tries to restore a sense of balance.

Food as a Reward

Mo's Tiny T Eating was clearly wrapped around his relationship with his family – but it wasn't just that food can be a demonstration of love, as it can also be a reward throughout life. We learn through experience which actions are associated with rewards, and on the other hand punishment. This is similar to our exploration of the stress response and how this response can happen automatically when in similar situations to the initial stressful event, but reward and punishment are seen in psychological terms as association by proxy. In other words, we learn the association for how others treat us, rather than from our innate survival reactions. The technical term for this is 'operant conditioning', or associative learning, and here our feelings, thoughts and behaviours are reinforced either by praise, the giving of treats and rewards or other positive experiences. Negative experiences are also part of associative learning in the form of punishments and recriminations, which shape our understanding of the world and how we fit into it. Punishments can in themselves create Tiny Ts, when carried out indiscriminately, but even rewards can strengthen patterns of Tiny T Eating as food is so often used and has an immediate and pleasurable effect.

Food was indeed employed as a reward during Mo's childhood and adolescence for just about any good behaviour he could think of – but particularly when he was a 'good boy' protecting his brother and abiding by the societal norms within his environment. Again, this is far from unusual – I remember vividly being given sweets or an ice cream after behaving well at a doctor appointment, boring family events and church!

Parents have a blooming difficult job, so, frequently, food is the quickest and most effective way to modify behaviour!

But unlike receiving a gold star, eating activates the 'reward system' of our brains.[51] Behaviours that increase our chances of survival (whether of the individual or the species) trigger our reward system. The reward system functions when a particular set of structures in the brain are activated in response to the neurotransmitter dopamine. Dopamine makes us feel good ... so anything that triggers the release of the dopamine pathway feels rewarding to us. The reward system affects our behaviour as it is hardwired to drive us to actions that release dopamine – i.e. we want to do the same thing again to get the pleasurable feeling. So, by being a 'good boy' Mo learnt that he would receive rewards, mostly in the form of highly palatable foods that triggered his brain's reward system, thus wanting him to continue these types of behaviours not only as a child, but also as an adult. However, always looking after everyone else is a heavy burden, so by the time Mo came to me he was over-eating so much it was severely damaging his health and wellbeing.

AAA Approach Step 2: Acceptance

We are *why* we eat

By adolescence, Mo had completely internalised his role as protector not just for his brother, but for everyone he cared about in his life. The positive reinforcement he had received in terms of praise, love, worth and food was so rewarding to him that even when the negative side of Tiny T Eating started in the form of high blood pressure, cholesterol and pre-diabetes, Mo could no longer see the distinction between his eating behaviour and his sense of self. He was *why* he ate. Accepting this as a starting point for change, the second of the AAA Approach was helped by a large dose of self-compassion. Next is an exercise you can do with Tiny T Eating and also when trying to disentangle aspects of your identity that no longer serve you.

Exercise: Mindful self-compassion

Mo was struggling with acceptance and was giving himself a hard time for so many things, including letting his family down, not being strong enough, and of course his weight, so I suggested a mindfulness exercise that focuses on self-compassion. Many aspects of mindfulness stem from more traditional meditation within Buddhism, and here we concentrated on 'metta', which means a sense of platonic love, kindness, goodwill, benevolence, peace and harmony. But there's a twist, so read on.

- Start as always with a few deep breaths through the diaphragm to still your body and mind.
- Next, notice your presence by allowing your mind to tune into your physical sensations. The easiest way is to start with the breath – simply notice how it feels to inhale and exhale. Explore this sensation with curiosity and openness. Then scan your body for any other sensations such as tension, tightness or heaviness.
- Now, think about someone you care for profoundly. Gather together these feelings of metta, the compassion, love, warmth, kindness, and wrap them around yourself, imagining that you are embracing this person that you regard so deeply in a gentle hug.

- Next, focus your thoughts on the following statements:

  May _____ (add name) feel happiness and freedom in their life's journey.

  May _____ experience calm, harmony and serenity as they walk through life.

  May _____ believe in their inner strength and be able to cope with the challenges life brings.

  May _____'s personal suffering diminish and be no more.
- Then refocus on your bodily sensations. How do you feel now? What physical sensations are present in your body? Perhaps your breathing has slowed down or the tension in your back has melted away. Perhaps you feel somewhat lighter, brighter. You may even be smiling or have a smile in your mind's eye.
- Next, return your attention to the images you can see when thinking of this person. Can you see them smiling, laughing and feeling free? Again, approach this mental picture with non-judgemental curiosity.
- Now, here's the surprise. Remove your loved one, and place yourself in the frame. Replace the phrases from above with yourself inserted:

  May I feel happiness and freedom in my life's journey.

  May I experience calm, harmony and serenity as I walk through life.

  May I believe in my inner strength and be able to cope with the challenges life brings.

  May my personal suffering diminish and be no more.
- Finally, end the session by bringing your attention back to your breath. Focus on the feeling of drawing your breath in, and steadily letting it out for a few moments before ending the exercise.

This can be an incredibly powerful, if at first uncomfortable, technique to develop self-compassion. Mo was rather irritated when we redirected the sense of metta onto him as he wasn't used to thinking about himself at all, let alone with love and tenderness! But he stuck with it, in the beginning for his family's sake, but over time his posture, eye contact and general presence altered, and it was clear that Mo was nailing the second part of the AAA Approach.

Suffix your identity

Researchers Amanda Brouwer and Katie Mosack conducted a fascinated study that shows us another way to tackle the Tiny T Eating Theme by tweaking our sense of identity through subtle modifications of internal self-talk.[52] The aim was to test whether simply adding the '-er' suffix to a healthy intention could actively influence people's behaviour. One group of volunteers was asked to create a list of identity statements around their health goals – i.e. if the goal was to eat more fruit, they became the 'fruit eater', if it was to increase exercise they became 'exercisers', and so forth. By tacking on the '-er' suffix, the participants became active 'doers' within each of their goals. The result was that the 'doers' ate healthy foods more often, and increased their other goal-related behaviours in the month following this identity tweak, compared to those in the control group who had only been given standard nutritional advice.

Managing self-talk and then communicating this new script to others is yet another formidable tool when it comes to shifting identities. This is much more than 'fake it until you make it' because our self-beliefs drive our behaviours. However, you may feel nervous about trying out your new identity for the first time - understandably so - therefore it can be helpful to prepare and test the water with a behavioural experiment in the Action phase of the AAA Approach.

AAA Approach Step 3: Action

Short-term, solution-focused strategies for beating cravings

Food cravings can feel overwhelming, but they are brief, normally only lasting for a matter of minutes - which is why distraction can be a good short-term method to change eating patterns.[53] Although distraction is sometimes seen as an unhealthy way to deal with life's challenges, when it comes to cravings this is a great strategy as it helps to pass the time until the urge to eat eases. Here are some short, sharp ways to use distraction effectively to shift your attention until the snack-attack impulse passes.

Game it away

This is one time where I will suggest getting your smartphone out, as playing a mentally challenging game such as *Wordle* or *Tetris* will direct attention and cognitive resources away from your preoccupation with food. Of course, you can go retro and find a paper crossword, whichever works for you!

Give your willpower a clench

Research has demonstrated that tensing or clenching muscle groups can in turn firm up your willpower, helping to overcome foodie temptation, as well as increasing tolerance for physical pain, make it easier to gulp down yucky medicines and focus on emotionally difficult messages.[54] This form of embodied cognition can help particularly when you truly want to make sustainable, long-term changes to eating patterns. So, next time you feel a craving hit, clench a fist and embody your inner Rocky Balboa!

Press the pause button on your mental remote control

Eating mindlessly on autopilot is a common symptom of the Tiny T Eating Theme, but we can regain control of what we put in our months by using a mental remote control. This is quite a fun technique that you can really play around with. Prepare by imagining you have a remote control in your brain – think about what it looks like, conjure up the buttons including pause, play, fast-forward and rewind. Then, next time you have a craving and find yourself reaching for soothing snacks:

Mentally press the pause button of your internal remote control and freeze the real-life frame – in other words, stop what you're doing!

Take a moment and step outside yourself by imagining that you're an observer of this scene.

Next, mentally press 'play' and see how this Act 1 plays out – watch yourself from above scoffing the chocolate and think about how this feels. There may be a brief moment of instant gratification, but what follows?

Then, take a deep breath and fast-forward this scene to sometime after succumbing to the craving, perhaps an hour or so after.

You are now in Act 2 of your inner movie. Here, ask yourself: how do I feel? Are you disappointed in yourself?

Frustrated, experiencing a sense of self-loathing or guilt? Be honest with yourself about how you usually feel following this eating behaviour. These emotions can be strong but try not to push them away, as they can help you.

Now that you have seen the future, press 'rewind' on your remote control and bring yourself back to the present. Replay Act 1 but this time *don't* give in to the craving. Instead, evaluate whether you are truly physically hungry or if you're about to engage in some Tiny T eating, remembering that cravings pass in a matter of minutes.

Ask yourself again: how do I feel? Strong, in control and grounded maybe?

Finally, it's time to press 'play' for real and make a conscious decision on the action you want in your real-life movie. You truly have the ability to change the third Act here and give yourself the final say.

This exercise is all about bringing our thoughts, feelings and behaviours back into our conscious awareness to regain control of our actions, which will impact on our whole life. Hence, you can use this remote control technique not only to overcome zombie-like, mindless eating but also to change everyday habits that no longer serve you.

Longer-term Action for Overcoming Emotional Eating

Because eating is such an integral part of our social world, and intertwined with our sense of identity in relation to others, we can often be fearful of changing how and what we eat in front of our friends, family or other groups of people. Apprehension around teasing, humiliation, worries about offending loved ones or merely wanting to avoid having to explain oneself can be tangible barriers to change. However, these concerns are seldom as bad as we think - so a good way to challenge these perceived obstacles to change is a behavioural experiment.

Try your new identity on for size with a behavioural experiment

The biggest challenge for Mo was changing his eating patterns in family situations - he didn't want them to worry about his health as he was the provider and protector. He also didn't want to upset his mum by turning down food, and these concerns acted as a significant mental wall to Mo overcoming his Tiny Ts Eating - and this was the important part, these family reactions were Mo's expectations and predictions. He didn't have any direct experience of what would happen if he said no to dessert, as he hadn't yet refused a pudding at a social meal. I so often see similar scenarios, and I have, without a doubt, had to encourage myself to engage in behavioural experiments to test my own assumptions about situations and my own and others' reactions! Some of the most common issues I see are around saying 'no' and building healthy boundaries - for example, people who are at their wits' end due to people-pleasing tendencies, who fear that they will lose social connections and their roles if they ever say no. Alcohol is also a frequent sticking point for people, where there is a concern that you can't have fun without a drink, or that a party will be boring, stressful or tedious without oiling the conversational wheels with a drink. Therefore, the behavioural experiment is one of my favourite exercises. With Mo, then, we devised a plan to test his assumptions, which you can do yourself too by following these steps:

First grab a piece of paper and split it into five columns – it's useful to write this down as the act of putting pen to paper helps to clarify beliefs. It's also useful to have a hard-core record, as we are experimental scientists here!

Now start by noting down your **experimental situation** – this is the petri dish in which you will test out your prediction, which is next. See the situation Mo decided to test in the table below.

Next is your **prediction**, i.e. how you think the situation will unfold. Jot down any difficulties you believe you might face, from whom and in what way they may emerge.

Now that you have your experimental condition and predictions, consider what **resources** you might also have to handle any of the difficulties that may occur. This is important as we don't want you to jump in the deep end without a life jacket!

Then, once you've carried out the experiment, reflect and document the actual **outcome** – this should include what happened on the day, others' reactions and how it all made you feel.

Finally, summarise the take-home message from this behavioural experiment – was there a difference between your prediction and the outcome? This should be what you've learnt from the experiment and can carry forward on your journey.

Experimental situation	Prediction	Resources	Outcome	Take-home message
We're going over to my mum's for our regular Sunday family lunch – everyone will be there including my brother, sister and her family.	Mum will have spent all morning preparing the food, and she will expect me to eat as I normally do. I could see my brother getting confused and maybe upset if he sees a difference in my behaviour. I think my sister would be worried too and it might cause everyone to be uncomfortable.	My wife is my greatest resource, so I'll tell her what I'm doing before we go to lunch so that she can support me if these predictions come up.	My mum and wider family did notice that I wasn't eating as much – but what shocked me was that they were relieved. Turns out they were already worried about my weight but thought they'd hurt my feelings if they mentioned it. It was emotional, so it was a bit uncomfortable in that sense as I'm not used to opening up like that. It really opened my eyes to how much pressure I'd been feeling.	I don't have to be the strong one all the time. I am strong, but my family want to help me. Maybe I don't have to wear this mask all the time.

Mo discovered that his expectations, and his predictions, were far from accurate. Also this experience was not easy; it was definitely challenging for Mo to be vulnerable in front of those he cared for and protected for so long – but he found out that what he thought he was protecting them from was causing some harm in his relationships as he'd prevented his family from being as close to him as he actually wanted.

Therefore, this 'scientific' method of prediction testing can allow us to see that even people we think we know inside and out may also be hiding their true feelings from us for the very same reason: to prevent perceived hurt. Taking that first step by experimenting in this way can be a vital part of setting yourself, and your loved ones, free from Tiny Ts.

Dr Meg's journaling prompts for emotional eating

1. What do I want food to do for me?
2. What could you do more of to nourish yourself – explore at least three non-food options.
3. I feel like 'me' when ...

CHAPTER 7 TAKE-HOME TINY T MESSAGE

Food and eating is intertwined with Tiny T in so many ways – as a form of self-soothing, reward and identity – and is one Tiny T Theme that usually has its starting point in early life. This is unsurprising as we need food to survive, but in a world of easy, round-the-clock access to energy-dense foodstuffs, it has become harder and harder to moderate our consumption. Because so much of our eating behaviour is on autopilot, creating awareness of our eating patterns, developing acceptance and taking action to regain control is key in this Tiny T Theme.

CHAPTER 8

What's love got to do with it?

In this chapter we will explore:

- the different types of love
- betrayal trauma
- envy and jealousy
- how our perceptions of love can be damaging
- methods to relearn love.

Like so many people, I grew up watching Hollywood films and similarly sanitised fairy tales - most of which present true love as the cure to all ills. While I've been relieved to see some of the stereotypes (particularly in gender norms) change over time, the notion of romantic love - that there is one person out there for you who will understand and complete you - prevails. Yet there are many different types of love, and therefore love lost ...

Olivia was heartbroken - utterly grief-stricken from the breakdown of a long-term relationship. But it might not be the kind of break-up that first comes to mind - Olivia wasn't let down by her knight in shining armour; she was experiencing a profound sense of loss from a friendship break-up. Here's what Olivia had to say about her Tiny T Love:

I feel so silly even bringing this up. I know it shouldn't be such a big deal but when you asked me to think about something that had changed me, this is it. And I just can't seem to get over it.

A couple of years ago I had this close female friend - we spent a lot of time together and would definitely WhatsApp or chat every day. I was going through IVF at the time and her support was amazing to me as the treatment didn't work out, and that has been a whole 'nother journey for me. So, this is the thing I can't get my head around - that was a big deal, a huge loss and one which I've had to adjust to, that's wreaked havoc on my life, but I feel ok with it now, I found some peace with it. What I'm finding so difficult to get over, and why I've come to you, is that this friend - who I thought of as a true friend - became pregnant after all this and didn't tell me. I found out from a post on Facebook where another one of her friends mentioned it - she hadn't posted a scan or anything like that. And it crushed me, absolutely crushed me - not that she was having a baby, I was thrilled for her, but that she hadn't told me, and I had to find out like that. I can't describe how painful this was and it still bothers me - I don't feel like I can trust anyone any more and I don't go out and meet people, no one new anyway. And I can't talk about it to anyone because even as I'm saying these words, I think most people would assume I'm just bitter and jealous - but I promise you I'm not, I just feel devasted that I was talking to her all that time, and she didn't mention it. So now we really don't even speak.

This description of Tiny T is classic – we know deep down that something had affected us but disregard the trauma as unworthy of attention and compassion, or feel that negative judgements and assumptions will be made by others. And as has been mentioned throughout this book, Tiny Ts are cumulative and often act as dominoes – one Tiny T can instigate a cascade of thoughts and actions that keep us from progressing in our lives. In Olivia's case, we began by exploring whether her friend's omission about her pregnancy would be perceived as a betrayal, but she herself questioned the validity of this: 'It wasn't like we were a couple, and she was cheating on me or anything.' But there are many types of love, all of which can cause us heartache and trigger a sense of betrayal.

Focus on Tiny T: Betrayal trauma

When we have been betrayed by someone it can feel as if the ground is suddenly pulled from under our feet – what we believed was a solid basis of trust and security is shattered and it can have a major effect on an individual. The emotional pain that emanates after a betrayal can feel as acute as a physical injury and leave enduring psychological scars if not processed properly.

Betrayal trauma can occur in childhood, which is a key time for the establishment of attachment. In psychological terms, if early-life caregiving is inconsistent or neglectful this can result in an insecure attachment style that can make it hard for people later in life to form emotional bonds in a number of ways. However, betrayal trauma can also occur later in life, in romantic relationships, close friendships and within grown-up families too. We often only think of betrayal in terms of our romantic partners but breaches of trust in other close relationships can have just as much impact as infidelity.

In this sense, betrayal trauma can be associated with many incidents, including disloyalty, lying, cheating (physical or emotional), gossiping, or other behaviours that damage the bonds of a relationship. This is because in evolutionary terms we are social creatures that rely on our groups for safety, security and survival. In this day and age, we may not necessarily need others to fend off dangerous predators, but we are still hardwired in the same way as early humans. This is why a betrayal can feel so overwhelming, as it is a perceived threat to survival.

The Philosophy and Taxonomy of Love

Like Olivia, we often think that the only love that really matters is the glamorised romantic type of love – the falling into someone's arms and immediately feeling like you're home, the 'you had me at hello', the love at first sight, 'the one'. But this understanding of love does a significant disservice to our emotional wellbeing as there are many types of love connection.

Within philosophy, theology, mythology and popular consciousness there are categories of love – some commentators cite four, others seven – all of which can help us understand the intricacies of our relationships. These are partly just for fun, as the below categories aren't used in psychology so much, but they are useful sociocultural information as you will see these various love types portrayed over and over again in film, art, music and other media that we all consume on a daily basis:

Eros (romantic love) – did you ever wonder where the phrase 'falling in love' came from? In Greek mythology, the little cherub that we now call Cupid was originally named Eros, the god of romantic, sexual love. With his golden arrows, cheeky Cupid could bring about this intense, passionate form of love – so fervent in its yearning, it was seen as a kind of madness, leading to the fall of Troy in the infamous case of Helen and Paris.[55] Hence, when the arrow strikes, this irrational type of lust and wanting possession of another can lead to our downfall too.

Philia (friendship) – this is a type of friendship-based love that centres on aspiring for the best in another person's life. This form of shared goodwill is equitable and founded on a firm sense of trust and companionship. Philia can be part of a sexual partnership or a platonic relationship. We often think about this type of companionship love as coming after Eros in romantic relationships, but it can come first too and lead to increased self-awareness, authenticity and insight. This type of true friendship is believed to protect both physical and mental health in the form of positive social support.

Storge (familial love) – pronounced 'store-jay', this type of love is all about the family and is the unconditional love that parents have for their children. Storge is similar to Philia in that the giver wants only good things for the recipient, but it is asymmetrical as children are by their nature egocentric and cannot offer in return this type of caregiving love. This kind of love is vital for species survival, as babies and children need to be loved and cared for regardless of behaviour that probably wouldn't be acceptable in other relationship dynamics.

Agape (love for the world) – this is universal love, for instance love for humankind, the natural world or a religious love for one's god. A central characteristic of Agape is altruism, helping others without any expectation of return, and so it is seen as a selfless type of love.

I find these categories of love useful to help us move away from the notion that love is all about 'the one'. Indeed, we have many 'ones' throughout life, in all of the above groups, which means that we needn't succumb to the Hollywoodified pressure of locating our Prince (or Princess – interesting that there isn't yet a non-binary version of this!) Charming who will magically make everything alright in our lives.

Focus on Tiny T – toxic friends

Just like romantic and family relationships, friendships can also be toxic – but we usually discuss this much less than toxic partnerships, which is why it's a tell-tale Tiny T. Not all friendships end because they are toxic, so sometimes it can be tricky to see if the relationship has soured, especially when it's happened gradually over a lengthy period of time. Here are some key signs, red flags if you will, that your friendship may have become unhealthy:

- Your friend has started to belittle your beliefs and values, which they know you cherish.
- Your friend has crossed a personal boundary for you, resulting in betrayal trauma.
- You're starting to feel your friend judges you – this can be exemplified by bitchy comments on the way you look or dress, your other relationships or work, or even minute things that you barely notice.
- Your friend accuses you of being 'over-sensitive' when you find their actions or remarks upsetting, undermining your feelings and lived experience.
- You've started to feel put down or humiliated by your friend, particularly in front of other people or on social media.
- When you talk you don't feel you're being listened to, or your friend appears visibly bored with the conversations to the extent that you don't want to speak.
- The friendship feels very one-sided, where the only contact is that which you follow up on.
- Breadcrumbing occurs: this is when a friend gives you just enough 'breadcrumbs' to keep you engaged in the relationship – for example, the occasional text message, call or meet-up – resulting in confusion and disappointment as it's not enough to maintain a solid relationship.

Toxic friends can drain your self-esteem, confidence and emotional energy so it is worth identifying these destructive relationships in your life and removing them if appropriate (see Action below). Friendships should energise and soothe, not suck the life out of you.

When Olivia and I explored her friendship, the only issue that jumped out was breadcrumbing. This is an interesting one, as inconsistent contact can be a pink flag, rather than red flag. A pink flag is like a pre-warning signal; for example, when the petrol tank for your car is running low and lights up, but you know you still have about a quarter of a tank left to get you to a filling station. Pink flags in relationships *might* be the indication of toxicity, although not necessarily so, but they are signs that you need to explore in your relationship to find out for sure – just as the petrol gauge running low isn't something to be ignored. In the case of breadcrumbing, the lack of communication and contact could be due to other factors, and so it's always worth checking out (which we will explore later in this chapter).

For now, this gave us an important starting point for unpicking Olivia's unique constellation of Tiny Ts. This will be different to everyone, even siblings, close friends or those we identify most with. So, to start to give us some clues, we began with the first AAA Approach phase of Awareness to uncover *how* Olivia loves.

AAA Approach Step 1: Awareness

Although not all Tiny Ts stem from early life, love is one area that is intrinsically linked to our formative experience of receiving care. Therefore, it's valuable to reflect on an area that is backed by a huge volume of research: attachment style.

Attachment is everything

As babies, infants and young children we absolutely need, and completely require for our survival, someone to look after us. We're not mammals that can walk an hour after being born or feed ourselves instantly, so this first relationship sets the scene for our perception of the world. How responsive our caregivers are to us in our early life forms what is known as our 'attachment style'. There are different types of attachment styles that we develop from childhood, and which go on to mould how we feel about ourselves and others, and how we behave. As young children we learn about human relationships and concepts such as trust, security and the confidence to explore the world from our primary caregiver - often our mothers, but fathers, grandparents and other adults can also fill this role. This attachment is helped along by physical touch and the bonding hormone oxytocin, which soothes and comforts. The four main categories of attachment style are:

Secure attachment: This provides a person with the inner belief that others will respond and reciprocate, meaning the world is a generally safe place. Adult relationships tend to be trusting and enduring, and in all types of love true feelings are shared, hence this secure foundation allows for vulnerability. Securely attached people also find it relatively easy to seek out support when they need and have developed adaptive coping mechanisms.

Ambivalent attachment: This may develop from inconsistent experiences of love, and at times caregiving was sensitive to one's needs, and at others there was a lack of comfort and attention. Ambivalent adult attachment can result in clinginess or neediness, where there's an underlying worry that partners, and to some extent friends, do not really, truly care for them. This fear can make a person wary of forming bonds with others, and if bonds are forged and then broken, the intensity of a break-up can be overwhelming.

Avoidant attachment: This is where care needs have not been appropriately met and so the expectation is that others will not respond and return affection. Adults with this type of attachment may develop issues with closeness and intimacy and find it hard to be open about their feelings with loved ones. Avoidant attachment may also lead to little perceived interest in creating social and loving bonds and such a person may appear aloof to others.

Disorganised attachment: This can come from an erratic environment, swinging from intrusive to passive caregiving, which can be disturbing for an individual. This less common form of attachment may be expressed as a combination of avoidant and ambivalent traits, in a mirror of the love experienced in early years – i.e. clingy, then cold.

Factors that affect the type of attachment we develop include the quality of parenting and caregiving, but many other influences also play a part - the characteristics and traits of infants themselves can have an impact on attachment style and so it's important to remember that this process is an interaction between child and caregiver. This explains how different children in the same family can have completely separate attachment styles. So, let's not wholly blame the parents for our attachment style! As we've seen throughout this book, understanding and awareness is generally a more helpful strategy than assigning blame. Family circumstances, including major life events within the family, environment and culture, all play their part too, and even as babies we form multiple attachments that may result in differing styles.

When Olivia and I reviewed these attachment styles, she noted that overall, as a child, she had a secure attachment. She felt in general that her caregivers were responsive and reliable, and she felt supported – '*but I wouldn't say mum was a big hugger – if anything, she was tepid, not cold but not warm like other mothers I knew*'. This was a small hint, as we all crave physical touch (see the box on page 196), so we were beginning to build up Olivia's Tiny T canvas. I suggested that Olivia might have different forms of attachment with her mother and father, and this seemed to shine some light on the situation; she revealed that, yes, her attachment with her mother seemed more ambivalent than the secure attachment she had with her dad.

For a long time in psychological and developmental research and practice we thought that people had a single, fixed attachment style from childhood – in other words, you could only have one style and it would stay with you throughout your life. But now there is greater understanding of the complexities of the human experiences and, basically, life just isn't like that – Tiny Ts can occur at the same time as secure foundations are being built in early life. These experiences are not mutually exclusive, which again is why Tiny T can feel so confusing – someone may feel that overall they have a secure attachment, 'so why am I having problems?' Furthermore, we can have different attachment styles in the different kinds of love - for example a secure attachment in Eros love, but an anxious attachment in Storge love.[56] But this also offers us a great deal of hope - just as Tiny T can metamorphosise a positive type of attachment into something that makes relationships more challenging, understanding and overcoming Tiny T can transform all types of love into secure attachments. This is the power of acknowledging Tiny T in your life.

Focus on Tiny T: Skin hunger

Human touch is vital for the development of attachment. This is why newborn babies are placed on their mother's skin after delivery, and parents are encouraged to practise skin-to-skin contact with their little ones. In Chapter 1, Harlow's seminal work on maternal deprivation with rhesus monkeys was noted, which suggests that infants have an innate (biological) need to touch and cling to something for emotional comfort, known as 'tactile comfort'. The comfort and perception of care that touch gives us is therefore vital for our functioning, not only when we are young but throughout life. Human touch releases the neurochemical oxytocin, sometimes called the 'love hormone', which helps in the bonding process. We also know that oxytocin boosts mood, increases feelings of trust and reduces the stress hormone cortisol - hence, when we engage in physical contact, such as hugging, we're likely to feel less stressed as oxytocin rises and cortisol levels dip. Physical touch seems also to help our immune system – one study of over 400 healthy adults found that hugging boosted feelings of social support and protected against the risk of contracting a common cold.[57] In those that did come down with a cold, greater frequency of hugs and perceived social support led to less severe symptoms.

However, this can produce challenges for those who live alone or need to isolate for periods of time, such as many of us experienced during the Covid-19 pandemic. It's likely that many people developed skin hunger or 'touch deprivation' at this time, but research has also found that stroking and cuddling pets triggers a flood of oxytocin,[58] so for people who either feel more comfortable with animals, or cannot interact with other people, physical touch with pets can also help.

Love on the move

We turned back to the original AAA Approach question (Chapter 1) about which aspects of life most formed who Olivia was today, and here is where the Tiny T Love Theme became clearer. Olivia revealed that, as a kid, she had moved home every couple of years as her dad was in the Forces. Although at home she did feel loved, she was aware on some level that all the moves had put a great deal of pressure on her mum – 'perhaps that's why she was tepid; she did have to sort everything out every time we moved and it must have been tough'. It was also hard to form friendships when you know you'll be posted somewhere else shortly. While in some ways technology had helped, as she could stay in touch with people around the country, and indeed the world at times, it was also hard to see other kids and then teenagers carry on their lives without this disruption. Now geographically settled, Olivia felt wary of making friends, particularly female friends, but because this one mate seemed so genuine, she jumped in with heart and soul. This made the breakdown of the friendship feel so debilitating, and Olivia did recognise the ambivalent attachment type she'd developed with her mother in this situation - she felt clingy, almost desperate at the thought of losing this friend.

Furthermore, Olivia admitted that she felt a dull, aching sense of loss when she saw the post of her friend's pregnancy, at the same time she felt a warm glow of happiness for her friend. If we think about the Emotobiome from Chapter 2, we can acknowledge that it's possible, indeed probable, that we can experience a variety of emotions at the same time, even those that may be perceived as contradictory. Both emotions - a sense of envy and of joy at her friend's pregnancy - were real and genuine for her.

Jealousy, envy and the greened-eyed monster

Although both jealousy and envy can feel unpleasant, there are important differences in these emotions when it comes to the green-eyed monster. Put simply, jealously is when we fear losing something that's important to us, and is associated with other emotions such as anxiety, anger and distrust in the face of this potential loss. Envy is wishing that you possessed what someone else has, and there are two sides to envy, one of which would take this desired object or experience away from someone else in order to obtain it, and the other being that you'd just like both of you to have it. Hence, envy can create feelings of longing and inferiority (e.g. 'What a wonderful holiday you had; I wish I could afford to get away too!'), but the darker side is that resentment can rear its head ('He doesn't deserve the career he has; I work so hard and should be in that position instead').[59] The latter, more negative type of envy is where the green-eyed monster phrase from Shakespeare's *Othello* comes in, and this more destructive type of emotional experience can be met with both internal and external disapproval, and sometimes feelings of shame and guilt.

Overall, the difference between jealously and envy is the contrast between 'loss' and 'lack'. This can be particularly evident when it comes to female friendships, where research shows biological females do tend to experience higher levels of 'friendship jealousy' compared to males at the prospective loss of best friends to others. In Chapter 1, we mentioned the concept of the tend-and-befriend stress response that females have, in which women are more evolutionarily programmed to want to keep the group close and intact as per their survival role. This is one reason why women and girls find it so hard when their friendships break down, especially if that friend is seen to be developing new Philia relationships. There are, of course, many subtleties in this, but often simply being aware that these feelings are somewhat ingrained can help release and accommodate the unpleasant feelings of jealousy and envy, and allow their exploration in the Emotobiome.

AAA Approach Step 2: Acceptance

To move on now from the initial stage of Awareness to Acceptance and progress through the AAA Approach, it can be helpful to deep-dive into this type of Philia love, as we tend to have quite a lot of ideas about how friendships work, and indeed how many friends we should have, which sometimes plays into our Tiny T.

Focus on friendship and Philia love

One of my closest friends mentioned the quote 'Friendships are for a reason, a season or a lifetime' and, like so many well-known adages, it's hard to know exactly its origin. But I adore the sentiment as it made me feel ok about some friendships that had fizzled - or imploded!

Research shows that there is a limit on the number of friendships we can maintain at any one time.[60] The number of close friends, the ones you bare your soul to, stay up late at night talking to until somehow the sun comes up - you know the ones - is usually no more than you can count on one hand. For good, but not your closest friends, the magic number is around 15. These are the buddies who you enjoy activities and share time with, but not your most intimate secrets. Next are the people who you look forward to seeing at parties or other major life-event celebrations like birthdays, weddings and even sombre events such as funerals, but whom you probably don't connect with on a regular basis - these friends usually number between 35 and 50. Finally, there is the outer circle of friends who you have an interest in on socials, and like to occasionally see how they're doing (or if you're a bit older, would be on your Christmas card list) but you only communicate with rarely, and this numbers around 150. You may have many hundreds more friends and connections on socials, but actually, were you to prune down your online friend list to the ones that you still care and think about, it would probably be around this 150 mark.

But it's totally fine also if you have nowhere near this many connections – it's much more about quality than quantity. Friends can come in different shapes and sizes too. A client of mine named Quinn consulted me as they had lost their best friend – in a break-up with a partner, their beloved cockapoo Chewy went with Quinn's ex as he had owned the dog first. In most countries, animals are seen as 'chattels' within the law, i.e. possessions, just like a sofa or piece of jewellery. This is starting to change but, nevertheless, I have seen Tiny T develop time and time again at the loss of an animal. I work with colleagues on the burgeoning field of animal-assisted therapy, and it is clear just how much unconditional love another living, non-human, being can give – and hence how devastating it can be to part from such selfless creatures.

So, what's the reason for the numerical estimates of friends we have in different friendship zones? We only have a finite amount of space and time in our lives – it would be impossible to maintain a deep friendship with everyone who walks through the door, and anyway many of us wouldn't want this! Also, as we progress through life and our hopes, dreams and circumstances change, in line with this so do our friendships. It may not be the Hollywood idea of Philia love, but it is a realistic and hopeful one.

Dealing with the breakdown of a friendship

In psychological therapy, the rupture of a relationship is only half the story - the repair, or attempts at repair, are just as, if not more, important. All types of relationships experience ruptures, although friendships can fizzle out or morph into something toxic over time - but of course a spectacular break-up can happen after a significant argument, event or situation, just as with any close connection. The latter is without doubt easier to spot, whereas the slow erosion of what was once a trusting, enjoyable and loving bond often leaves people like Olivia feeling completely adrift. The longer this goes on, the deeper the indentation of Tiny T. So if you feel a friendship souring, consider this three-step OWN process, which is all about being accountable for your own experience and being proactive with Tiny T Love:

O is for open: Have an open conversation that focuses on you – i.e. how you feel about what's happening by using 'I' statements to avoid defensiveness – and give your friend a chance to come to the table, such as: *'I feel that our friendship has been a bit one-sided lately ...'*

W is for wonder: Next, build on this first-person statement by using a bit of wonder and curiosity – even our closest friends may keep difficult circumstances from us, especially people that seem really strong and together from the outside (these are often the ones who need good, non-judgemental friends the most). If your friend's behaviour towards you has changed markedly and seems out of character, this will be particularly important. So, building on the first step, this could look like: *'I feel that our* *friendship has been a bit one-sided lately, and I was wondering if you're ok ...?'*

N is for No: If you've been open, amiable and warm but your friend has responded in a toxic manner (see box on toxic friendships), it is probably time to respect your peace and your boundaries, and just say 'no' to the relationship. This person may have just been a friend for a reason or a season, but not a lifetime – and that's ok. However, if your friend responds positively, this can be a real turning point for a deeper, more fulfilling connection, and the 'no' here in this process is more about maintaining your personal boundaries when it comes to relationships.

Sometimes friendships re-emerge when your reasons or seasons are more aligned, so by using the OWN process you can give yourself space and time to nurture other connections that are more beneficial to you, without completely burning the bridge. Even thinking about this process can bring on a sense of grief, however, so do go gently with yourself and allow your feelings of loss and sadness to be part of your Emotobiome. Finally, seek emotional support from other friends but try not to criticise your old friend for too long as this can lead to the types of resentment and rumination that deplete your quality of life and optimism for the future.

Olivia took the courageous step to have an OWN conversation with her friend, and it was an emotionally challenging and exhausting interaction to say the least - there were tears, hugs and some glimmers of hope. Olivia's friend admitted how bad she'd felt about the way her news had been spread and said she just didn't know how to let Olivia know about the pregnancy after all her fertility struggles. Olivia's friend revealed also that, when the baby was born, she struggled with new motherhood much more than she expected but didn't feel she could express this to someone who wasn't fortunate enough to have these problems. Juggling the demands of motherhood, work and life in general had almost floored Olivia's mate, and she felt inundated with WhatsApp NCT groups, trying to continue a career as a freelance writer and simply attempting to keep all the plates spinning - and this was the real cause of the breadcrumbing pink flag. What also came across in this OWN conversation was that her friend had felt that Olivia hadn't listened to her properly in the past, which she understood, as Olivia had been going through such an awful time. Olivia found this hard to hear but did her best not to react and instead sat with her friend's honesty. When we get to grips with Tiny T Love, it is important to take ownership of our part of the equation, as hard as that might be at first.

The powerful influence of what we see

Now we are building a much more comprehensive picture of the Tiny T Love Theme, and there was one more vital piece of the puzzle. Social learning theory is basically 'I do what you do', or modelling others' behaviours, often our primary caregivers or people we value and respect.[61] This theory was introduced in the late 1960s by psychologist Albert Bandura, who built on earlier theories of conditioning (see Chapter 4), but Professor Bandura noted that to make associations we don't need to directly experience something ourselves - these linkages could also be formed through vicarious learning.

Bandura's now-famous 'Bobo doll' experiments did indeed find that after witnessing someone else hitting this doll, children themselves were more likely to whack the plastic toy in a similar way. At the time there was a huge concern about the influence of TV on and children viewing violence, and indeed in 1972 the United States Surgeon General declared that television violence was a public health problem. There have been many critiques of these experiments to date, but the base theory that our experiences afford some social learning still stands, which is why the world around us and information we consume is part of Tiny T.

For Olivia, like many of us including myself, she grew up on books and movies about how best friends were friends forever, and this gave her a model of what she believed friendship should be. And in her own family, even though they often moved, her mum kept a close friendship with her bestie throughout. In fact, Olivia and her siblings referred to this friend as 'auntie', who had been present throughout her life no matter how many times they moved. This set a high bar for the standard of Philia in Olivia's belief system, so that when her friendships didn't quite match up, they did indeed feel disappointing.

AAA Approach Step 3: Action

The strategies in this Action stage of the AAA Approach can be helpful for all types of loving relationship – from romantic Eros relationships to Storge family-type love, and indeed Philia friendship love.

Longer-term approaches for all types of love

Learn to LISTEN

Psychologists are taught a skill called 'active listening' and it is something that you can also learn and use to improve the quality of your loving relationships. Active listening is not the same as hearing - hearing words is a rather passive form of communication, whereas active listening takes some concentration and effort. This effort is without doubt worth it and can completely transform close relationships. The purpose in active listening is to uncover the emotional meaning of what is being communicated, not just the literal meaning of the words uttered. Try this LISTEN technique that I devised, based on teaching of the late, great humanistic psychologist Carl Rogers:

L is for look – active listening involves both verbal and non-verbal communication. So, first start paying attention to what you can see – your loved one will be communicating a range of information with their amount of eye contact, gaze, display of small gestures, bodily posture, facial expressions and even micro-expressions.

I is for incongruence – one aspect of active listening that is incredibly useful is whether what someone is saying to you verbally is incongruent, i.e. contradictory, with their non-verbal cues. Usually, the non-verbal signals are the more accurate reflection of how someone is feeling. So if your partner or friend is saying 'Yeah, I'm fine, it's fine, everything is totally fine' but their shoulders are hunched, arms folded in front and eye contact is not maintained, then you can safely conclude that they are not fine at all!

S is for silence – when we are merely hearing another's words, rather than listening actively, our minds tend to rush ahead and think about how we're going to respond. This often leads to a hasty response or outright interruptions – there is no headspace for the active part of listening to occur. Leaving space for silence can feel intimidating at first, but this will allow you to process both the verbal and non-verbal messages (what is being said and how it is said) *and* it creates the opportunity for your partner to be more open.

T is for touch – humans have an intuitive, non-verbal way to communicate known as 'social touch'. A simple hand placed on an arm or shoulder squeeze can convey more compassion and understanding in few seconds than a long monologue. Social touch is particularly effective when the intent is to calm and settle a companion, but can also be used to share a range of emotional experience.

E is for emphasis – the voice is of course important in communication and you can attend to many aspects such as tone, pitch, speed, volume and articulation. It's not that you have to think about all these features individually; you will know from experience of interacting with others what certain speech patterns may be telling you. For example, if someone is shouting in quick succession like a machine gun then it's unlikely they're just fine! Everyone has their personal speech patterns, though, so it can be more useful to watch out for emphasis if it appears different than in your usual conversations.

N is for noticing yourself – another clue to deciphering the emotional meaning of your loved one's communication is to notice what's happening in your body during the interaction. For example, are you experiencing tension in your body that wasn't there before you started this exchange? What are you feeling emotionally, physically and perceptually now? Often our innate and immediate internal reactions can tell us a great deal about what's going on for others.

Active listening is a skill and so it will take a bit of practice - you and your loved one might want to try practising this skill together. Regardless, I challenge you to have a go at it and see how it changes the outcome of your social interactions!

Relearn to LOVE

I'm not sure why but this chapter seems to be full of mnemonics! I do like to use these easy-to-remember techniques, because when life is busy it can be challenging to remember how to show affection to those we care about the most. This is my way to remind myself of the foundations of love:

L is for LISTEN: This first aspect of loving is so important it has a technique all of its own above!

O is for OPENNESS: Relationships thrive on honest and open communication, but sometimes it isn't clear how to do this. Think about those moments when your relationships have deepened – was it when you both were putting on your best face, or when the mask has slipped and revealed something tender inside? This is all about leaning into feelings of vulnerability, which will allow your closest connections to become even stronger.

V is for VALUES: When we acknowledge and respect one another's values, bonds will also strengthen. This doesn't mean you have to agree on every topic with your friends and loved ones, but having some shared values helps you to agree to disagree on more surface issues.

E is for ENABLE your loved one to be themselves: True love (not Hollywood love) comes from profound acceptance. People do change, they grow and transform before our eyes and can be supported by us – but it is not up to us to try and change those we love. This is not about knowingly accommodating abuse, major or Tiny T – rather, if someone has overstepped one of our red lines or boundaries in life, even someone we love deeply, we cannot impose change on them. In this instance, self-protection is imperative, and you may need to walk away from a relationship – we cannot change someone else. In healthy relationships, however, allowing our loves to be who and what they are in the context of a safe and trusting space is the pinnacle of human love.[62]

Learning these love skills was a real turning point for Olivia and her friend, and although I can't report that their friendship was magically mended overnight, mainly because they were indeed on quite different paths, there was now some hope for repair. Acknowledging that they were going through different seasons in life at the time allowed Olivia to exhale her held breath on this relationship and focus on what she could do to improve the quality of all her love bonds.

Finally on love ...

Think about all the people who have loved you into being – hold this for one minute of reflection.

Dr Meg's journaling prompts for love

1 Note down three qualities you have in relationships and how you demonstrate each to your loved ones.

2 What are the most important things you have learnt from relationships? Think about different types of love here and explore each.

3 In what ways do you draw strength from loved ones?

CHAPTER 8 TAKE-HOME TINY T MESSAGE

We've only touched lightly on the Tiny T Theme of love here, as love really has got everything to do with it. However, being aware of the Tiny T involved with all forms of love in addition to romantic Eros love can start to help you navigate difficulties that arise with other bonds, such as friendships. While early attachment styles are important, they are not set in stone and we can create fulfilling future bonds in the manner we choose – once we develop a sense of acceptance and take action.

CHAPTER 9

To sleep, perchance to dream

In this chapter we will explore:

- the basics of sleep physiology
- sleep revenge procrastination
- labelling theory and the highly sensitive person
- how to rest your body clock through sleep restriction
- reprogramming the brain for good sleep quality and quantity.

Do you have trouble sleeping? Problems during the witching hour are yet another Tiny T Theme I see and, like many others, once people come to me, they've often tried a hundred and one remedies, potions, tinctures and all manner of products and habit change. But if you ask someone who sleeps well what they do to capture slumber, the answer is usually 'nothing' – which is as infuriating as it is compelling. The global sleep economy is worth hundreds of billions and is a fast-growing industry, so this is big business. But logic tells us that if any of these products really did work, then there wouldn't be such fierce competition for our night-time suffering. Tiny Ts, however, may lead us to some answers.

Let's start by peering into Harper's narrative:

I know I'm too sensitive – that's why I can't sleep. I was told all throughout my life that I was too sensitive – my dad called me the Princess and the Pea after that fairy story where the princess could feel a teeny-tiny pea under about 20 mattresses. He said it warmly, almost as a boast like it was proof that I was different, special maybe, but my sensitivity is completely ruining my life now.

My mum says I've always been this way – not just about sleep but about everything. At primary school I do remember being upset when my friends fell out – not even with me, that didn't happen much, but with each other. And I wasn't too keen on the screaming in the playground or the kids that pushed into you. I was definitely happier during the quiet reading times.

But sleep wasn't so much of a problem then – it really started after I had surgery. The pain during recovery would keep me up at night so I spent hours and hours online, not watching Netflix or anything like that but researching and listening to free courses. But my sleep pattern ended up so out of whack and I know the tiredness makes me feel even more sensitive to things that don't even bother other people. So I looked into how to fix it and I really have tried. Nothing seems to help me though.

I desperately need to sleep as I feel like I'm losing my mind – can you please help me be less sensitive?

Harper knew a lot – and I mean *a lot* – about sleep already. And if you've ever had trouble catching up with the Sandman, you will probably know a great deal too. Extremely poor sleep can make people feel delirious, which is why it's been used as a method of torture, so people often spend hours and hours online researching everything they can about sleep – to the point that it becomes an obsession. But I would not say that this satisfies the Awareness stage of the AAA Approach as the preoccupation with sleep is often a maintaining factor in sleep dysfunction.

Why Are We So Obsessed with Sleep?

Sleep is a natural state of rest and restoration for both the body and mind, but for a long time it's been a bit of a mystery to us. There are countless fables, fairy tales and folklore about sleep, showing how fascinated we as a species have been with slumber since the dawn of humankind. Harper's narrative included just one such children's story about a prince's great search for his princess – he would only know he'd chosen correctly if the lady in question experienced a horrendous night's kip. Although this is not exactly romantic in this day and age, as the princess would most likely have been in a terrible mood the next morning, it is interesting that light sleep is viewed as something superior. In this tale, being a poor sleeper was the very measure of royalty, yet anyone who's had chronic sleep problems would probably find this association rather abhorrent. And anyone who perceives themselves as a light sleeper will attest to the fact that disturbed sleep is definitely not a blessing. Yet, throughout the ages, and in particular for women, being seen as a sensitive sleeper has been demonstrated in art, narrative culture and other societal depictions. You see, we've always been somewhat obsessed with sleep; it's just now that we can track every twitch and tremor at night.

What is insomnia?

On average approximately 10 per cent of people suffer from poor enough sleep to be diagnosed with insomnia, but a third of us experience troubled sleep to the extent that we have sleep-related difficulties in the day.[63] These can include lack of concentration and forgetfulness, irritability and a low threshold for stress, as well as daytime sleepiness and tiredness. The diagnosis of insomnia, however, is all about threes:

The three indicators of insomnia:

- problems initiating sleep
- problems maintaining sleep
- problems with early waking where you can't go back to sleep.

In general, for a diagnosis of insomnia, one or all of these would need to occur for three days a week, for at least three months.

Also, the impact of this sleep disturbance must mean your ability to function in the day is decreased in the sense that you can't carry out your usual duties, roles and responsibilities – it has to be messing up your life, basically, for a firm diagnosis of insomnia to be given.

AAA Approach Step 1: Awareness

To start Harper's journey with her Tiny Ts Theme of poor sleep, I wanted to explore some of her beliefs around this physiological necessity. Hence, we started the Awareness phase with a little Sleep 101.

Sleep 101

During sleep, we are usually unaware of the world around us. But our bodies and brains are incredibly busy, even if we are unconscious of these processes, as numerous changes in the activity levels of our brain, muscles and other bodily systems have been studied and documented in the fields of sleep physiology and psychology. We know that within the brain, new memories are organised and there's a type of pruning process where mental debris from the day is cleaned away.

The benefits of sleep are countless – your mental and physical health rely on sleep to function. Studies show that consistent poor sleep is associated with cognitive decline, cardiovascular problems, anxiety, depression, chronic pain, and so on and so on, in pretty much every condition that's had a sleep study. This is because sleep, like eating, is necessary for survival, so lack of it is bound to worsen any underlying condition. However, hypersomnia can also be an issue, where too much sleep is also bad for our health. It's a bit of a Goldilocks-type scenario yet again – you need the right amount of sleep for *you*. Some people say they're raring to go after five to six hours a night, whereas others swear that they need ten hours to function properly. For most people, the amount of sleep you need depends on your age, with the average adult requiring around seven to nine hours per night, and older adults needing a bit less at approximately seven to eight hours.[64]

But it's not all about quantity - sleep quality is important too. Frequently disturbed sleep can result in a high level of disruptive daytime tiredness, even if you have eight or nine hours in bed. In fact, many people don't know they have disorders that wake them up throughout the night until they go to their doctors - they just feel tired all the time (TATT). If you ever see the acronym 'TATT' on your medical notes, this is what it means. These individuals may also be gaining weight, as rubbish sleep leads to additional calorie consumption, or they may generally feel that they're struggling on a day-to-day basis.

This is because sleep isn't just one process, it is a series of phases that work in cycles. We generally go through four or five complete cycles per night, with varying amounts of each sleep phase in each cycle (see the graph in the figure below). Like so many of the explanations in this book, we sleep in this way for evolutionary reasons. We were never meant to be in deep sleep for a solid eight hours, as this would have made humans exceptionally vulnerable to predators - rather our sleep evolved so that there are periods of lighter sleep and even wakefulness, just in case there was a threat in the environment. In the same way that our stress response hasn't caught up with our advanced worlds, our sleep is still physiologically very similar to early humans. Therefore some problems arise because we've convinced ourselves that we *shouldn't* wake up at all during the night - and when we do have periods of wakefulness, our minds start to race with ruminations and worries, thereby preventing us from getting back to sleep.

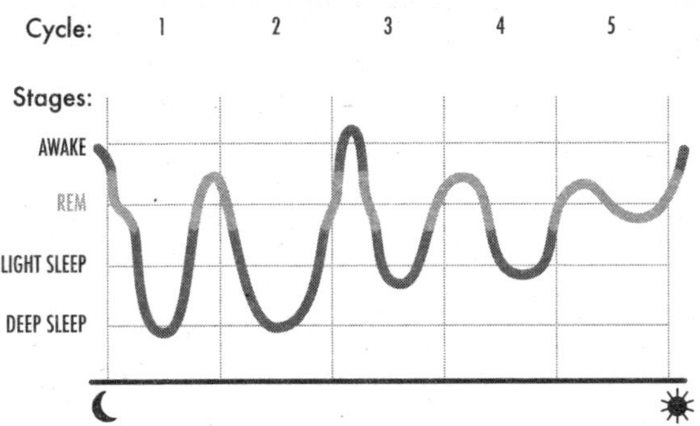

Figure 9.1: Sleep cycles and stages

This is exactly what happened with Harper. When we discussed the types of thoughts she had during those wakeful periods, she said they were often about sleep - how she was just too sensitive, how awful she was going to feel the next day and not be able to do X, Y and Z, and so on and so forth - until the early hours of the morning when she would fall back into an exhausted slump. Then of course, seemingly seconds later, Harper's alarm goes off and the situation she so dreaded has come to pass.

Sleep revenge procrastination

I'll just watch one more episode of this thrilling series ... or maybe scroll through socials for another few minutes ... whatever the method of delay, if you're putting off going to bed it's very likely to be a case of sleep revenge procrastination. The reason we do this – and it's incredibly common these days – is to essentially take 'revenge' on our daytime selves for ignoring some of our core needs. Life is hectic, and we tend to be on the go non-stop from the moment we wake until we fall asleep, with little space or consideration for moments of surprise, joy or even just daydreaming. So, at the end of a long day, the rebellious inner self in us all stands its ground and demands some 'me' time, even though we know this will impact on the next day in terms of tiredness, grumpiness and a general sense of had-enough-ness. Sleep revenge procrastination is more common in younger adults and women,[65] and is a response to daytime stress and lack of free time in our waking hours. But research has shown that we do have time in our day,[66] it's just not in one big chunk any more as it was in previous generations. We now have 'time confetti' that's peppered throughout the day[67] – the problem arises because we tend to fill these pockets of time with work, life admin or any other number of joyless tasks. Therefore, rather than giving yourself a hard time for going to bed too late, use your time confetti in the daytime to do anything that brings a smile to your face – play with your dog, use a short mindfulness technique, sit in nature – as this will satisfy the rebel inside.

Self-fulfilling sleep prophecies

Gone are the days (well, mostly I hope!) of a firm belief that dreams themselves can offer precognitive insight into the future, but I see many people predict their own sleep doom.

And this is where Tiny Ts really come into play. If we recall, Harper told us that she had always been sensitive - or rather, she had been told from a very young age that she *was* sensitive. This is how she further explained the way in which her perceived sensitivity affected her sleep, and quite frankly was consuming her life:

> *I don't drink caffeine any more - at all. I started by cutting back, then not having caffeine after midday, but now I don't even drink tea. I bought blackout blinds, eye masks, bespoke earplugs that were moulded to fit into my ears. I have white noise and natural sound players, downloaded every sleep app and tracker there is and have a full library of audio books with adult bedtime stories to try and help me drift off. I've tried melatonin, valerian, every root and tincture I can find. None of it helps - nothing. I don't eat food in the evening, and I've completely excluded spicy foods. I've bought any supplement that's been linked to sleep including CBD oil and have an entire bathroom full of Epsom salts and lavender drops. My doctor once gave me a week's prescription of sleeping pills, which did help, but I was so drowsy in the day I couldn't do anything anyway and I felt awfully hungover. I think I'd become addicted to them and one thing I do not want is an addiction to prescription pills.*

Ruminations and worries around sleep sensitivity marked every aspect of Harper's days. She had also developed quite strict routines around sleep, with any deviation from these rituals leading to such a state of stress that travel, holidays or even staying with her family were distant memories of the past.

This is why the next part of Harper's journey with me was somewhat of a surprise to her. I asked:

What if your sensitivity is actually your superpower?

AAA Approach Step 2: Acceptance

To move from Awareness of the AAA Approach into Acceptance, it wasn't enough to challenge Harper's knowledge about sleep and its physiology - this was because sleep was the symptom of her Tiny Ts, not the Tiny T in itself. Like all Tiny Ts Themes, sleep struggles had started as a trickle, then cascaded into a problem that was paralysing Harper's life. This is because Tiny T snowballs, but we often only start to sense the signs and signals of Tiny Ts after something happens in our lives that disturbs the delicately balanced house of cards. For Harper, this was her surgery, but the tendrils of Tiny Ts reached back to *The Princess and the Pea* - Harper had been labelled as 'too sensitive' for this earthly world.

In our work, Harper revealed that she had heard the sentence '*You're just too sensitive*' more times than she could count, so much so that she had internalised it to her very core. Often it felt like an accusation - a personal and unavoidable failure. Hence, when I reframed this as a superpower, Harper looked at me with deeply fatigued eyes that prickled with tears - and the path towards acceptance began to materialise for her.

Focus on Tiny T: Labelling Theory

Labelling Theory has most frequently been used in sociology and criminology to account for criminal acts and offender behaviour, but it has its place in mental and psychological healthcare too. Put simply, this theory explains how a particular type of behaviour develops from external judgements in the forms of labels, which then go on to shape someone's actions. In other words, if you tell a kid they're bad, naughty or no good enough times, the chances are they will live up to this label and show you exactly how naughty they are. The same can apply to a trait like sensitivity when it comes to sleep – although some people might be more sensitive than others, if you highlight how lightly someone sleeps, they will probably become hypervigilant to any slight noise, movement or other environmental factors, and therefore have a poor night's kip. This is particularly true if the label has some social gains for an individual – for example, a young child primarily wants their caregivers' attention, so by incorporating such a label, he or she may have more time with their caregivers at bedtime. Also, these labels may be reinforced if any deviation from this categorisation is ignored or even prohibited. Finally, when this label is given publicly, it can be too risky for someone to act against it as it might cause emotional pain (in the form of embarrassment) to those valued most, e.g. parents, particularly when we are forming our sense of identity.[68] Hence, a label can very quickly and easily turn a good kid into a delinquent, but it also works the other way round and we can resolve challenging behaviour by using Labelling Theory in a positive way.

The highly sensitive person

In the 1990s, a gentle wave was gathering far off in the seas of academia. Dr Elaine Aron, an American research psychologist, started to conduct studies that reflected her own experience. Dr Aron had found certain areas of life challenging. During a psychotherapy session, her therapist pointed out that she was a 'highly sensitive person' or HSP[69] - not in any derogatory way, but as an observation. This incredibly significant moment led Dr Aron to collect data and later devise a scale to see whether others had this trait. Over the course of her career, Dr Aron has estimated that 15 to 20 per cent of the population are highly sensitive.[70] Aspects of this trait include:

- being affected by other people's moods and atmosphere in a social context
- being sensitive to noise, light, coarse textures, strong smells, pain, hunger and stimulants (e.g. caffeine) and, as such, making efforts to control these stimuli
- nervousness or anxiousness when demands are high, performance is being observed or plans are changed with short notice
- high levels of conscientiousness, a strong desire to avoid making mistakes, and ruminative thought patterns if a perceived error is made
- having a heightened awareness of the details of an environment and being able to appreciate the subtleties and beauty of the external world
- having and enjoying a rich and intricate inner world as well as art, music and other creative areas.

Nowadays this concept is much better known, and although Dr Aron originally conceptualised the HSP as a neutral personality trait, the term 'sensitive' is frequently still used as a type of insult or microaggression to undermine people. If we look at definitions of this word, it can mean to be easily offended or upset, yet it also refers to the speediness of detection or response to slight changes, signals or influences - and in an evolutionary sense that would be advantageous. The ability to notice subtle differences in the environment would have undoubtedly protected not just an individual but the group, and so would have been a prized asset in early humans. But now, in a noisy, bright and constantly changing world, this trait has been rather turned on its head to become a weakness - only I don't think it is.

At this point, Harper and I carried out an exercise - we brainstormed different superheroes and their superpowers onto some massive pieces of paper stuck onto my office wall. It looked a bit like this:

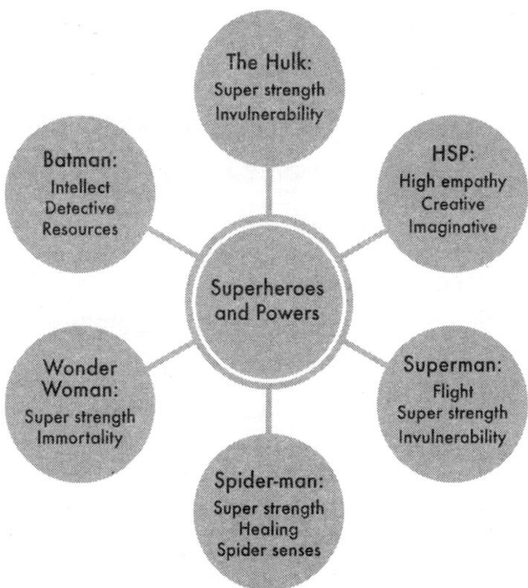

Figure 9.2: Strengths mind-mapping

When we stepped back, it was clear that many of our most loved superheroes had finely tuned strengths - and it was this attunement that made them extraordinary. Next, we worked a bit more on the reframing exercise to help with the Acceptance phase, by listing the positive attributes Harper had. And many were in the form of Dr Aron's HSP - her ability to notice others' feelings, which made her a wonderful friend and confidante; how she could become immersed in music to such an extent that it felt like an out-of-body experience; and her affinity with animals. Then, finally, we looked back at our superhero mind-map and explored whether these fictional characters were able to use their exceptional capabilities in *all* situations or whether they had to manage their abilities somewhat. I think you know the answer here, and it's backed up in observations across cultures and societies. Many parts of the world celebrate the quieter, more reflective, and indeed more sensitive individual - it's really only in Western societies that being brash, loud and overly extroverted has been seen as a strength to trump all others. And this is yet again the cumulative effect of Tiny Ts - it's not that there was anything 'wrong' with being sensitive, Harper was just in an environment that made it challenging for her and because of this she built up a belief system that constantly told her this trait was troublesome.

Dream therapy

As human beings, we have been fascinated by our dreams throughout history – but what do they mean, if anything? While the area of dream analysis is not grounded in science, there are now many studies that give us some clues about the purpose of dreams. Famously, Sigmund Freud, the father of psychoanalysis, suggested that dreams are a way for the subconscious mind to tell us the nature of our deepest desires and wants. Another notable psychoanalyst, Carl Jung, countered this argument by proposing that dreams communicate our waking-life problems to the conscious mind via universal images and themes, which he referred to as archetypes. Both of these seminal figures therefore believed that dreams do indeed have a purpose, and current research suggests this might be true when it comes to emotions – and Tiny Ts.

Most studies carried out in the latter decades of the twentieth century found that the vast majority of dreams seemed to be negative – around a quarter of recalled dream reports were associated with unpleasant feelings.[71] It has been theorised that this is a way for the brain to process these more difficult emotions that people may find hard to express in waking life – in other words, our minds may be mentally dealing with Tiny Ts while we sleep. Indeed, neuroscientist Rosalind Cartwright studied divorce trauma and found that these unpleasant dreams – nightmares even – appeared to allow people who developed depression after a break-up to recover from their emotional trauma more successfully.[72]

So next time you have a bad dream, have a go at reframing it from a horrid experience to a bit of free therapy! This might just put a spring in your step for the day ahead.

AAA Approach Step 3: Action

It's true to say that not everyone with disturbed and poor sleep is highly sensitive; as with all Tiny T, everyone will have their own unique set of life's cuts and scrapes that lead them to a life less lived - but there is a universal way to deal with Tiny T Sleep in my view. It's all about deactivation and association, and in this hectic 24-hour world we live in, the former can be particularly transformative. Here are ways to move through the day to make sleep an effortless process again.

AAA action: Strategies for bedtime

It's all about efficiency: how to use sleep restriction to improve sleep quality

If your sleep is now at the point that you're feeling it's hopeless and you'll never get back into a natural pattern again, a technique called 'sleep restriction' can reset your body clock. This is a challenging method, so I would advise that you only take it on board when you have a clear schedule, so that you will have the best possible chance of sticking with the below steps. I used this technique with people who've had the worst Tiny T Sleep, and it's proved to be a game-changer in their lives. Here's how it works:

Phase 1

To start, you need to know your sleep efficiency, so keep a pen and pad by your bed for at least a week to find out:

the amount of **time you spent in bed,** averaged over the week each night, whether you are awake or asleep;

the estimated amount of **time you were asleep**, even if this is disturbed.

I don't recommend using a sleep tracker or apps as these tend to increase a maladaptive preoccupation with sleep – the old-fashioned pen-and-paper method works just fine.

Next a bit of maths for you, as we need to use the info above to compute your sleep efficiency score. It's really simple; all you need to do is divide the average amount of time you sleep by the amount of time you've spent in bed. Then multiply by 100 to give a sleep efficiency score like this:

(TOTAL TIME ASLEEP ÷ TOTAL TIME IN BED) X 100 = Your SLEEP EFFICIENCY

This was Harper's example:

(5.5 hours asleep ÷ 10 hours in bed) X 100 = 55 per cent sleep efficiency

No one has 100 per cent but a good sleep efficiency is around 80 to 85 per cent (for those without long-term health conditions), so Harper's sleep problem was without a doubt causing her significant problems in the daytime due to sleep deprivation.

Phase 2

So now that you know where you stand with your sleep efficiency, we can move on to the sleep restriction phase:

Your SLEEP WINDOW is the amount of time you've slept on average, not the amount of time in bed. This will now be the total time you can let yourself stay in bed while carrying out this technique. For Harper this was 5.5 hours.

Next, set your THRESHOLD TIME, which is basically the time you go to bed to start your window of sleep. For Harper, who had been going to bed quite early, meaning she had a lot of time lying in bed worrying about why she couldn't sleep, we agreed her threshold time would be much later, at midnight.

Finally, combine this threshold time with your sleep window to give yourself an ANCHOR TIME, which is the time you need to get out of bed, even if you're still tired. In Harper's case this was 5.30am, which sounded pretty harsh! But the key was to improve sleep efficiency and revert some of the damaging sleep patterns that she had developed.

<table>
<tr><th>Time</th><td rowspan="3">THRESHOLD TIME

12 midnight – Bedtime, get into bed</td></tr>
<tr><td>10pm</td></tr>
<tr><td>11pm</td></tr>
<tr><td>12pm</td><td rowspan="6">SLEEP WINDOW

5.5 hours allowed in bed

(Your average time asleep)</td></tr>
<tr><td>1am</td></tr>
<tr><td>2am</td></tr>
<tr><td>3am</td></tr>
<tr><td>4am</td></tr>
<tr><td>5am</td></tr>
<tr><td>6am</td><td rowspan="3">ANCHOR TIME

5.30am – Wake up, get out of bed</td></tr>
<tr><td>7am</td></tr>
<tr><td>8am</td></tr>
</table>

The aim is to use this schedule for a week to give your body and mind a strong sleep drive. But during this week, stick to these three sleep restriction rules even if you feel fed up:

- Only allow yourself to get into bed once you've crossed your **threshold time**.
- Only stay in bed for the amount of time in your **sleep window**.
- Get out of bed in the morning at your **anchor time**, even if you're still tired or sleepy.

Phase 3

This final phase is where you can start to increase your sleep time, but first you need to recalculate your sleep efficiency and adjust your sleep window based on the following guidance:

- If your sleep efficiency is now above 85 per cent, you can add an additional 15 minutes onto your sleep window – for Harper this meant 5 hours and 45 minutes was her new sleep window.
- If you're between 80 and 85 per cent sleep efficiency, please keep your sleep window the same for another week.
- If your sleep efficiency is less than 80 per cent, please decrease your sleep window by another 15 minutes.

As you can see, this is a gradual process and so takes some patience - if you feel like you've tried everything, give this a go as it's a powerful method to break free from poor sleep.

Practical action steps to physiologically deactivate the mind and body

The following tips are usually included in general 'sleep hygiene' guidelines, which is simply good sleep practice - it's about sleep being spotless! These general rule-of-thumb-type suggestions help to dial down physiological activation of the mind and body so that it's possible to drift off to sleep at bedtime. Early humans wouldn't have needed all the guidelines, but now that we live in a technological world where food, for example, is heavily processed, it can be useful to be mindful of all the stimulants that we are exposed to on a daily basis - and reduce these where necessary. However, do bear in mind these should also be flexible to fit in with your life, travel and family - if you start to feel anxious or rigid about any of the below, it's worth looking at your thought patterns (see Chapter 4).

The old saying of keeping the bedroom for sleep and sex still holds weight, so ditch the screens, including smartphones and tablets. 'But I use my phone as an alarm clock!' I hear you cry - well, a bit of tough love here ... I'm calling you out on this. It's cheap and easy to purchase a traditional alarm clock or dawn simulator to ease you into the day. The resistance towards leaving your phone outside of the bedroom is much more to do with sleep revenge procrastination and Tiny Ts, so if you're finding it difficult to forgo your messages, socials or emails at night, work on these underlying themes.

Caffeine, chocolate and some types of food (spicy, aromatic and piquant) are stimulating, so replace these with more deactivating food and drink from mid-afternoon. Caffeine has a half-life of around five to six hours, depending on your genetic capability to metabolise it - so if you have a caffeinated drink in the afternoon to perk you up during the dreaded mid-afternoon dip, it's equivalent to having a small cup of coffee just as you're going to bed.[73]

Heavy and calorie-laden meals - breads, pasta and other starchy foods - can initially make us feel drowsy, as our digestion system must process all this; but because these meals are heavy our tummies need to work extra hard to digest them, which can activate the body and wake us up. Of course, the odd curry for dinner with mates is not harmful; these suggestions are about giving you a firm foundation in sleepiness that will support good-quality and restorative slumber so that sleep is no longer a battleground for the mind and body.

It's a common misconception that a boozy nightcap aids sleep. In fact, although a tipple may make us feel drowsy, alcohol actually disrupts sleep as the body metabolises it. The rule of thumb is that every measure of alcohol consumed (even during the day) equates to an hour's loss of sleep. As our drink measures have steadily grown, and the potency of wine, beer and ciders has increased, it can be difficult to know exactly how much we're drinking. A large glass of wine, for instance, is now equal to a third of a bottle – so if you have three large glasses of wine in the day you would have guzzled an entire bottle down! This is around nine to ten units of alcohol, meaning it's unlikely that you will have any good-quality sleep at all during the night.

Many prescribed and over-the-counter medicines can also interfere with sleep. Commonly used medications such as beta-blockers, corticosteroids and SSRI antidepressants all alter our physiology, so it isn't surprising that they can disrupt sleep. For example, corticosteroids mimic the effects of the hormones our bodies produce naturally in the adrenal glands, which is part of the nervous system, and so activate the mind and body. If you need to take medicines, have a chat with your doctor to see if you can use them earlier in the day to give yourself time to deactivate.

In general, the optimal bedroom temperature is around 18°C, but what this really means is an overly hot or cold room can hamper sleep, as the body will need to work harder to cool off or warm up. Our bodies naturally start to cool down in the evenings to encourage sleep, and we can use a trick to induce these feelings even more. By taking a warm bath before bedtime, your core temperature will rise and then fall as your body cools off, producing a sensation of sleepiness. Ride this wave and use this as part of your sleep ritual (below) to lull yourself naturally into a state of drowsiness.

We've evolved to move our bodies around every day, so if your job is desk-based and/or sedentary, as most are in our modern world, try to integrate some movement into your schedule - otherwise, your body won't have the chance to physically burn off some of its energy. However, avoid strenuous exercise in the three to four hours before bedtime, as this will reactivate the body.

Deactivating troublesome thoughts at bedtime

Intrusive thoughts *about* sleep can be difficult at bedtime, but many of us also replay events from the day over and over again in their minds - sometimes this isn't even daily events but things that have happened weeks, months or years ago. These mental perceptions and projections of a *faux pas*, error or slight activate the innate stress response in the form of both rumination and worry about doing it again. You might recall, perhaps, forgetting someone's name at a wedding ten years ago and feeling the blood rush to your face, hands trembling from the weight of pitying eyes in the conversation circle. So often our minds play out endless stories of faults as soon as we slide beneath the sheets - it generally happens immediately, and people state they feel powerless to stop these internal narratives. Research shows that these unhelpful thoughts patterns are the nemesis of sleep,[74] as **sleep will never override the stress**

response[75] - our desire to survive in the face of threats (real or perceived) is simply too strong. But there is a simple technique to deactivate these thoughts, which is one of my favourites for bedtime and during the night.

Say in your head the word 'the' about every other second. 'The' has no emotional connotation so it won't trigger the stress response, but the act of concentrating to mentally utter the word will keep the mind focused just enough to stop it going down a sleep-depriving rabbit hole of past mistakes and future fears.

Using the power of associations and programme your bedtime routine

In Chapter 4 we saw how associations can affect us negatively, leading to an activated stress response and avoidance-type behaviours via Tiny Ts. But we can harness the power of associations and use them for good, not evil!

We instinctively know that children need a wind-down routine to deactivate, but we somehow forget this when we are adults. Really, we're all just big kids wandering around in life so we can take some lessons from a child's bedtime routine as a way of making associations between certain activities and time for sleep. By setting up a series of cues, we can gently deactivate the mind. Although many of us would love our brains to work like a light switch with an on and off button, we're simply not programmed this way. But we can programme a bedtime routine to gradually shut down that whirring computer in our heads.

Bedtime routine

Around 60 to 90 minutes before it's time to go to bed, start your bedtime routine by turning off the TV, tablets and computers and any other stimulating activities.

Instead, choose a deactivating wind-down activity such as reading, listening to soothing music, a recorded meditation, or a form of artwork.

You may want to try the bath cooling-down trick. Why not make your own mini-spa with soothing lighting, candles, scents, etc.?

Gentle stretching and breathing exercises can also be part of your wind-down routine.

You can also download your mind by writing a to-do list for tomorrow – this way, when you have a phase of wakefulness during the night, your mind won't rush to remind you of the tasks for the next day.

Other forms of writing can also be beneficial – journaling as part of a bedtime routine is another way of releasing the activation of the day.

Experiment and find out what works for you; remember that it can take time to develop different associations and rewire the brain with new neural pathways. But once these associations are strengthened, you'll find that just starting your bedtime routine will make you feel sleepy.

Dr Meg's journaling prompts for sound sleep

1. Your word of the day is ... Explore why you've chosen this word also.
2. Write down what you'd like to leave here in this day.
3. Next, write what you'd like to take with you into tomorrow.
4. Designate a 'word of the day' for tomorrow. Think about what this word means to you.

CHAPTER 9 TAKE-HOME TINY T MESSAGE

There is an epidemic of sleep issues across the world, and because we need sleep for recovery and everyday functioning, it's central to physical and psychological wellbeing that we get to the bottom of the Tiny T that may be contributing to this theme. While the HSP may be highly attuned to their environment and so woken more easily, as well as being prone to intrusive thoughts at bedtime, sleep disturbance is by no means exclusive to the HSP. Knowing the drivers of poor sleep, accepting your uniqueness and taking strategic action to reset your body clock will all help you to get a good night's sleep.

CHAPTER 10

Transitions, transitions, transitions

In this chapter we will explore:

- life stages and the social clock
- moral injury
- moving through transitions within liminal space
- menopause and the sandwich generation
- letting go and moving on.

When I was an undergraduate studying psychology, there was a huge focus on child development, but less on development throughout the lifespan. Developmental psychology tended to use stage theories, where children progress sequentially through phases that were very much set within defined age brackets. I remember at the time thinking that this can't be totally accurate and that even if a child was outside of these ranges it didn't mean there was something wrong with them or they were 'delayed', as surely we as humans vary quite a bit. Now, most of my colleagues would agree that stage theories are more guides than rigid milestones, although we are so used to using developmental benchmarks they can actually create a huge amount of anxiety. Parents in particular can become understandably preoccupied with milestones, but some kids simply exhibit certain signposts when they damn well please! This goes beyond childhood however, and in most cultures there is a common view that as adults we 'should' reach certain landmarks at particular times in our lives. If we haven't crossed these invisible lines, this sense of 'missing the mark' can be a form of Tiny T in itself, as we look at others and believe they somehow have it all figured out. At this point, I'd like to introduce you to Freya, a lovely young woman who came to me on the cusp of her thirtieth birthday:

> *I know it's silly but I'm finding the thought of turning 30 terrifying - I don't feel like I've done anything at all by now, and I don't even know what I should be doing, not with work, whether to stay in my relationship or anything. I don't think I'll ever be able to afford to buy a house, and without a stable home how can we even start to think about having babies? Everything, I mean everything, seems out of reach and when I try to talk about it with my family they just fob me off and say it will all work out - but how? I'm not even sure who I am, or supposed to be any more - it's like I'm going backwards, as I knew when I started working, or at least I thought I knew, and now I just don't know. I don't know what I should be doing with myself, or my life - what should I do?*

Of course, I couldn't answer that for Freya, as it was she herself who had the solutions - we just need to lean into the AAA Approach to uncover them.

Whose Stage Is It Anyway?

I would say the most famous stage theories include Erik Erikson's *Psychosocial Stages of Human Development* and Daniel Levinson's *Seasons of a Man's Life* (see the table on pages 240–1).[76] Both theories saw adulthood as developing from the age of 18, with a number of defined stages of development including early adulthood, middle adulthood and late adulthood. Quite a bit of our sociological and psychological understanding of people has been based on these sorts of theories, but it's worth considering for a moment the context in which such concepts were created. Erikson's theory was published in 1950, and Levinson's in 1978. If we think for a minute how life was in these decades - how gender roles played out, for example - we can start to see why perhaps we should take these now widely accepted stages with a pinch of salt. Also, even the title of Levinson's theory is rather biased - a 'Man's Life' - and reflects the fact that he and most psychologists, researchers and scientists based their conclusions on research carried out predominantly with cis male participants. Indeed, Levinson later conducted interviews with women and found some differences, unsurprisingly. However, as the aim of such models was to identify the common themes over the adult lifespan, they did by their nature plonk people into boxes and exclude the complexity and variety of human experience, as well as the influence of a person's context.

Focus on Tiny T: Sex bias in scientific research

When Levinson published his theory, the title probably didn't raise an eyebrow at all – until relatively recently the belief that women's bodies (and minds for that matter) were rather too complex to study was widespread in scientific and medical research. It seems astonishing now, but the vast majority of ground-breaking research is based on male biology – in humans, animals and even cells.[77] [78] This undoubtedly spilled over into psychological research and theory formation, a problem that we've been aware of since the 1970s[79] although many models of adult life transitions and development are very much still based upon these ideas, so it is worth us always bearing this and other demographic biases in mind.

Adult psychosocial development

Period of development	Erikson's psychosocial conflicts	Levinson's transition/ crisis points	Social and biological clock tensions
Early adulthood (20–40 yrs)	Intimacy vs isolation	Early adult transition (17–22 yrs)	Finish education; first job; search for partner
		Age 30 transition (28–33 yrs)	Concern over partner and career choice; parenthood
Middle adulthood (40–65 yrs)	Generativity vs stagnation	Midlife transition (40–45 yrs)	Unrealised dreams in sharp focus, both family and career; perimenopause

Period of development	Erikson's psychosocial conflicts	Levinson's transition/ crisis points	Social and biological clock tensions
		Age 50 transition (50–55 yrs)	Empty nest; menopause; sandwich generation pressures
Late adulthood (65 yrs–death)	Ego integrity vs despair	Late adulthood transition (60–65 yrs)	Acceptance of life choices, retirement, forced or otherwise; health deterioration; grandparenthood

Despite the biases, we can't overlook that there were many valuable findings from this body of research and theorising – mainly that throughout life we move through various phases of development, and within these periods there are numerous transitions, often referred to as a 'crisis'. If we compare Erikson's and Levinson's theories side by side, particularly the former's psychosocial conflicts and the latter's transition points, we can start to build a picture of how transitions relate to Tiny T. In general, it is not the transition per se that causes Tiny Ts, but rather Tiny Ts may make it much harder for people to work through a transitional crisis or psychosocial conflict in their lives. What Freya was describing certainly sounded like a crisis – a transitional crisis in fact – and we needed to do some work on the Awareness phase of the AAA Approach to discover if some Tiny Ts were making this journey more difficult for her.

'I'm too young to feel this way!' – The transitional crisis

Levinson's theory clearly included an 'age 30' transition, sometimes referred to as a quarter-life crisis. But, of course, not everyone who approaches 30 will have a crisis, or it may happen later - we do, though, all experience transitions in our lives at various times. However, the main body of research on transitional crises has unsurprisingly focused on the 'mid-life crisis' - a phrase that was first coined in 1957 by Canadian psychoanalyst and social scientist Dr Elliott Jaques, who observed middle-aged people (but mostly men) in his practice demonstrating the now classic mid-life crisis behaviours of trying to look young, buying a sports car and sleeping around in an effort to hold on to youth and avoid inevitable bodily decline and eventual death.[80]

But what was most interesting in Dr Jaques' report was that people who hadn't met their own and society's expectations of life's milestones seemed to experience this state of crisis more intensely than others and struggle with this transition to a greater extent than people who had neatly met all life's sociocultural markers at specific timepoints. In other words, the question 'How am I doing for my age?' often rings in people's ears as they look over at friends, loved ones and social media, and this also happens in early adulthood around the age of 30.

The social clock – a benchmark for comparison

We often talk about the biological clock when debating life's milestones - well, child-bearing at least - but rarely the social clock.[81] Like the biological clock, the social clock is a race against time, with age-checked social and cultural expectations for major life events such as securing your first job, being in a committed relationship or getting married, buying a home, moving up the career ladder and retiring, to name a few. The social clock appears to be a universal phenomenon, to the extent that a board game was made out of it! I had completely forgotten about *The Game of Life* by Hasbro until last Christmas when my niece and nephew wanted to play it - there are more than just blue and red play figures, but otherwise it hasn't changed much at all. It is a spot-on demonstration of how pervasive the social clock is in many cultures. However, what you'd never be able to understand from this children's board game is the way in which the social clock affects people, and how widely this can vary.[82] Like so many things in psychology, if you believe it's important then it will be so - but often when you look behind the curtain all is not as it appears.

If we look back at Freya's narrative, there are lots of 'shoulds', 'supposed tos' and 'sures' - which are all forms of all-or-nothing thinking (Chapter 4). But this way of conceptualising our lifepath is not some miscalculation on Freya's part; it is the type of Tiny T that stems from living in an environment that supports the notion of a social clock. To help Freya peek behind this sociocultural Tiny T curtain we started her AAA Approach journey with an exercise that enabled her to take a bird's-eye view of her life course to date.

AAA Approach Step 1: Awareness

Exercise: Life-mapping

I often use a life-mapping technique with clients such as Freya who are at a crossroads in their lives, as it's helpful to zoom out to increase Awareness. We grabbed a blank sheet of paper and placed Freya's date of birth on the left-hand side of a straight line, like this:

DoB ⟶

Then I asked Freya to think about her experiences and jot these on her life-map – you can do this too by noting down:

- milestones or events that have been significant *to you* – not worrying about societal conventions of what should have been achieved by certain dates;
- achievements or realisations that you're proud of, or have changed you in some important way.
- plot the positive events on the top half of the life-map, and more negative ones below. The height of each line should reflect how much the event affected you so that you can start to see what's been most transformative in your life (both the good and the not-so-fun). You can also add the age it occurred to get a clearer picture of your chronology.

For each of these, it's useful to write a few words of phrases as a descriptor.

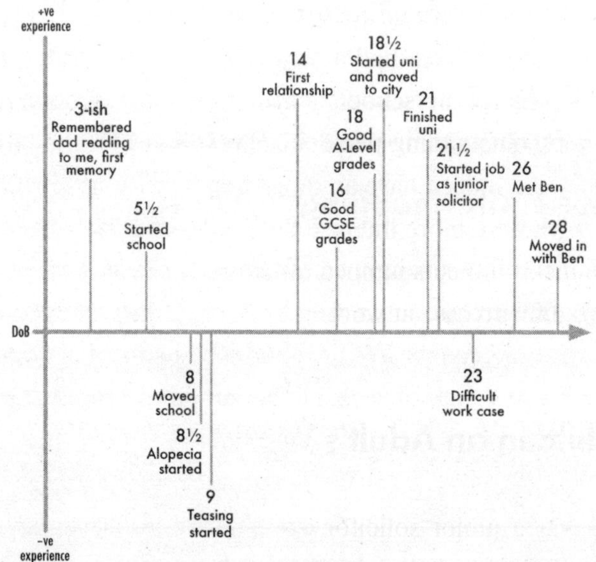

Next, consider these probing questions to help you uncover more detail in this Awareness phase of the AAA Approach:

- What obstacles did you overcome during your journey? How?
- What did you discover about yourself during both the highs and lows?
- Can you see any common or frequently occurring values on your life-map?

Now, take a step back and take an overview of your life-map, but look at the map as if it belongs to someone else. How do you feel about this person when looking at their life-map from afar?

From looking at Freya's life-map, both her Tiny Ts and some major life events came into focus. If you remember in Chapter 1, we briefly touched on the difference between Tiny Ts and life events – the latter being more obvious and notable experiences that most people would recognise as being challenging and/or transformative. Freya had already gone through quite a few of these – change in school, starting/finishing school/college/ university, outstanding personal achievement, moving house – and they did indeed have an impact on her. But it was the Tiny Ts that we were more interested in and a couple of these more subtle nicks and cuts jumped out at me – one in particular was Freya's difficult case at work.

A Child in an Adult's World

Freya was a junior solicitor, specialising in family law, when she was asked to help with an acrimonious divorce involving two children. She was well aware that any type of split in assets can get a bit ugly, but she said she wasn't prepared for how vicious this case turned out to be. Freya's client was 'using every trick in the book' to get the settlement she wanted, and Freya said it was at this point that a hefty doubt about her life-path started to rear its head. She had studied hard and was now in significant student-loan debt - Freya knew that she earned pretty well for her age, but it started to feel like it was at a high cost to her moral compass. She mentioned that she felt like a little girl at this time - supposedly an adult but utterly helpless in the situation, because as a junior solicitor she had no choice but to work on the case or potentially lose her job, career and never be able to find the financial security she required to start a family of her own.

Focus on Tiny T: Moral injury

The concept of moral injury originally emerged from situations such as armed combat and emergency medical cases, where someone witnesses, fails to act or even carries out something that goes against their core moral values and beliefs.[83] There were many reports of moral injury doing the Covid-19 pandemic from healthcare workers who had to ration treatment that impacted on the survival of some severely ill patients, going against their oath of 'do no harm' for all patients. Yet moral injury can occur in anyone, in any setting, where there is injustice, perceived cruelty, degradation of one's status or any other breach of a valued moral code. The Tiny T that forms is one that often starts with bewilderment, then morphs into resentment towards others, and the pairing of guilt and shame towards oneself. Like all Tiny Ts, if this was to happen in a war zone, we'd be able to spot it much more readily – but when a subtle moral injury occurs such as Freya's case, people find it hard to discuss and come to terms with.

My fellow coaching psychologist Sheila Panchal has carried out some illuminating research into the 'turning-30' or quarter-life transition, which found that Freya's review of her career trajectory was not uncommon at this point in life.[84] [85] Having invested both significant time, and these days money, into that trajectory, realising that it was not all it was cracked up to be was challenging. Along with this, there is an urge to supercharge salary and status to move up a level – which appears even stronger in times of high costs of living. The heady days of late teens and twenties hedonism tends to fade, as people approaching their thirties start to lose the assumption that they're physically invincible and can get away with burning the candle at both ends. Indeed, I would say that at this point in history, the turning-30 crisis is experienced as particularly daunting.

For Freya, the moral injury she experienced also made her question her career choice, and to an extent her relationship. If we look at the table on pages 240–1 again, we can think about both of these internal battles as the conflict between intimacy and isolation. At some point in our lives – it may be when we're around 30 but may be earlier or later – there is emotional and psychological tension between the need for closeness and the desire to be independent. It's evident that Freya's experience at work made her feel isolated when she needed support, yet she did want to appear that she was coping independently. This tension left Freya with a feeling of floating in space, untethered and confused.

AAA Approach Step 2: Acceptance

To move on to the Acceptance phase of the AAA Approach when it comes to Tiny T Transitions, it's helpful to pause a moment and contemplate this space that Freya found herself in.

Liminal space

'Liminal space', or liminality, is the in betwixt and in between, wherein we can get rather stuck.[86] This 'stuckiness' feels uncomfortable and is characterised by a sense of confusion, ambiguity and lack of understanding - as Freya revealed in our first meeting. It's a bit like the ground falling away beneath your feet and you observing it, caught in the moment - what was known about the self, social roles and structures is questioned and often agonised over as there is one foot stuck in the past (pre-liminal) and one tentatively grasping for a future, post-liminal state. Culturally, we know that people can become trapped in the liminal space, which is why we have many ceremonies and rituals to help us move as smoothly as possible from one state to another - often called 'rites of passage'. But even with these it can be challenging to find our way through the haze of liminality, and these traditions can be attached to outdated notions of age and stage, as above.

Exercise: The Transition Onion

To help you though this liminal space and into the Acceptance Stage of the AAA Approach when you're dealing with a tricky transition, there's a technique I like to call the 'Transition Onion' (see Figure 10.1). In the centre of your onion is the transition you're going through right now – note it down. Next, draw the layer in your onion from the example below – add what you feel has been important to you with regards to this transition; this could be a mixture of experiences and Tiny Ts. Think about the following categories and explore what is influencing your experience of the transition at the centre of your onion:

- Your relationships, attachments and bonds: these can be from early life or connections that you have in the present that you feel are influential in your transition phase.
- Your life experiences, including your Tiny T: you may have discovered different examples of Tiny T in this book and reflected on some of your own that may be keeping you stuck.
- Your cultural context and the society you in live in: depending on the transition you're exploring, this can include a workplace organisation (for example, if you're pivoting career or retiring), your community, which might include religion and spiritual beliefs (this is often relevant when dealing with the transition into a partnership, parenthood or the death of a loved one), or even wider societal views that may be influencing how you feel about this transition.

The point here is to highlight how the different levels of our lives impact on how we experience a transition – in other

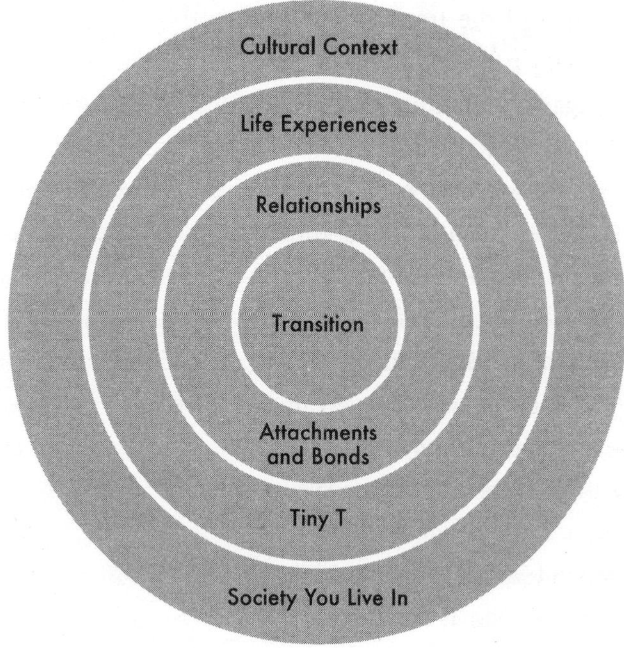

Figure 10.1: Transition Onion

words, it is rarely, if ever, *you* in and by yourself creating the sense of stuckiness; rather, it is this broader context of our existence that places social-clock expectations on us.

This is where Acceptance as a concept really comes into its own as well, and like so much of the Tiny T work we've been doing in this book, the purpose here is to connect the dots between our lived experience and the things that impact on that experience. It's only when we make these links that the sense of isolation ebbs away, and we can start to work towards the third Action stage of the AAA Approach. Although these personal factors, social expectations and associations often seem so obvious after the exercise, we frequently miss out the Acceptance phase in life – often to our detriment. Let's take the example of the transition into parenthood – or not. I've seen so many people who have chosen to remain child-free yet have struggled within liminal space with this decision until we had the opportunity to explore some of these social-clock expectations and how each layer of their context (as per the onion) was making it difficult for them to move from a pre-liminal state to post-liminal acceptance. The cultural and societal pressure to have children can be difficult for everyone. On the other side of the spectrum, I've worked with individuals who have had kids at different chronological points in their life course and felt as if they were too early/too late/doing it at the wrong time in relation to the social clock. This tells us something important about how our beliefs, expectations and our environment affect our experience of transitions. In other words, maybe there is no 'correct' time, just a good time for *you*.

If we go back for a moment to Freya, another key element of her turning-30 crisis that emerged from the Transition Onion exercise – one that hadn't been in her life-mapping – concerned her family context. When we were discussing both the relationships and attachments layer within the sociocultural circle, Freya mentioned that she was finding it hard to think about what she was going through, as her mum was struggling with the menopause – in other words, like so many Tiny Ts, she didn't feel that her feelings were worthy as her mum seemed to be having a 'real transition'. On top of this, Freya's mum was having problems securing HRT (hormone replacement therapy) for the menopause and so was struggling with a range of symptoms including anxiety and irritability. Freya's mum was also having to look after her parents (Freya's grandparents) a lot more, as well as work and support her younger brother – she did seem to have an awfully full plate. Therefore, in Freya's mind, her mother's transition negated her experience to such an extent that she hadn't shared her feelings with her mum for fear of burdening her further. This contributes to an overwhelming sense of isolation.

Menopause and the sandwich generation

There are some transitions in life that are defined by definitive changes in human physiology – menopause is probably the most obvious example in adulthood. Humans are living much longer – since the 1840s, life expectancy in the most privileged countries has been increasing almost linearly by 2.5 years per decade,[87] yet the average age for the onset of the menopause hasn't changed, at 51 years. However, the perimenopause can start ten years before this, beginning in the early- to mid-forties. Considering we now live into our eighties and beyond, it is feasible that half of a biological female's life could be spent within the process of perimenopause, menopause and then post-menopause, rather than say a quarter when average lifespans were shorter. In many areas of the world, people are also having children later in life, all of which has conspired so that menopause symptoms, older kids either still at home or boomeranging back and elderly parents requiring additional care happen at the same time, under one roof.

About a third of symptoms are severe enough to disrupt everyday activities during this physiological transition – and for many, this could be for over a decade. Some of the early symptoms of the perimenopause include high levels of anxiety and feelings of being overwhelmed, and I have seen countless clients who come to me after having been diagnosed antidepressants by their primary care doctors. Although drugs have their place, recognising that the co-occurrence of a symptomatic menopause with being part of the so-called sandwich generation can be an extremely challenging time can help a great deal and lead to more sustainable ways of coping.

What we mean by 'sandwiching' is akin to Freya's explanation, where there are dual caring responsibilities - and this is often where the conflict between generativity and stagnation, from Erikson's theory, comes in. Generativity is all about making your mark on the world and contributing to the next generation, and this was often seen as the goal. But we also need to look after ourselves to reduce the chances of stagnation, which can be tough when sandwiched between parents who need more assistance and children still requiring support. Freya seemed intuitively aware of this and so didn't want to overload her mum with more problems.

However, Freya didn't factor in the fact that the menopause isn't all bad - one study from the University of Cambridge reported that during the menopause and post-menopause women felt more able to be open and speak their mind.[88] The menopause can also trigger a surge in confidence and strength, with people reporting that they are more in tune with their feelings and less constrained by inhibitions.[89] Once symptoms are adequately addressed, that is. I cannot stress enough how real and debilitating the physical and psychological symptoms of the menopause can be - and also how appropriate treatment gives people their lives back. Hence, discussing these topics and the type of conflict that Freya's mum might be going through was helpful, as it opened a door back to intimacy through open conversation with her mum.

AAA Approach Step 3: Action

The Action phase in the Tiny T Transitions is very much about moving through the liminal space and taking the learnings from previous transitions to new ones. The exercises can be used for any transitional crisis, so focus on what you're going through right now.

Exercise: Transitional-crisis tug-of-war

This is an exercise that can result in a profound shift during liminality, helping us move through the Acceptance phase to the Action stage of the AAA Approach.[90] Start by thinking of what you've been struggling with – then work through the following:

Visualise this battle as a superhero nemesis – you could, instead, imagine a monster, demon or any other kind of powerful, nefarious character, but it must be something that has the ability to destroy you.

You are both standing at the top of a volcano, on opposite sides of the deep, black and fiery red pit beneath. You can feel its heat on your face and know the gorge travels down to the molten centre of the earth.

You and the supervillain are in an almighty tug-of-war over the volcano, both pulling and tugging on a thick rope.

Your desire to drag your opponent into the crater feels overwhelming, as your life depends on it. You are using every ounce of energy that you have, but you and your nemesis are well matched in terms of strength and power. It feels like a true battle.

Now ... drop the rope.
How does that feel?

I absolutely love this exercise as the mental shift is often immediate. How did that feel for you when you were reading the description? If you can't find the words, go back to page 80 and have a look at the Emotions Wheel or doodle what you're feeling – whichever works best for you.

This exercise helps us to see that the struggle is often within ourselves – with our own thoughts and expectations, which can become the focus of the transitional crisis. When we are focused only on the battle – the tug-of-war – it is impossible to see the solutions that exist to help us move through a transition. This is why moving through the AAA Approach is so very important – without Awareness, Acceptance, then Action, we can get lost in the struggle and use all our energy and resources fighting to stay in the same place. Running to stand still or continually pulling on a tug-rope with only ourselves at the other end isn't fun for anyone – quite frankly, it's exhausting, often not only for you but also for the people who love you too.

Letter from the future exercise

To figure out *how* to move into Action, think about a time in the future, in the post-liminal space where everything has turned out pretty darn well. Consider different aspects of your life - both the big and small, the seemingly insignificant to the substantial areas - and imagine how these all would look in a time machine.

Now, take a pen and paper (it's important that this is handwritten) and write a letter from your future self to the current version of you. You might want to look back at Chapter 2 and think about each area of the Life Assessment - what would each of these areas feel like from the standpoint of fulfilment? Remember, some components may be more important to you than others - family and personal freedom might eclipse financial security and career or the other way round; it's completely down to what you value.

Explore in detail in your own words what it's like to be in this future point to your current self - describe how it feels, the context and surroundings, what kind of thoughts you have and the sorts of actions you take on a daily basis. Here are some coaching psychology prompts to help with your letter writing:

Think about your dreams in the life areas that are most important to you – what do these look like?
If you had unlimited resources (not just financial but time, support and encouragement), what would you set out to do?
Try not to just consider your heartfelt dream and ambitions in the frame of your current capabilities, but rather in terms of your potential.
How would this transform the quality of your relationships, work and health?

I use this exercise a great deal as it helps to close the gap between 'then' and 'now' and progress through the liminal space.

For Freya, this exercise illustrated that she still loved her career, but mostly needed more emotional support from family (including her mum) and at work. Not all stories have a fairytale ending though - not in real life anyway - so I wanted to share with you that during the time we worked together Freya broke up with her partner. She confessed that a great deal of the social-clock pressure she was feeling was to do with his expectations of how life 'should' pan out, and in her work on the intimacy–isolation conflict Freya felt the need to be free of this romantic, Eros relationship that she felt was expected of her. Indeed, Freya leant into the isolation side of the transitional crisis point, which gave her more independence and helped her to have closer and more meaningful relationships with other people in her life. She stopped caring so much about the ticking of the social clock, and this helped her to become 'unstuck'.

Longer-term planning for transitions

One of the hardest aspects of a transition is that it can feel unexpected – Tiny T has a lot to do with this as it can trigger a liminal phase such as was the case with Freya and the moral injury she experienced. However, we do know that there are certain transitions that the majority of us will go through, of course bearing in mind individual cultural and societal differences. One example of this in late adulthood is retirement, which usually occurs within the final conflict in adult development proposed by Erikson – that of ego integrity versus despair. Ego integrity is all about reflecting back on one's life and feeling satisfied with our achievements, whereas a sense of despair comes if we are laden with regrets or feeling that life was wasted.

Whether paid or voluntary, labour in the home or within an outside organisation, work provides us with a sense of purpose, gives structure and routine to our days and can also be an important aspect of our self-identity. Also, most jobs provide social networks and friendships that are fundamental to our wellbeing. These are some reasons why it can be challenging to retire, and indeed many people experience depression post-retirement, particularly if they are forced to retire due to ill health, caregiving responsibilities, or are not able to find another job.[91] Even though the world of work has changed from 'jobs for life' to more fluid types of careers, most of us will see a close to our working lives at some point. While there are many ways to reinstate the psychosocial elements and structure that work provides, including volunteer work, hobbies and developing new relationships, there are mental barriers that stymie our ability to truly enjoy these years.

Research shows that people with a negative view about growing older tend to struggle more with retirement,[92] so if you feel worried about retirement, getting older, or any other transition, here are some ways to make the passage somewhat smoother:

- If you're about to retire (or even just thinking about a career change), ask others who are now 'job-free' to name the three best aspects of their retirement, and three things they'd wished they'd been prepared for. The same goes for every transition – don't sit in the dark and fear the unknown; take action by seeking out others' experience and wisdom.
- Discover positive role models within wider culture and media – we tend to only think about role models for young people but they are helpful at any age. Observe the qualities you admire in each role model and how they exhibit their values during this transitional stage, and

consider how you can assimilate these characteristics into your daily life. For example, you may follow a fellow retiree who has taken to the stage with stand-up comedy – this doesn't mean you need to perform a 30-minute set, but you could explore your own sense of humour with your family.

- Finally, look at the transitions that you have successfully navigated in the past and pinpoint the personal resources within *you* that have helped you traverse sometimes bumpy roads – perhaps your humility, loyalty or integrity helped you move through a transition. Maybe it really was your sense of humour that got you to the other side. Dig deep – you may not have experienced the same transition in the past, but you will have experience that you can draw from based on your core values that will guide you to the next stepping stone of life.

Dr Meg's journaling prompts for transitions

1. What aspects of life have surprised you most? In what ways?

2. Think about yourself as a teenager – what three questions would you ask your present self?

3. What do you know to be true now that you didn't know a year ago?

CHAPTER 10 TAKE-HOME TINY T MESSAGE

Transitions are part of life – but this doesn't mean they are always easy. Normalising transitional phases by having an awareness of what other people also go through is a good starting point for navigating this Tiny T Theme. Accepting that there is a process of letting go of who and what we once were, to enable the next stage of life, is also helpful. Finally, forward planning for the transitions that you will face in the future is a good way to support your psychological immune system in relation to this Tiny T Theme.

CHAPTER 11

Jumping, not staring, into the abyss: Your Tiny T prescription for life

In this chapter we will conclude with:

- the AAA Approach for life
- how to follow your arrow
- how to limit choice overload
- why kindness is key
- your prescription for a life less sh*t.

So here we are, the final chapter of our journey together. My hope is that you will be able to use some if not all of the Tiny T exercises in this book - now and in the future. Even just being aware of Tiny T as a real, valid and tangible concept can be of significant benefit. There are far too many Tiny Ts to cover in this book, so what I would say is that if you've experienced something that makes you feel uncomfortable, unworthy of support or leads you to question your grasp on yourself, it could very likely be a form of Tiny T.

But there comes a time to jump, rather than stare, into the abyss. The idea of staring into the abyss until the abyss gazes back at you was introduced by the German philosopher Friedrich Nietzsche - and like all great philosophical quotes, there are various interpretations, including losing oneself as a result of looking too deeply into the dark areas of the inner human psyche. If we explore this notion in relation to Tiny T, we can see that there is a danger in spending too much time contemplating the harsh realities of our life course, and the difficult circumstances we have experienced - this is the risk of Awareness without Acceptance and then Action. Therefore, my challenge to you now is to combine what you have learnt with the final teachings of this chapter, to take control of your past, live fully in the present and jump unabashed into your flourishing future.

The AAA Approach – for Life

Throughout our time together in this book, we've used my Awareness, Acceptance and Action - or AAA - Approach. You can take this method and apply it for whatever difficulties come your way - and the more you use it, the more you will hone these vital psychological skills. Like any skill, using the AAA Approach will also become easier with practice, as your mind will seek out Awareness more readily, you will be more open to Acceptance of life's tricky problems that are both complex and everyday, and will be empowered to take Action to live life to the fullest.

AAA Approach Step 1: Awareness

What's your purpose?

Ahhhh ... such a short question for such a massive concept. Some people spend their entire lives trying to figure out their purpose, and there's something to be said for this journey. Often, when people have children, they express that they finally know their purpose: to care for and raise other human beings. Other people find purpose within their work and community activities, or a combination of all these things. Yet this can be the sticking point - with so many options, what can we do to help us find our purpose?

Exercise: Follow your arrow

To help narrow these choices down, let's play the *Follow Your Arrow* game. Each of the below is a core value that you either care deeply or aren't that bothered about. For each category, move the arrow to the right if you value it deeply, or nearer the left if you couldn't care less about it.

⟶

Artistic skills
Athletics/sport
Business/earning money
Creativity
Independence
Musical ability/appreciation
Politics/community

Relations with friends or family
Religious values
Sense of humour
Spontaneity/living life in the moment

The above list isn't exhaustive, and you can add your own categories too.

Now, which arrows are pointing towards the future? Take a moment to reflect on why these are important to you.

These are your core values – your unique set of stars that will help you find meaningful purpose in life and light your way home if you ever run off-course. And this is the secret: you can have more than one – we can have numerous values, purposes and paths in life. So much of the time we're told that we must find our one true purpose – kinda like our one true love – but that's far too miserly. Life is generous, when we view it as such.

Next, ask yourself:

'In what ways does my life move in this (or these) direction(s)?'

Keep this in mind as you read on.

Purpose Venn diagram and the Westernisation of *ikigai*

When thinking about following your arrow, you may have heard of the Japanese concept of *ikigai* - and the figure below may be familiar to you. If not, this theory states that your purpose can be found within the overlap of a Venn diagram, where what you love, what you're good at, what the world needs and what you can get paid for all meet in the middle.

Figure 11.1: Venn diagram of ikigai

My mum spent a significant part of her life in Japan, so I asked her about this framework. She said she recognised some parts of it, but felt it was too rigid and would be surprised if meeting all of these conditions was truly faithful to the original concept. From my professional standpoint, I would tend to agree and believe that the necessity of meeting all four of these circumstances sets the bar unrealistically high for most people. If we think more in terms of psychological flexibility, which is a core part of the psychological immune system in terms of its adaptive function, your purpose may be something you love to do and are good at, but not what you are paid for (i.e. a passion). So, you might then also need to dedicate some time to something that the world needs, and that you can draw an income from (in the above *ikigai* model, this would be a vocation), making sure you still have some time to devote to your passion projects.

As with so many societal Tiny Ts, the insistence that all the stipulations must be met for a well-lived life puts us under so much pressure, and as such is counterproductive. This is an outcome-driven, Westernised view of *ikigai*, whereas a more traditional view would take these aspects of one's purpose as a lifelong continuum, which changes and develops over a lifetime. However, you may be able to add a sprinkling of your own arrows to more areas of your life to enhance the time you have on this earth.

Takeaway dice and choice overload

If there's one thing I've learnt during my bumbling life, it's that humans are fascinating. And although we desire endless choice, this multitude of options doesn't actually serve us very well. Choice overload is a term we use in psychology where too many options lead to a decision paralysis.[93] But there's an easy way to narrow down your possibilities and it's something I use at home - my partner and I occasionally get takeaway food and because there are so many choices, we were spending half the evening debating what we'd like to eat. So, one Christmas, unbeknown to both of us, we bought one another takeaway dice! I must admit that my partner did a better job at selecting the gift, which was a lovely personalised wooden cube, whereas I picked up a plastic toy version from a gift shop (read into that what you will!), but we had both come to the realisation that we needed some help with this trivial issue. However, the interesting thing about using a random selection tool is that it focuses the mind - some days the dice might land on 'curry', but we'll look at each other and say, 'Nah, let's get pizza.' What this means is that, by limiting your options, you'll be in a better position to know what you truly desire. Therefore, when you're thinking about your life choices, strike all but three off and chuck the others in a metaphorical f*ck-it bucket and on to the remaining areas in life that you now have the headspace to truly consider.

Try before you buy

Do you remember that store Build-A-Bear®? I think they were actually called workshops, and this probably shows my age yet again, but kids loved the concept - parents, perhaps, didn't like this shop quite as much, since the toys were rather expensive! But you could go into the workshops and choose the type of stuffed toy, its clothes, accessories and many other add-ons *before* you bought one. What if you could do this with your *ikigai*, and 'try before you buy' in your life?

Adjunct Professor and Executive Director of the Design Program at Stanford Bill Burnett suggests just this.[94] Instead of ditching your entire life, which in his research he found usually did not turn out very well, add components of your arrows to your existing life and see how it feels. For example, one of your arrows may be 'artistic skills' but you feel overwhelmed by the thought of going to an adult learning centre to train in fine art. Instead, think of places where your artistic desire could be more a part of your life - perhaps adding your artsy flare to your home through some redecoration, or trying a few crafting activities via Pinterest. Just like constructing the plush bear, you can see what fits, feels right and is workable *for you*, as we only really know if something will bring us fulfilment if we've actually tried it for ourselves. Selling your suburban semi and moving to the woods off-grid might seem like a fantastic life change, but it's only when you're out there and you remember how much you hate spiders and discover how hard it is to grow anything remotely edible that it becomes real. Instead, maybe you can take a sabbatical from your jobby-job and try that idyllic-looking off-grid lifestyle for a few months in a caravan before selling-up lock, stock and barrel. This change may or may not be all it's cracked up to be, but like the takeaway dice, trying before you buy a whole new life gives you much more clarity and direct experience of your options, without the risk of losing your shirt.

AAA Approach Step 2: Acceptance

I would say again that Acceptance can be the most difficult phase of the AAA Approach, and one that often gets overlooked. This can be because we conflate bad things happening in our lives to *being bad people* - but this is not the case. It's true we may feel unloved, unworthy and undermined, and these experiences are incredibly tough to sit with. Instead, we often rationalise Tiny T in the sense that we must have done something terrible to deserve this treatment - but when we move to a place of acceptance, rather than resignation, we are able to build a strong psychological immune system and be that little bit kinder to ourselves. Here's a reminder of the difference between resignation and acceptance - it can be helpful at this juncture to explore whether you feel more comfortable with the idea of acceptance, and how important it is to your sense of self:

Resignation	Acceptance
Psychological rigidity	Psychological flexibility
Feeling disempowered and frozen	Feeling empowered to act
Self-judgement and recrimination	Curating a deep sense of self-compassion
A mindset of scarcity	A mindset of abundance
Giving up/giving in	Recalibrating to take positive action
Tolerating difficulties	Learning from difficulties
Soldiering on	Up-skilling
Avoidance of change	Open to change
Resistance	Recognition
Judgement-led	Value-led

Tiny T and the psychological immune system in perspective

Revisiting the concept of the psychological immune system, at the end of Chapter 1, we compared it to the human physical immune system that protects us against a range of harmful pathogens such as viruses and bacteria throughout our lifespan. We are born with some immunity, but much of the immune system develops over a lifetime - particularly in early childhood - when it comes into contact with these microscopic invaders. Our bodies then mount a response to the interloper, and it is this physical response that gives us symptoms such as a cough, runny nose and fatigue in the case of a common cold. The psychological immune system works in much the same way and gives us unpleasant feelings when we experience Tiny Ts, in the form of the stress response and emotions that we'd rather not feel. But both the physical and psychological symptoms are important as they allow our immune systems to grow and adapt to our environment. Without some challenges, we would only have the basic immunity that we're born with - and considering how tough such major life events can be, this may not be sufficient for good psychological health.

Hence, by being **aware** of Tiny Ts, **accepting** that these scrapes and scratches happen in life and taking positive **action** to manage well with these experiences, we can transform small traumas into *emotional antibodies* - otherwise known as coping skills.

In other words, the concept of Tiny T is not about a mindset of passivity or resignation, but rather a way to take control of your past so that you can own the present and develop a future in which you thrive, not merely survive.

Mind your 'buts' – Tiny Ts are not excuses

In this sense, Tiny Ts are **absolutely not excuses**. One way to make sure that you aren't allowing Tiny Ts to take over your life in a negative manner is to mind your use of 'but' and 'because' - both in your inner narrative and in the way you communicate with others.

For example, mind your 'buts' if you hear this:

'I'd like to talk to my friend, but she upset me - so much that I don't think I can talk to her.'

Change to this:

'I'd like to talk to my friend, and she upset me - so I will talk to her even though I was upset.'

By replacing the 'buts' with 'ands', we open up different possibilities for the future. This also gives a much more realistic version of the complexity of life and human emotion - we can be simultaneously upset with a friend and still care about them deeply. However, when we use 'buts' we are preventing forward progression and trapped behind the 'but' wall. When this is replaced with 'ands', we can break down this wall and move forward.

Also, keep an eye out when using 'because':

'I don't want to apply for the promotion, because I had a bad experience at work in the past.'

Tweak like this:

'I want to apply for the promotion, although I had a bad experience at work in the past.'

Simply softening the language here doesn't change the past - we cannot change the past of course - but it loosens the hold our Tiny T has over the present. Also, being mindful of your intention and altering it in both your internal narrative and discussion with others will allow for forward movement, so tune into this mental script and try to replace words such as 'can't', 'won't' or 'don't' with more empowering terms.

Be the editor in this blockbuster called life

This tweaking of the way we tell our story, either to ourselves or others, can be extended. The above examples can be seen as lines within the script of your blockbuster - i.e. your life. Just like any blockbuster movie, the role of the editor is central to the story that makes it to the screen. Different kinds of shots, frames and pace will all affect the mood of the film, and the editor uses these tools to focus our attention on the story they want to tell, as well as including more or less screen time for a particular scene. To see how this works, first write your outline script including events, experiences, Tiny Ts and any other key moments that have made you who you are today (this links back to our opening Tiny T question in Chapter 1). These are the touchpoints of your movie, not the interpretations, so it's usually the information before any 'buts' or 'becauses' when you're writing. In the example in the previous section, our protagonist wanted to see their friend – this is the touchpoint in this simple scenario. Now, play around with it to give the action a variety of meanings and outcomes. We have two possibilities above; what others can you come up with?

I hope this exercise helps you to see that you have agency, not just over the future but over the way you interpret the past and live your life today.

AAA Approach Step 3: Action

In this final Action stage of our Tiny T expedition, I want to share with you some everyday actions that support both the body and mind, the physical immune system and the psychological immune system. Whichever condition, presentation or theme I've studied, from chronic fatigue to emotional eating, from anxiety to heartbreak, these fundamentals are unwavering.

Your daily prescription for life

If there's one insight I've taken from 20 years of researching and working in the field of health, it's that the more we live our lives in harmony with the natural world, the more grounded we feel and at peace with our experience of existence. This may sound pretty hippy-dippy, but it makes scientific sense – we are part of the natural world, no matter how far technology takes our minds and bodies away from it. Our inner workings and physiological processes are synched with the circling of the sun in a 24-hour circadian rhythm. This is not just to do with sleep, although sleep is indeed a life-or-death issue, as we have many biological rhythms that are driven at a molecular level in response to the environment. There are other, longer rhythms too, for example the menstrual cycle.

Working with, rather than against these rhythms generally supports both physical and mental health as we need then to stimulate or sedate ourselves less with synthetics - be this via information, substances or unhelpful thoughts. Therefore, below are my Action tips to help you live that life that is best *for you*.

Make light a friend, rather than foe

Light is by far the most important environmental factor when it comes to the 24-hour circadian rhythm - our minds and bodies work best when we sleep during darkness and are active in daylight. Yet with the invention of artificial light, we are able to see what we're doing no matter what time of day it is. This is no criticism of Thomas Edison, as the development of the lightbulb was a moonshot in the Industrial Revolution, stimulating economies around the world and raising living standards for billions of people. But like so many of the tools we create, the human tendency is to push a good thing rather too far. In our current non-stop societies, we find it very hard to switch off, literally and figuratively. Now, we spend much of our daytime indoors with artificial light, which is qualitatively different from natural light and does not give our brains the same signals. Research has found that artificial light impacts on us as individuals, on our environments and on our health.[95] For a long time, we've mainly focused on sleep disturbance and seasonal affective disorder (SAD), but we are increasingly learning that a lack of daylight can be a perpetuating factor in a variety of mental health conditions and physical wellbeing.

Are you SAD? Seasonal affective disorder as Tiny T

Seasonal affective disorder is a much talked about condition as soon as the nights begin to draw in. But there is rampant debate about whether it is 'real' or not. SAD is a subcategory of recurrent major depressive disorder, differing only by the extent it is tied to specific seasons. Most people who report seasonal depression have symptoms in the winter but about 10 per cent of cases appeared to be associated with summer. To be diagnosed with SAD, you'd need to see a clear start and end point that can be tracked with the changes of the seasons, then be symptom-free at other times of the year for at least two years, with more symptomatic episodes in your lifetime than without.

While some research has shown a link between natural light and mood, the physiological mechanism for this is still up for grabs. We know that daylight does affect the production of melatonin and serotonin, which then influences the sleep/wake cycle (circadian rhythm), and poor sleep often leads to waking up on the wrong side of the bed. And indeed, when digging further into the research, studies in the USA report that only 1 per cent of people who live in Florida experience SAD compared to 9 per cent of Alaskans. Yet researchers in countries like Norway and Iceland found few instances of SAD considering their extremely short winter days. So what's the deal? Well, this could be more about our expectations and societal beliefs than anything else – in the USA, hot, sunny weather is often associated with 'good' feelings such as happiness, but in Scandinavian countries where the weather is more consistent across the entire country there may be a greater appreciation of the beauty of darker seasons. How we cope with bitterly cold days in different parts of the world might be a factor too – the Norwegian word *friluftsliv* can be directly translated as 'free-air life', where we embrace the outdoors no matter what the weather. So perhaps SAD might be in part to do with our beliefs – beliefs that have been built over our lifetime and as such formed a type of Tiny T.

I think the next type of 'wellness wearable' technology will have something to do with this – I wouldn't be surprised to see a natural-light sensor fitted to the body, which will feed data to your smartphone and ping you an alert to go outside and absorb some natural light. But you don't need to wait for this bit of tech – instead, make sure you get outside every day, even if only for 20 minutes or so to soak up some mood-boosting vitamin D.[96]

The art of REST

Rest is the poor relation of sleep in our full-on lives. Researchers from Durham University surveyed over 18,000 people from 134 countries and asked them how much rest they had on a daily basis and also what types of restful activities they practised. Perhaps unsurprisingly, a majority – over two-thirds of the sample in fact – said that they would like more rest. The researchers also discovered that people who had less rest reported lower overall wellbeing.[97]

Highly demanding jobs, juggling multiple care responsibilities, trying to see friends, have some fun and generally live life all contribute to our restless society. We're not just burning the candle at both ends – we've thrown the entire thing into a roaring fire so all that's left is a waxy mess on the floor. Or at least that's what modern life can feel like by the end of the week!

But there's also the Tiny T of societal norms, expectations and labels that often prevent us from resting – one client who was clearly exhausted told me she thought of herself as 'lazy' if she rested in the day, no matter how tired she was. If we turn to the natural world, however – which we are an intricate part of – it's clear to see that nature knows how to rest. The seasons change, day turns into night and all the while our environment regenerates, restores and renews itself continually – without resistance.

Likewise, it is important to build rest periods into our daily lives. This doesn't necessarily mean sleeping or napping, but rather activities that allow us to 'switch off' from the stressors of life such as reading, listening to music or spending time in nature.

REST: Restore Energy (with) Space (and) Time

I like to use the above mnemonic as an easy reminder of how to rest, as it reminds me about active rest – and that we need to dedicate space and time to achieve recovery in the same way that we'd dedicate these precious resources to work or to an objective goal. Although it can feel hard to find time in our daily lives, these suggestions only take a few minutes and can be used as part of your 'time confetti' – those little snippets of time we have that tend to be filled with mindless scrolling and clicking. It can also be useful to clarify the different types of rest that we all need to feel deeply restored and rejuvenated.[98]

Physical – this is the most obvious category, but this doesn't just mean sleeping or sitting passively – breathing exercises (see Chapters 1 and 4) help to activate the parasympathetic nervous system, which moves the body into a 'rest-and-digest' state. Also, if your job is sedentary, physical rest is more about giving your body a rest from the constant static sitting position that causes pain and discomfort, in the form of gentle desk-based stretching or getting up from the chair once an hour to move your body around. However, if your days are physically active, developing moments of complete stillness will act as rest.

Mental – 'brain fog' is a pervasive issue right now. Mental rest is about overcoming the urge to multitask, and instead focus on uni-tasking. Turn off app and phones alerts, log off email and shut the door so that you can create chunks of time when you concentrate on just one task. This takes a bit of practice as many of us are ingrained in the myth of multitasking – but it's worth the effort.

Social – social rest doesn't necessarily mean solitude – although it can if that's what you need – but rather, spending time with people who need no airs or graces, where you can be completely and utterly *you*. These people are your battery chargers, so hold on to them for dear life! Importantly, sometimes these people are acquaintances rather than our loved ones, as it can often be easier to be ourselves with those we only see every once in a while.

Sensory – we all require differing amounts of sensory stimulation, and those of us who are highly sensitive (Chapter 9) may need more quiet time than others. Simply taking a few moments to close our eyes during the day to give the sense of sight a rest can be helpful. Again, this is not about going into solitary confinement, as the less artificial sensory input we receive when in nature is also restful.

Emotional – look out for the emotional vampires in your life that drain your emotional energy, and limit (or cut all together) the time spent with these people. The exercises in Chapter 2 will also help to feed your Emotobiome and offer respite from restless emotions.

Creative – our minds spend so much time on analytical work these days that few of us get a chance to nurture the creative parts of ourselves. I feel profoundly creative after visiting my favourite galleries and endeavour to schedule a visit regularly. If this isn't possible or not your bag, give yourself time and space to doodle for three slots of five minutes throughout the day. Adult colouring is also restful, particularly intricate mandala patterns.

Spiritual – you don't need to be religious to benefit from the restful qualities of spirituality. Feeling embedded in the world we occupy is the secret and this can be realised through helping others. Indeed, we know that assisting our fellow human beings increases our own wellbeing, as this acts as rest from self-focus – too much of which can be exhausting.[99] Feeling restored via spiritual sources also has to do with feeling secure in our purpose (above), which is another reason why aligning yourself with your arrows can be so beneficial.

The trick here is to tailor the rest to the life you live – the type of rest you need will be different from your partner, friends and family, so respecting this personalised approach is the key for true rest.

Eat stuff from the ground and move your body around

Although this isn't a nutrition or exercise book, it would be totally remiss not to mention the impact of what we put into our mouths and how we burn off this energy has on our psychological immune system – so my humble suggestion is:

Eat stuff from the ground and move your body around.

There are more diets than I can count, or even contemplate. The weight-loss industry was one of the only wellness sectors that grew during the Covid-19 pandemic and, like our waist-lines, it just keeps on expanding.[100] Hence, there's a very real financial imperative to keep us confused about what we should – and should not – be eating. Then there are numerous research studies about the effectiveness of all of these diets, and in my opinion it boils down to this: try to eat stuff that looks as close as possible to its natural form. It really is that simple – fruit and veg, nuts and seeds, some fish and maybe a bit of white meat (if you eat meat that is)[101] that looks like it's just been harvested, picked or plucked is a safe bet. Of course, if you have medical requirements this may differ somewhat, but the vast amount of brain hours that have been spent on this issue seems rather excessive. If your great-grandmother would recognise it, it's probably ok! If, however, it's an ultra-processed form of Frankenfood, steer clear or eat it in very small amounts.

In addition to this, keep in mind that humans didn't evolve to consume 24/7, day in, day out. There were no app-based delivery services in prehistoric times, so we fasted for long periods during every 24-hour cycle, and faced even lengthier fasts when food was scarce. All the trillions of microbes in our guts need time to do their work - and they need you to leave their environment alone to get the job done, which is one reason why overnight fasting of a minimum of 11 to 12 hours is now recommended. Indeed, the word 'breakfast' means just that: to break your nightly fast.

The second part of my little ditty is about movement - and I use the word movement purposefully as 'exercise' can have all sorts of connotations and Tiny Ts attached! As I've said, our bodies didn't evolve to sit at desks all day - we need to move to maintain both a healthy mind and body, but this doesn't mean a two-hour gym session every day (unless that's your thing of course!). An easy way to think about it is:

- If you can do X sitting, can you do it standing? For instance, computer work: could you use a standing desk? if the answer is no, that's fine – it's worth asking the question.
- If you can do it standing, can you do it walking? This might be talking on the phone – could you take a walk-and-talk instead?

The wonderful thing about walking is that it helps maintain physical fitness *and* mental health, and you don't even need to expect it to do you any good for it to work. Researchers at Iowa State University found that it doesn't matter where or why people walked, as simply getting up and putting one foot in front of the other makes us feel better mentally and physically.[102]

Walking is one of the easiest ways to increase your daily activity and it really does make a difference. We tend to get caught up in the numbers, but the 10,000 steps a day is at best a guesstimate of the ideal figure - now we know that the number is more like 7,000, but I still think the most important aspect of this is to just get moving. If you can challenge your body, up your heart rate and get a little puffed out on a regular basis then you will see improvements in your fitness levels and overall health.

Connection is a non-negotiable

We need human connection. Fact. In Chapter 1 we highlighted the loneliness epidemic and how harmful this is to both mental and physical health. As social creatures, we have evolved to live in groups, and although we may not necessarily need others these days for food, shelter and safety from predators, we do still need other people to add to our sense of belonging, as social support and often as a vehicle to our purpose. Hence, feeling a sense of connectedness absolutely is about our health as a whole, not 'just' emotional wellbeing. This doesn't have to be a deep and meaningful marathon conversation; even micro-interactions like a chat while waiting for a bus or at the till also help us to feel connected. Although this might at first feel awkward, be aware that we tend to underestimate how much strangers like us after a bit of small talk - a phenomenon called the 'liking gap'.[103]

It is great if you can see people face to face, but sometimes this isn't possible. Talking on the phone, even just about seemingly trivial things like the weather, can create that sense of being allied in the big bad world. There are so many ways to reach out to people now, but mind yourself on social media - research tell us that passively liking posts or scrolling without interaction leads to depressed mood and feelings of inadequacy. Use these amazing technological tools for good instead and genuinely connect and communicate with friends, family or even just people who have common interests. Whatever you like, no matter how abstract, there will be a page for that. Guaranteed.

Fur, feather, scaly or leafy connections as a proxy

Ok, ok, I'm a bit biased here as an animal lover but there is data that shows time spent with creatures help us to feel connected to another living being. For those of you who do love the felines, studies have shown that purrs help to lower stress levels by activating our innate rest-and-digest parasympathetic nervous system.[104] Somewhat crazily, even watching videos of cats could offer benefits - in fact, there are now festivals where people come together to watch cat vids! And this is indeed backed up by evidence that found those of us who watch cat clips in our spare time felt more positive overall and had more energy.[105] But more than anything, animals can also give us a sense of connection. So, if for whatever reason you can't connect with people, think about spending time with other living creatures instead - cats, dogs, reptiles, whatever! I would go so far as to say that even tending to and looking after plants can create a sense of calm, as research shows that interacting with indoor plants reduces stress.[106]

Cultivate gratitude every day

My partner and I do this every evening, but you can practise gratitude any time of day. I do think it's useful to use this exercise at the same time each day, however, so that it becomes a habit. In the field of positive psychology, a good deal of research has found that cultivating a firm sense of gratitude improves wellbeing and gives us a broad perspective on life.[107] This technique is so easy it's hard to believe that it really works - but I suggest this frequently, and when I follow up with them months later, their views have indeed changed. Traditionally, psychologists and therapists suggest that you think of three things that you are grateful for - these needn't be major positive life events like having a child or getting a new job, but rather the little things in life. My partner and I list five things, though, as the first two always stay the same - one another and family. But otherwise, the aspects of the day we are thankful for are tiny, such as a nice walk in the park or a compliment at work. Your gratitude can be about absolutely anything, as this method is a way to retrain your brain to see the good in life - as we saw in Chapter 4, we are programmed to search the environment for threats to our survival, so it does take a bit more effort to notice the silver linings. But they are there, however small.

Why You *Don't* Have to First Love Yourself ...

But you don't have to wait to do all this until you love yourself - I meet so many people who feel like they can't take action until they 'love themselves first'. This idea, peddled by seemingly well-meaning people, leaves individuals isolated and lonely, stuck waiting until the magical day arrives when they experience self-love. But if you weren't shown unconditional love in early life, it can be bloody hard to love yourself, as you have no model for that love (see Chapter 8). I'm telling you from a place of compassion and experience that loving yourself *first* is not the greatest love of all, it's the greatest myth of all. Therapy, counselling or allowing someone to love you first can all help. So please don't wait to start this process, as by working through it you will be showing yourself love, even before you feel it.

... but you can start with self-kindness – and stay youthful in the process!

It costs nothing to be kind - well, nothing in terms of cold, hard cash - but many people do find it challenging to be kind to themselves, much more so than showing others generosity and compassion. If you're not yet in a place of self-love, it can be helpful to start by working with self-kindness, as some fascinating research suggests that it may turn the clock back and keep us youthful. One study looked at telomere length, which is a marker of biological ageing, in groups of people who practised loving-kindness meditation similar to that on page 173, and those who did not. The researchers found that people who practised this type of kindness had a longer relative telomere length than the control group - telomeres shorten with age and are associated with earlier mortality.[108] Hence, developing a sense of kindness to oneself is central to my prescription, even on those days you might not love yourself.

Life is a marathon, not a sprint – but you have to be in the running

As we come to the end of our time together, I want to wholeheartedly encourage you to use what you've learnt and leap forward into the unknown abyss - it's usually not as scary as we fear. And even if additional Tiny Ts come your way, you will now have an arsenal of tools, emotional antibodies and skills to use to cope with what life has to throw at you. But here's one last exercise if you're feeling at all nervous about this ...

Exercise: 'The nearly missed it!' diary

Have you ever looked back on your week and found it almost impossible to recall anything notable at all? We can miss out on so much of what life has to offer if we're constantly in our own heads. My suggestion here is to be engaged in the world for a week by writing a 'nearly missed it!' diary of the things that you would have missed out on if you'd been too far in the black hole of your own thoughts. These are often small, mundane but utterly fascinating occurrences such as sunshine on a cloudy day, a sweet moment between a mother and child in a café who you can hear behind you – or any number of tiny things that make life interesting.

Life really is all about the tiny things – whether this is Tiny T trauma or finding those magical moments in the mundane. It's our choice what we hold on to, and what we let go of.

Dr Meg's journaling prompts for developing a life in which you flourish

1 What makes you feel most alive when you're doing it?

2 If you can't change something in your life, in what ways can you make peace with it?

3 If not now, when?

Final Note ...

I want to thank you for coming on this Tiny T crusade with me. One of the reasons I wrote this book was to allow more people to feel seen – and you can help with this too. If you feel comfortable, please share your Tiny Ts with me and others with the hashtag #tinyt on @tinytraumasbook or my @drmegarroll account on Insta. The more we all shine a light on Tiny T, the easier it will be to talk about and process this type of low-grade, yet insidious trauma. Thank you again and all the best on your continuing journey.

Notes

1 Holmes, T. H. and Rahe, R. H. 'The social readjustment rating scale', *Journal of Psychosomatic Research*, 11(2) (1967), pp. 213–18.

2 Lackner, J. M., Gudleski, G. D. and Blanchard, E. B. 'Beyond abuse: The association among parenting style, abdominal pain, and somatization in IBS patients', *Behaviour Research and Therapy*, 42(1) (2004), pp. 41–56.

3 Bretherton, I. 'The origins of attachment theory: John Bowlby and Mary Ainsworth', *Developmental Psychology*, 28(5) (1992), p. 759.

4 De Schipper, J. C., Oosterman, M. and Schuengel, C. 'Temperament, disordered attachment, and parental sensitivity in foster care: Differential findings on attachment security for shy children', *Attachment & Human Development*, 14(4) (2012), pp. 349–65.

5 If you haven't seen *Ferris Bueller's Day Off*, or indeed the entire back catalogue of John Hughes films, then stop reading this book immediately and go to your nearest streaming service! So many examples of Tiny T can be found in 1980s movies ...

6 Passmore, H. A., Lutz, P. K. and Howell, A. J. 'Eco-anxiety: A cascade of fundamental existential anxieties', *Journal of Constructivist Psychology* (2022), pp. 1–16, DOI: 10.1080/10720537.2022.2068706.

7 Seligman, M. E. *The Hope Circuit: A Psychologist's Journey from Helplessness to Optimism*, Hachette UK, 2018.

8 Layard, P. R. G. and Layard, R. *Happiness: Lessons from a New Science*, Penguin UK, 2011.

9 Agarwal, S. K., Chapron, C., Giudice, L. C., Laufer, M. R., Leyland, N., Missmer, S. A., Singh, S. S. and Taylor, H. S. 'Clinical diagnosis of endometriosis: A call to action', *American Journal of Obstetrics and Gynecology*, 220(4) (2019), pp. 354–364.

10 Chen, E. H., Shofer, F. S., Dean, A. J., Hollander, J. E., Baxt, W. G., Robey, J. L., Sease, K. L. and Mills, A. M. 'Gender disparity in analgesic treatment of emergency department patients with acute abdominal pain', *Academic Emergency Medicine*, 15(5) (2008), pp. 414–18.

11 Diener, E., Seligman, M. E., Choi, H. and Oishi, S. 'Happiest people revisited', *Perspectives on Psychological Science*, 13(2) (2018), pp. 176–84.

12 Brickman, P., Coates, D. and Janoff-Bulman, R. 'Lottery winners and accident victims: Is happiness relative?', *Journal of Personality and Social Psychology*, 36(8) (1978), p. 917.

13 Kraft, T. L. and Pressman, S. D. 'Grin and bear it: The influence of manipulated facial expression on the stress response', *Psychological Science*, 23(11) (2012), pp. 1372–8.

14 Wilkes, C., Kydd, R., Sagar, M. and Broadbent, E. 'Upright posture improves affect and fatigue in people with depressive symptoms', *Journal of Behavior Therapy and Experimental Psychiatry*, 54 (2017), pp. 143–9.

15 Keyes, C. L. 'The mental health continuum: From languishing to flourishing in life', *Journal of Health and Social Behavior* (2002), pp. 207–22.

16 Affleck, W., Carmichael, V. and Whitley, R. 'Men's mental health: Social determinants and implications for services', *The Canadian Journal of Psychiatry*, 63(9) (2018), pp. 581–9.

17 Check permissions in Lomas, T. 'Towards a positive cross-cultural lexicography: Enriching our emotional landscape through 216 "untranslatable" words pertaining to well-being', *The Journal of Positive Psychology* (2016), pp. 1–13. doi: 10.1080/17439760.2015.1127993.

18 Jiang, T., Cheung, W. Y., Wildschut, T. and Sedikides, C. 'Nostalgia, reflection, brooding: Psychological benefits and autobiographical memory functions', *Consciousness and Cognition*, 90 (2021). doi: 10.1016/j.concog.2021.103107.

19 Cheung, W. Y., Wildschut, T., Sedikides, C., Hepper, E. G., Arndt, J. and Vingerhoets, A. J. 'Back to the future: Nostalgia increases optimism', *Personality and Social Psychology Bulletin*, 39(11) (2013), pp. 1484–96.

20 Sedikides, C., Leunissen, J. and Wildschut, T. 'The psychological benefits of music-evoked nostalgia', *Psychology of Music* (2021). doi: 10.1177/03057356211064641.

21 Cheung, W. Y., Hepper, E. G., Reid, C. A., Green, J. D., Wildschut, T. and Sedikides C. 'Anticipated nostalgia: Looking forward to looking back', *Cognition and Emotion*, 34(3) (2020), pp. 511–25, doi: 10.1080/02699931.2019.1649247.

22 Vervliet, B. and Boddez, Y. 'Memories of 100 years of human fear conditioning research and expectations for its future', *Behaviour Research and Therapy*, 135 (2020), pp. 1–9.

23 Pittman, C. M. and Karle, E. M. *Rewire Your Anxious Brain: How to Use the Neuroscience of Fear to End Anxiety, Panic, and Worry*, New Harbinger Publications, 2015.

24 Rozlog, L. A., Kiecolt Glaser, J. K., Marucha, P. T., Sheridan, J. F. and Glaser, R. 'Stress and immunity: Implications for viral disease and wound healing', *Journal of Periodontology*, 70(7) (1999), pp. 786–92.

25 Scholey, A., Haskell, C., Robertson, B., Kennedy, D., Milne, A. and Wetherell, M. 'Chewing gum alleviates negative mood and reduces cortisol during acute laboratory psychological stress', *Physiology & Behavior*, 97(3–4) (2009), pp. 304–12.

26 Gallup, A. C. and Eldakar, O. T. 'The thermoregulatory theory of yawning: What we know from over 5 years of research', *Frontiers in Neuroscience*, 6 (2013), p. 188.

27 DeBoer, L. B., Powers, M. B., Utschig, A. C., Otto, M. W. and Smits, J. A. 'Exploring exercise as an avenue for the treatment of anxiety disorders', *Expert Review of Neurotherapeutics*, 12(8) (2012), pp. 1011–22.

28 Powers, M. B., Asmundson, G. J. and Smits, J. A. 'Exercise for mood and anxiety disorders: The state-of-the science', *Cognitive Behaviour Therapy*, 44(4) (2015), pp. 237–9.

29 Stonerock, G. L., Hoffman, B. M., Smith, P. J., and Blumenthal, J. A. 'Exercise as Treatment for Anxiety: Systematic Review and Analysis.' Annals of behavioral medicine: a publication of the Society of Behavioral Medicine vol. 49,4 (2015): 542–56. DOI: 10.1007/s12160-014-9685-9.

30 Abramowitz, J. S., Deacon, B. J. and Whiteside, S. P., *Exposure Therapy for Anxiety: Principles and Practice*, Guilford Publications, 2019.

31 Burcaş, S. and Creţu, R. Z. 'Perfectionism and neuroticism: Evidence for a common genetic and environmental etiology', *Journal of Personality*, 89(4) (2021), pp. 819–30.

32 Lopes, B. and Yu, H. 'Who do you troll and why: An investigation into the relationship between the Dark Triad Personalities and online trolling behaviours towards popular and less popular Facebook profiles', *Computers in Human Behavior*, 77 (2017), pp. 69–76.

33 Avast, 2021. 'Avast Foundation survey reveals trolling becoming an accepted behaviour for younger generations'. Available at: https://press.avast.com/en-gb/avast-foundation-survey-reveals-trolling-becoming-an-accepted-behaviour-for-younger-generations?_ga=2.256764171.1422491308.1638966148-989583476.1638875314 (Accessed: 29/05/2022).

34 Cheng, J., Bernstein, M., Danescu-Niculescu-Mizil, C. and Leskovec, J. 'Anyone can become a troll: Causes of trolling behavior in online discussions', in Proceedings of the 2017 ACM Conference on Computer Supported Cooperative Work and Social Computing (February 2017), pp. 1217–30.

35 Suler, J. 'The online disinhibition effect', *International Journal of Applied Psychoanalytic Studies*, 2(2) (2005), pp. 184–8.

36 Rosenbaum, D. A., Fournier, L. R., Levy-Tzedek S., et al. 'Sooner rather than later: Precrastination rather than procrastination. *Current Directions in Psychological Science*, 28(3) (2019), pp. 229–33, doi:10.1177/0963721419833652.

37 Wiehler, A., Branzoli, F., Adanyeguh, I., Mochel, F. and Pessiglione, M. 'A neuro-metabolic account of why daylong cognitive work alters the control of economic decisions', *Current Biology*, 32(16) (2022) pp. 3564–75.e5. doi: 10.1016/j.cub.2022.07.010.

38 STEM is an acronym for the professional fields of science, technology, engineering and mathematics.

39 Sakulku, J. 'The impostor phenomenon', *The Journal of Behavioral Science*, 6(1) (2011), pp. 75–97.

40 Gravois, J. 'You're not fooling anyone', *Chronicle of Higher Education*, 54(11) (2007).

41 Bernard, D. L., Hoggard, L. S. and Neblett, E. W. Jr. 'Racial discrimination, racial identity, and impostor phenomenon: A profile approach', *Cultural Diversity and Ethnic Minority Psychology*, 24(1), (2018), pp. 51–61.

42 Cokley, K., Awad, G., Smith, L. et al. 'The roles of gender stigma consciousness, impostor phenomenon and academic self-concept in the academic outcomes of women and men', *Sex Roles*, 73 (2015), pp. 414–26; https://doi.org/10.1007/s11199-015-0516-7.

43 Bravata, D. M., Watts, S. A., Keefer, A. L., Madhusudhan, D. K., Taylor, K. T., Clark, D. M. and Hagg, H. K. 'Prevalence, predictors, and treatment of impostor syndrome: A systematic review', *Journal of General Internal Medicine*, 35(4) (2020), pp. 1252–75.

44 Sue, D. W. *Microaggressions in Everyday Life: Race, Gender, and Sexual Orientation*, John Wiley & Sons, 2010.

45 Feiler, D. and Müller-Trede, J. 'The one that got away: Overestimation of forgone alternatives as a hidden source of regret', *Psychological Science*, 33(2) (2022), pp. 314–24.

46 Carney, D. R., Cuddy, A. J. and Yap, A. J. 'Power posing: Brief nonverbal displays affect neuroendocrine levels and risk tolerance', *Psychological Science*, 21(10) (2010), pp. 1363–8.

47 Kerr, M. and Charles, N. 'Servers and providers: The distribution of food within the family', *The Sociological Review*, 34(1) (1986), pp. 115–57.

48 Evers, C., Marijn Stok, F. and de Ridder, D. T. 'Feeding your feelings: Emotion regulation strategies and emotional eating', *Personality and Social Psychology Bulletin*, 36(6) (2010), pp. 792–804.

49 10 = Starving (weak, dizzy); 9 = Ravenous (irritable, low energy); 8 = Very hungry (stomach rumbling, preoccupied with food); 7 = Slightly hungry (thinking about food); 6 = Neutral (neither hungry nor full); 5 = Slightly full (pleasantly satisfied); 4 = Full (somewhat uncomfortable); 3 = Very full (bloated, trousers feeling tight); 2 = Overly full (very bloated and slightly nauseous); 1 = Full to the point of pain (painfully bloated and feeling extremely sick).

50 Parker, G., Parker, I. and Brotchie, H. 'Mood state effects of chocolate', *Journal of Affective Disorders*, 92(2) (2006), pp. 149–59.

51 Cota, D., Tschöp, M. H., Horvath, T. L. and Levine, A. S. 'Cannabinoids, opioids and eating behavior: The molecular face of hedonism?', *Brain Research Reviews*, 51(1) (2006), pp. 85–107.

52 Brouwer, Amanda M. and Mosack, Katie E. 'Motivating healthy diet behaviors: The self-as-doer identity', *Self and Identity,* 14(6) (2015), p. 638.

53 Skorka-Brown, J., Andrade, J., Whalley, B. and May, J. 'Playing Tetris decreases drug and other cravings in real world settings', *Addictive Behaviors*, 51 (2015), pp. 165–70.

54 Hung, I. W. and Labroo, A. A. 'From firm muscles to firm willpower: Understanding the role of embodied cognition in self-regulation', *Journal of Consumer Research*, 37(6) (2011), pp. 1046–64.

55 Please forgive me as these are very simplified versions of complex and intricate stories!

56 Stein, H., Koontz, A. D., Allen, J. G., Fultz, J., Brethour, J. R., Allen, D., Evans, R. B. and Fonagy, P. 'Adult attachment questionnaires: Disagreement rates, construct and criterion validity', Topeka, Kansas, The Menninger Clinic Research Dept, 2000.

57 Cohen, S., Janicki-Deverts, D., Turner, R. B. and Doyle, W. J. 'Does hugging provide stress-buffering social support? A study of susceptibility to upper respiratory infection and illness', *Psychological Science*, 26(2) (2015), pp. 135–47.

58 Hodgson, K., Barton, L., Darling, M., Antao, V., Kim, F. A. and Monavvari, A. 'Pets' impact on your patients' health: Leveraging benefits and mitigating risk', *The Journal of the American Board of Family Medicine*, 28(4) (2015), pp. 526–34.

59 Parrott, W. G. and Smith, R. H. 'Distinguishing the experiences of envy and jealousy', *Journal of Personality and Social Psychology*, 64(6) (1993), p. 906.

60 Dunbar, R. *How Many Friends Does One Person Need? Dunbar's Number and Other Evolutionary Quirks*, Faber & Faber, 2010.

61 Grusec, J. E. 'Social learning theory and developmental psychology: The legacies of Robert R. Sears and Albert Bandura', in R. D. Parke, P. A. Ornstein, J. J. Rieser and C. Zahn-Waxler (eds), *A Century of Developmental Psychology*, American Psychological Association, 1994, pp. 473–97.

62 McGill, J. M., Burke, L. K. and Adler-Baeder, F. 'The dyadic influences of mindfulness on relationship functioning', *Journal of Social and Personal Relationships*, 37(12) (2020), pp. 2941–51.

63 Cunnington, D., Junge, M. F. and Fernando, A. T. 'Insomnia: Prevalence, consequences and effective treatment', *The Medical Journal of Australia*, 199(8) (2013), S36–40. doi: 10.5694/mja13.10718.

64 Hirshkowitz, M., Whiton, K., Albert, S. M., Alessi, C., Bruni, O., DonCarlos, L., Hazen, N., Herman, J., Katz, E. S., Kheirandish-Gozal, L. and Neubauer, D. N. 'National Sleep Foundation's sleep time duration recommendations: Methodology and results summary', *Sleep Health*, 1(1) (2015), pp. 40–3.

65 Herzog-Krzywoszanska, R. and Krzywoszanski, L. 'Bedtime procrastination, sleep-related behaviors, and demographic factors in an online survey on a Polish sample', *Frontiers in Neuroscience* (2019), p. 963.

66 Sturm, R. and Cohen, D. A. 'Free time and physical activity among Americans 15 years or older: Cross-sectional analysis of the American Time Use Survey', *Preventing Chronic Disease* (2019), p. 16.

67 Schulte, B. *Overwhelmed: How to Work, Love, and Play When No One Has the Time*, Macmillan, 2015.

68 Sjöström, S. 'Labelling theory', in *Routledge International Handbook of Critical Mental Health*, Routledge, 2017, pp. 15–23.

69 Aron, E. N. *The Highly Sensitive Person: How to Thrive When the World Overwhelms You*, New York, Harmony Books, 1997.

70 Lionetti, F., Aron, A., Aron, E. N., Burns, G. L., Jagiellowicz, J. and Pluess, M. 'Dandelions, tulips and orchids: Evidence for the existence of low-sensitive, medium-sensitive and high-sensitive individuals', *Translational Psychiatry*, 8(1) (2018), pp. 1–11.

71 Domhoff, G. W. 'The content of dreams: Methodologic and theoretical implications', *Principles and Practices of Sleep Medicine*, 4 (2005), pp. 522–34.

72 Cartwright, R. D. *The Twenty-four Hour Mind: The Role of Sleep and Dreaming in Our Emotional Lives*, Oxford University Press, 2010.

73 https://sleepeducation.org/sleep-caffeine/.

74 Schmidt, R. E., Courvoisier, D. S., Cullati, S., Kraehenmann, R. and Linden, M. V. D. 'Too imperfect to fall asleep: Perfectionism, pre-sleep counterfactual processing, and insomnia', *Frontiers in Psychology*, 9 (2018), p. 1288.

75 Akram, U., Ellis, J. G. and Barclay, N. L. 'Anxiety mediates the relationship between perfectionism and insomnia symptoms: A longitudinal study', *PloS one*, 10(10) (2015), p. e0138865.

76 Erikson, E. H. *Insight and Responsibility*, Norton, Levinson, D. J. *The Seasons of a Man's Life*, Knopf, 1994.

77 Kim, A. M., Tingen, C. M. and Woodruff, T. K. 'Sex bias in trials and treatment must end', *Nature*, 465(7299) (2010), pp. 688–9.

78 Beery, A. K. and Zucker, I. 'Sex bias in neuroscience and biomedical research', *Neuroscience & Biobehavioral Reviews*, 35(3) (2011), pp. 565–72.

79 Doherty, M. A. 'Sexual bias in personality theory', *The Counseling Psychologist*, 4(1) (1973), pp. 67–75.

80 Jackson, M. *Broken Dreams: An Intimate History of the Midlife Crisis*, Reaktion Books, 2021.

81 Neugarten, B. L. 'Time, age, and the life cycle', *The American Journal of Psychiatry*, 136 (1979), pp. 887–94.

82 Rook, K. S., Catalano, R. and Dooley, D. 'The timing of major life events: Effects of departing from the social clock', *American Journal of Community Psychology*, 17(2) (1989), pp. 233–58.

83 Shale, S. 'Moral injury and the COVID-19 pandemic: Reframing what it is, who it affects and how care leaders can manage it', *BMJ Leader*, 4(4) (2020) pp. 224–7.

84 Panchal, S. and Jackson, E. '"Turning 30" transitions: Generation Y hits quarter-life', *The Coaching Psychologist*, 3(2) (2007), pp. 46–51.

85 O'Riordan, S., Palmer, S. and Panchal, S. 'The bigger picture: Building upon the "Developmental Coaching: Transitions Continuum"', *European Journal of Applied Positive Psychology*, 1(6) (2017), pp. 1–4.

86 Wels, H., Van der Waal, K., Spiegel, A. and Kamsteeg, F. 'Victor Turner and liminality: An introduction', *Anthropology Southern Africa*, 34(1–2) (2011), pp. 1–4.

87 Oeppen, J. and Vaupel, J. W. 'Broken limits to life expectancy', *Science*, 296(5570) (2002), pp. 1029–31.

88 Rubinstein, H. R. and Foster, J. L. '"I don't know whether it is to do with age or to do with hormones and whether it is do with a stage in your life": Making sense of menopause and the body', *Journal of Health Psychology*, 18(2) (2013), pp. 292–307.

89 Hvas, L. 'Menopausal women's positive experience of growing older', *Maturitas*, 54(3) (2006), pp. 245–51.

90 Hayes, S. C., Strosahl, K. D. and Wilson, K. G. (2011). *Acceptance and Commitment Therapy: The Process and Practice of Mindful Change* (2nd edn), Guilford Press, 2006.

91 Lee, J. and Smith, J. P. 'Work, retirement, and depression', *Journal of Population Ageing*, 2(1) (2009), pp. 57–71.

92 James, J. B., Besen, E., Matz-Costa, C. and Pitt-Catsouphes, M. 'Engaged as we age: The end of retirement as we know it', The Sloan Center on Aging and Work, *Issue Brief*, 24 (2010), pp. 1–20.

93 Chernev, A., Böckenholt, U. and Goodman, J. 'Choice overload: A conceptual review and meta analysis', *Journal of Consumer Psychology*, 25(2) (2015), pp. 333–58.

94 Burnett, B. and Evans, D. *Designing Your Life: Build a Life that Works For You*, Random House, 2016.

95 Chepesiuk R. 'Missing the dark: Health effects of light pollution', *Environmental Health Perspectives*, 117(1) (2009), A20–A27. https://doi.org/10.1289/ehp.117-a20.

96 Anglin, R. E., Samaan, Z., Walter, S. D. and McDonald, S. D. 'Vitamin D deficiency and depression in adults: Systematic review and meta-analysis', *The British Journal of Psychiatry*, 202(2) (2013), pp. 100–7.

97 Callard, F. 'Hubbub: Troubling rest through experimental entanglements', *The Lancet*, 384(9957) (2014), p. 1839.

98 Dalton-Smith, S. *Sacred Rest: Recover Your Life, Renew Your Energy, Restore Your Sanity*, FaithWords, 2017.

99 Piliavin, J. A. and Siegl, E. 'Health benefits of volunteering in the Wisconsin longitudinal study', *Journal of Health and Social Behavior,* 48(4) (2007), pp. 450–64.

100 Global Wellness Institute (no date). Wellness Industry Statistics & Facts. Available at: https://globalwellnessinstitute.org/press-room/statistics-and-facts/#:~:text=The%20healthy%20 eating%2C%20nutrition%2C%20%26,during%20the%20 COVID%2D19%20pandemic (Accessed: 29 May 2022).

101 Longo, V. D. and Anderson, R. M. 'Nutrition, longevity and disease: From molecular mechanisms to interventions', *Cell*, 185(9) (2022), pp. 1455–70.

102 Miller, J. C. and Krizan, Z. 'Walking facilitates positive affect (even when expecting the opposite)', *Emotion,* 16(5) (2016), p. 775.

103 Boothby, E. J., Cooney, G., Sandstrom, G. M. and Clark, M. S. 'The liking gap in conversations: Do people like us more than we think?' *Psychological Science*, 29(11) (2018), pp. 1742–56.

104 Aganov, S., Nayshtetik, E., Nagibin, V. and Lebed, Y. 'Pure purr virtual reality technology: Measuring heart rate variability and anxiety levels in healthy volunteers affected by moderate stress', *Archives of Medical Science*, 18(2) (2022), p. 336.

105 'Emotion regulation, procrastination, and watching cat videos online: Who watches Internet cats, why, and to what effect?' *Computers in Human Behavior*, 52 (2015), pp. 168–76.

106 Lee, M. S., Lee, J., Park, B. J. and Miyazaki, Y. 'Interaction with indoor plants may reduce psychological and physiological stress by suppressing autonomic nervous system activity in young adults: A randomized crossover study', *Journal of Physiological Anthropology*, 34(1) (2015), pp. 1–6.

107 Wood, A. M., Froh, J. J. and Geraghty, A. W. 'Gratitude and well-being: A review and theoretical integration', *Clinical Psychology Review*, 30(7) (2010), pp. 890–905.

108 Hoge, E. A., Chen, M. M., Orr, E., Metcalf, C. A., Fischer, L. E., Pollack, M. H., DeVivo, I. and Simon, N. M. 'Loving-kindness meditation practice associated with longer telomeres in women', *Brain, Behavior, and Immunity*, 32 (2013), pp. 159–63.

Acknowledgements

When I first revealed my idea for *Tiny T* to my utterly amazing agent Dorie, she was treating me to an afternoon tea (with bubbles no less!) at the Wolseley on Piccadilly. You know, the olde-worlde kind of restaurant that could easily be a set out of *Harry Potter*, which certainly was exactly how I imagined London to be as a kid. I mention this because my tumbleweed-town ticker skipped a beat when I saw my darling agent's eyes shine a touch brighter after I mentioned this type of cumulative trauma that is so often ignored and disregarded as 'not bad enough' to warrant care and attention. We had only just started working together, and it was at this point in such cinematic surroundings that I knew my gut instinct was spot-on: the world needed to know about Tiny T. Hence, I want to thank from the bottom of my blue-sky Arizonian heart the firecracker that is my literary agent Dorie Simmonds for believing in me and Tiny T – I may have won the 'comma wars', but we will fight the global epidemic of mental health difficulties together.

However, on even-footing of support and encouragement are my two ginger boys, Neil Mordey and the Boobah, who both gave me real-time evidence of my hypothesis 'you don't have to love yourself first' and proved that countless cuddles and 'tru wuv' can indeed breathe life back into a withered soul.

You are my world #sofronge. It would be amiss not to include my bestie Tessa Lacey – you're a daily inspiration to me and, like Neil and Ginge, you are the beacon that guides me home in choppy waters. And if I must, I thank my big little sister Amy Roy, who keeps me grounded in round-the-clock 1980s nostalgia – honestly, what would I do without 20 retro memes a day?!

There are so many other people to sincerely acknowledge, including Lydia Good and the team at Thorsons and HarperCollins, all the amazing health journalists who I feel fortunate enough to call friends, my previous co-author Louise Atkinson who taught me how to slay the demon that is too much detail, and communication pros Mars Webb and Julia Champion for help in spreading the Tiny T word. To my supervisor Dr Siobhain O'Riordan – I bow to your encyclopaedic knowledge of coaching psychology! But I also immensely appreciate your warm and encouraging style of support, which has helped me in many more areas of life than work. In this sense also, David Smith my personal therapist, you have truly buoyed and guided me on this journey – thank you.

Speaking of motivation – Jennifer Kennedy, I have no idea how you always know exactly what to say but you are by far the best cheerleader ever! I also want to thank my family friend Charlotte Smyth, who knew that scraggly, rather shy girl in the desert, and who has also supported me in so many ways (usually accompanied by cake!) – you are without a doubt my 'acquired family'.

But I do want to tell the world again about my lovely dad, Graham Kinghorn Arroll, who was ripped away from us in the early days of the first Covid-19 wave. It gnaws at every ounce of my being that you passed just when you had been doing so well, after so many overwhelmingly difficult years. More than anyone, this book is for you and in honour of the unwavering and unconditional love you always gave me. You suffered so much, but it is my hope of hopes that through your battles I will be able to shine a light on the full scope of mental health challenges. I love you, Daddy.

Finally, to everyone who has been ignored, stigmatised, marginalised and gaslit when it comes to their mental health, your lived experience and constellation of Tiny Ts is as unique as you are - but you're not alone. Let's talk about Tiny T so much that they can't sweep it under the carpet any more and pave the way for better understanding and treatment of the spectrum that is mental health.